CORPORATE STRATEGY
AND PLANNING

CORPORATE STRATEGY AND PLANNING

Edited by

BERNARD TAYLOR, B.A.

Professor of Business Policy and Management Development,
The Administrative Staff College, Henley

and

JOHN R. SPARKES, B.A., M.Sc.(Econ.)

Senior Lecturer in Managerial Economics,
University of Bradford Management Centre

A HALSTED PRESS BOOK

JOHN WILEY & SONS
New York

Published in the U.S.A.
by Halsted Press,
a Division of John Wiley & Sons, Inc.
New York

© Bernard Taylor and John R. Sparkes 1977
First published 1977

Library of Congress Cataloging in Publication Data

Corporate strategy and planning.

   "A Halsted Press book."
   Includes index.
   1.   Corporate planning—Addresses, essays, lec-
tures. I.   Taylor, Bernard, 1931–   II.   Sparkes
John R.
HD31.C64474   1976   658.4'01   75-8310
ISBN 0-470-98935-1

Printed in Great Britain

Preface

The last ten years have seen a rapid growth in the use of Corporate Planning systems in private enterprises, large and small, in nationalized industry, and in central and local government both in the Western world and in developing countries. At the same time the study of corporate strategy and planning has been recognized as an important area for the development of theory and research, and within this field a great deal of work has been done to identify the possibilities and limitations of formal planning processes.

Presumably in all types of organization it is desirable to have a clear sense of purpose, commitment to agreed strategies or policies, the use of modern techniques for forecasting and planning, systems for coordinating and reviewing plans, and methods for comparing plans against results achieved. Various formal systems of planning and analysis are currently being used in a wide range of enterprises, and most current developments in economics and business are reinforcing the need for long-range planning.

This book sets out to review within one volume the state of the art in Corporate Planning and to suggest ways in which the planning process might develop in the 1980s. Its aim is to provide a conceptual basis for the acquisition of corporate planning skills. Experienced managers can regard the book as a guide to the use of Corporate Planning in managing their enterprises. Management students and researchers will find it a convenient summary of new developments in thinking and practice.

The book begins with a discussion of the concept and the role of Corporate Planning as an overall control system for an enterprise. It goes on to examine the practice of forecasting, both for economic factors and in technological, social and political areas.

The section on key strategies and plans starts with the con-

ventional analysis of corporate strengths and weaknesses and
the development of financial and marketing plans, and then
moves into new areas of corporate planning, e.g. strategic planning for resources, the development of strategies for international
expansion, and planning for technology, production and industrial relations.

The part of the book concerned with organizing and implementing corporate planning examines the problems of organizational
change and the evolution which has to take place in the management system as a whole if the corporate or strategic aspects of
an enterprise are to be given due attention. This last section includes five case studies written by senior managers who were
concerned in the implementation of planning systems in very
different organizations — manufacturing industry, construction,
local government, a bank, and a nationalized industry.

Given the multifarious nature of corporate planning we felt
it would be best to have authoritative chapters written by specialists on each topic. Our task has been to weld the text into a
book, rather than a symposium of articles. This we have tried
to do, and we are grateful for the forbearance of our contribu-
tors in the editing process. Any shortcomings which may remain
are our responsibility.

We hope it will be clear to the reader that we see planning
and policymaking as not merely a thought process, but as one
of the central social and political activities in an enterprise —
an arena in which important issues are identified and analysed,
and decisions made which are critical to its survival and long-term
viability.

Bernard Taylor
John R. Sparkes

Acknowledgements

Chapters 6, 15, 21 and 23 originally appeared in *Long Range Planning*. We are grateful to Gordon Wills, Adrian Buckley, Clive Rugman, and Neville Geary, and to Pergamon Press for allowing us to reprint these articles in the book.

Bernard Taylor
John R. Sparkes

Contents

The Contributors

ADRIAN BUCKLEY heads the financial planning function with a multinational group of companies whose profits are in excess of £20 million. He is a Chartered Accountant and a Business Graduate, and lectures frequently at Business Schools. Some of his recent articles have appeared in *Accountancy, Accounting and Business Research, The Journal of Business Finance,* and *The Journal of General Management.*

STANLEY CORLETT is Managing Director of Resource Planning Ltd, a company based in the Isle of Man which specializes in the design of in-company training and consultancy in finance and planning. He was formerly on the staff of Ashridge Management College, and previously held responsible positions in industry with Lever Brothers Nigeria, Associated Fisheries, and General Foods. He has recently carried out research into the impact of changing patterns of demand on resource networks.

NEVILLE R. GEARY is Head of the Policy Analysis Group of British Nuclear Fuels Limited. He graduated in chemistry at Queen's University, Belfast, and, after a period in private industry, joined the Department of Atomic Energy in 1950. From 1960 to 1963 he was the Atomic Energy Authority's senior representative in Canada, then become special assistant to the Member for Production. When the Production Group became British Nuclear Fuels Limited, he was placed in charge of long-term planning, from which he progressed to his present work on policy analysis.

A. J. GOODALL, Strategic Development Manager of Batchelors Foods Limited, has spent more than thirty-five years in the food-manufacturing industry, initially with J. Lyons and Co. and since 1947 with Unilever subsidiaries, principally Batchelors Foods. A chemistry graduate of London University and a Fellow of the Royal Institute of Chemistry, he is past chairman of the

BIM Sheffield Branch and president for 1975–6. In 1967 he founded the first regional group, now the N.W. Regional Group, of the Society of Long Range Planning.

KEVIN HAWKINS is Lecturer in Industrial Relations at the Bradford University Management Centre. He has published widely in the fields of industrial relations and corporate planning, and was deputy editor of the *Journal of Business Policy* from 1970 to 1972. He has also undertaken a large number of management-development and consultancy assignments on behalf of large business organizations.

J. CHRISTOPHER HIGGINS is Director and Professor of Management Sciences at Bradford University Management Centre. A Cambridge physics graduate, Professor Higgins served in the RAF, and later joined the Department of the Chief Scientist (RAF) in the Ministry of Defence. After a period as a consultant/ lecturer sponsored by the Metra Consulting Group, he joined IPC Newspapers Ltd and eventually became Director of Economic Planning and Research. He is the author of several textbooks and numerous papers on O.R. information systems and planning.

JAMES C. LEONTIADES is Senior Lecturer in International Management, Manchester Business School, and president of the European International Business Association. He has acted as consultant to General Motors and the Marketing Science Institute. His current research interests comprise the marketing adjustment of multi-national firms to foreign environments, and management implications of the E.E.C.; and he has published numerous papers on these subjects

RICHARD E. B. LLOYD is Chief Executive of Williams & Glyn's Bank Limited. He is also a Director of the National and Commercial Banking Group, The Royal Bank of Scotland, Legal & General Assurance Society and Kredietbank SA Luxembourgeoise. He was a non-executive Director of the Australia and New Zealand Banking Group from 1961 to 1975, and its Deputy Chairman from 1965 to 1971. Mr Lloyd is a member of the Industrial Development Advisory Board, and of the National Economic Development Council and has served on the London and South-East Regional Council of the CBI.

BRYAN LOWES lectures in Business Economics at Bradford University Management Centre. His research interests lie in business objectives and social responsibility. He is co-author of *Modern Managerial Economics* and of *Principles of Modern*

Management, and has contributed a number of articles to journals dealing with management and allied subjects.

CLIVE A. RUGMAN is Assistant Education Officer for Planning and Development in Kent. He took a classics degree at Cambridge and taught for several years in the south of England before joining the Kent Authority, where he was at first concerned with plans for secondary-school reorganization consequent upon the raising of the school-leaving age. In his present job with the Kent County Council he is concerned with corporate planning for education.

JOHN R. SPARKES is Senior Lecturer in Managerial Economics and Deputy Chairman of the Undergraduate School of Studies in Management and Administration at the University of Bradford Management Centre. He joined the Management Centre in 1965 from the University of Wales, and has taught economics and corporate planning to undergraduate, postgraduate and post-experience students. He is co-author of *Modern Managerial Economics* (Heinemann, 1974) and has contributed articles to books and journals in the management, economics, and industrial fields.

FRANCIS H. STOKES recently retired from the position of Corporate Planner at John Laing & Son, and now practises as a management consultant. He is also chairman of the Industry Structure Committee for the Building and Civil Engineering Industries. A civil-engineering graduate, he interspersed the career of an engineer in several parts of the world with technical marketing appointments. He became John Laing's chief engineer in Southern Africa in 1950 and later returned to the U.K. to become the company's Group Commercial Manager. Then in the early 1960s he became Corporate Planner, in addition to holding a number of board appointments.

BERNARD TAYLOR has been Director of Planning and Development and Professor of Business Policy at the Administrative Staff College, Henley, since 1972. He held responsible positions in business with Procter & Gamble and Rank Xerox before joining the University of Bradford in 1965. Professor Taylor is Editor of *Long Range Planning*, Founding Editor of the *Journal of General Management*, and co-author or editor of eleven books. He works as a consultant and teaches on a number of in-company and external management programmes in Europe and North America on policy and planning. In 1971 he was United Nations adviser to the National Council for Applied Economic Research in New Delhi. He has been Chairman of Study Groups and Working Parties on Policy Studies for the European Association of Management Training Centres and the Association of Teachers of Management, and is involved in international research projects in the policy field.

BRIAN C. TWISS is Assistant Director of Management Development Programmes at the University of Bradford Management Centre. He was previously Director of the Management Development Programme at Cranfield. With degrees in the mechanical sciences, economics and production, he spent several years in the management of advanced defence projects in the U.K. and Australia — which is reflected in his current work on the management of technical innovation. While he was Director of the Case Research Programme sponsored by the Department of Education and Science, he wrote a number of case studies on British management. He is co-author of three books on the management of production and the management of technological innovation.

GORDON S. C. WILLS, Professor of Marketing and Logistics Studies at the Cranfield School of Management, is also vice-chairman of MCB Publications, a director of Roles & Parker and Protocol Engineering Ltd, and editor of the *European Journal of Marketing*. A graduate of Reading University, Professor Wills has broadcast, lectured and written extensively in Europe and North America. He has worked as a marketing-researcher and acted as consultant on management and marketing to many organizations, including Dunlop, ICI and the BBC.

IAN H. WILSON is a Staff Associate with General Electric's (U.S.A.) Corporate Strategic Planning Department, which is responsible for developing environmental analyses for use in strategic planning. An Oxford graduate, he was first employed by ICI and went to the U.S.A. in 1954 joining General Electric, where he worked in public relations and manager education. In 1967 he joined the Business Environment Department, part of which was later transferred to Corporate Strategic Planning. He belongs to several American societies, is co-author of *The Business Environment of the Seventies,* and is a member of the editorial boards of *Intellect* and *Planning Review.*

Part I
Corporate Strategy and Planning: the Concept and the Need

1 The Concept and Use of Corporate Planning

Bernard Taylor

INTRODUCTION

The practice of corporate planning is now established on a worldwide basis and it continues to grow rapidly. Virtually every blue-chip company in the United States and Europe has a corporate planner, and in the leading companies — for example, IBM, Shell, ICL, ITT, Fiat, Ciba-Geigy — corporate planning has been practised for a considerable time. In the future it is to be expected that corporate planning will become as much a part of management in a progressive company as budgetary control is today.

This development is by no means confined to the private sector. Nationalized industries and public corporations have not been slow to develop comparable planning processes, many of considerable sophistication. And largely inspired by the 'Planning, Programming and Budgeting System', or P.P.B.S., originally used by Robert McNamara in the United States Defense Department, and thereafter in all United States Federal Agencies, central and local Government in Europe has followed suit. Formalized planning is now an established fact in both the private and the public sector.

What has brought about this surge of interest in planning? If pressed, most managers would probably claim that managing and planning are virtually synonymous. Up to a point this is, of course, true, but planning, in this broad sense, tends to be intuitive, sporadic and unsystematic. What is needed, in practice, is a consciously systematic approach that reflects a determination to start from first principles, to take decisions on the basis of facts, and to test the plan or hypothesis in action.

This view of management encompasses the following steps:

1 Define the problem or objective
2 Analyse the facts
3 Generate alternative proposals
4 Agree a plan and set performance standards
5 Implement the plan
6 Make periodic checks that the plan is being carried out
7 Take remedial action and review the objectives and
     the plan.

There are many benefits to be reaped from a more formal approach to planning. It forces a manager to think forward and anticipate problems before they occur. It provides a detailed forecast and plan that makes it easier to discover why the action taken did not produce the expected results. And detailed planning of this kind enables a manager to delegate with more confidence. Within the framework of the plan a subordinate can be given a fair amount of autonomy and independence, while his superior on the other hand retains general control.

CORPORATE PLANNING

Planning may therefore be seen as a natural part of the management process. Corporate planning, however, has come to bear a rather specialized meaning, with the emphasis laid on the regular review of *strategy*. One short and quite useful definition of corporate planning (by PA Management Consultants) is 'Planning systematically the *total* resources of the company for the achievement of *quantified objectives* within a specific period of *time*'.

This definition, however, does not sufficiently emphasize the relation of corporate planning to strategy. Peter Drucker's definition is, therefore, preferable. He defines corporate long-range planning as 'a continuous process of making entrepreneurial decisions systematically, and with the best possible knowledge of their futurity; organizing systematically the effort needed to carry out these decisions; and measuring the results against expectations through organized systematic feedback'. This gets the emphasis right: in a nutshell, corporate planning has come to mean a systematic approach to strategic decision making.

What benefits do companies foresee when introducing corporate planning? A study[1] of corporate planning in twenty-seven major U.K. companies suggests they wish:

1 To improve coordination between divisions
2 To achieve successful diversification
3 To ensure a rational allocation of resources
4 To anticipate technological changes.

The same study, however, made it clear that, in many of the cases where corporate planning had been introduced, profound and usually well-founded dissatisfaction had arisen with the level of profitability and the rate of growth. In addition, *in nearly half the cases, the introduction of corporate planning had been accompanied by a change of chief executive or of a member of the main Board.*

This illustrates perhaps more clearly than anything else that corporate planning is a philosophy of change. It is not so much a battery of techniques and systems as a style of management, and consequently the main benefits from planning derive from a continuing dialogue about the future of the organization, between top management and middle management, between line and staff, between the divisions and head office, even between management and unions, or the company and its major suppliers or major customers.

Once this process is accepted, corporate planning becomes part of the corporate approach to management. The annual long-range planning cycle becomes as much a part of management as the annual budget. The idea is born that it is necessary to measure the performance of the company and of its employees by criteria more sensible than one year's profits. The emphasis is therefore thrown on to manpower development, new product development and all the longer-term investments that are essential to the survival of the company.

Inevitably this means changes in attitude, particularly on the part of senior management. Often something of a crisis is required before corporate planning is accepted as necessary. The advantages are, however, considerable. Management gains a new sense of direction, there is a greater awareness of the business environment, the habit of forward thinking is encouraged, and a process for making a systematic and critical review of the business is developed.

How does the performance of companies using corporate

planning compare with those which do not? Studies in the U.S.A.[2] indicate that companies that use corporate planning significantly outperform companies that use informal planning methods. One finding was that companies with corporate planning performed around 30–40 per cent better in terms of earnings per share, earnings on common equity, and earnings on total capital employed. This better performance was not, of course, proof of the benefits of corporate planning, so the study examined the extent to which performance had improved after corporate planning had been introduced. The improvements were impressive: sales grew by 38 per cent, earnings per share grew by 64 per cent and the share prices increased by 56 per cent. The evidence therefore strongly suggests that corporate planning can lead to significant improvements in performance.

STRATEGY

Effective corporate planning is dependent on the development of a corporate strategy, and there is plenty of evidence that strategy is something management often tends to neglect. There are a number of reasons for this. Often the demands of day-to-day problems preoccupy managers, who leave too little time for thinking about the future growth and profitability of the business. This is not a new problem. Alfred Sloan, the architect of General Motors, was so afraid of it that he formed a separate 'policy committee' of top management whose brief was to be concerned solely with the general direction of the firm. But it is only in more recent years that the dilemma of top management has been studied. Professor Herbert Simon of Carnegie Mellon University invented Simon's Law to explain it. This states simply that routine drives out planning, that the urgent takes priority over the important.

There are other reasons. Research by Professor Warren of Columbia University suggests that it is not simply that senior managers are too busy 'putting out fires': they usually obtained their position because they were doers rather than planners; they were good at taking decisions and making things happen; they were men of action; in addition, their whole experience and training was probably in production, sales or finance, making sure of the profits *this year*.

The fact is that the system of management in most companies

encourages this myopia. Everyone talks about the importance of management development, staff training and investment in plant and equipment that will pay off in the long run. But when salaries are decided and promotions are arranged, there is a tendency to look at performance against the profit target this year.

Among companies practising long-range planning, the situation is not dissimilar. The average long-range planner spends his time developing a five-year budget. In fact, this is what most managers think long-range planning is — developing a three-year or five-year plan for the present business.

The corporate planner is usually required to assemble the divisional plans and the plans for different products and different countries or regions on the same basis, so that they can be consolidated into a five-year plan for the company as a whole. This is an essential and worthwhile job, but it robs the company of the major benefits of long-range planning — the opportunity to make a critical reappraisal of those few major decisions that can have an important effect on the company's future survival and profitability.

STRATEGIC PLANNING

A distinction needs to be drawn between operational planning, as described above, and strategic planning, which is a systematic process for guiding the future development of an enterprise. The most important elements in strategic planning are the *long-term* goals set by top management and the plans to achieve those goals in a thorough and systematic way. Strategic planning helps top management, on the one hand, to anticipate, and so lessen, the adverse influences of a rapidly changing business environment and, on the other, to take advantage of opportunities occurring in the environment.

This approach includes the following elements:

1 Setting company objectives
2 Appraising the enterprise's resources and capabilities
3 Analysing trends in the commercial, technological, social and political environment
4 Assessing alternative paths open to the business, and defining strategies for future development and growth

5   Producing detailed operational plans, programmes and
        budgets
6   Evaluating performance against clear criteria in the light of
        the goals, strategies and plans established.

The process has three important characteristics: first, it is
concerned with the development of integrated plans for the total
enterprise, not simply planning for a particular department or
division; second, it emphasizes long-term 'strategic' considerations as opposed to short-term 'operational' ones. A distinction
is made between extended budgets and forecasts, which often
assume little change in the status quo, and 'strategy', which typically implies a complete reappraisal of the business in relation
to its environment. Third, it envisages the establishment of formal procedures for strategic planning, which will exist in parallel
with the short-term budgeting operations. Objectives, strategies
and plans are written down and regularly reviewed, and full-
time or part-time specialists are appointed to coordinate the
planning process.

Research suggests that strategic planning has produced some
impressive results, especially in helping organizations to plan
for diversification into new fields and for expansion internationally. However, in many cases strategic planning has been rejected
or ignored by powerful groups in the enterprise, or has been
treated simply as a system of long-term forecasting or extended
budgeting, with no consideration of objectives and strategies.
Enterprises with strategic-planning systems frequently plan well
for products and markets, but are inclined to lack adequate
strategies and plans for personnel and organization, research and
development, purchasing and logistics, finance, and social and
political change.

There are, however, some who believe that even strategic planning can only be a partial answer to the problems posed by a
rapidly changing environment. In recent years the speed of
change has accelerated and it is becoming more and more important for managers at all levels to participate in the process of
altering the traditional relations between the enterprise and the
environment, creating entirely new businesses and closing down
old ones. Usually it requires a serious challenge from the environment — a major switch in demand, the appearance of a new
technology, a competitive threat, government legislation, social

protest, a takeover bid — to get management into making a
thorough reappraisal of the organization's general strategy and
implementing the radical changes necessary. The objective of
strategic management is to bring forward and carry through a
programme of change before the situation has degenerated to
the point of crisis.

INTRODUCING STRATEGIC MANAGEMENT[3]

It is suggested that managers in an enterprise have to operate in
two decision-making systems at the same time. They make
'operating decisions' that relate to buying, producing, selling and
distributing goods and services, and improving the efficiency with
which resources are used in this process. They also make 'strategic decisions', which are concerned with effecting major changes
in the 'linkages' between the enterprise and its environment. A
fundamental problem for management is to ensure that strategic
issues are not neglected owing to the pressures of the day-to-day
operation.

Strategic planning is apparently only a partial answer to this
problem. Strategic management suggests a number of ways in
which strategic planning may be developed for this purpose.

First, it suggests that the process should be viewed not as a
planning exercise by top management but rather as an organizational change programme aimed at affecting management attitudes and behaviour at many levels. This implies that a good deal
of work needs to be done in each enterprise to define in operational terms what strategic management means for each level of
management. A good example of this is provided by the American
General Electric Company which defines strategy in operational
terms as 'a statement of how what resources are going to be used
to take advantage of which opportunities to minimize which
threats to produce a desired result'. Three levels of strategic decisions are distinguished by the company: at the corporate level,
the investment decision; at the divisional level, the resource allocation decision; and at the unit level, the implementation decision.

Strategic management suggests that experiments will have to
be carried out with new organizational structures in order to discover how best to accommodate within the same enterprise:

1   Activities and staff necessary to improve productivity in the
    current operation.
2   Work and working teams specializing in the start-up and
    development of new activities.

Some writers have suggested that operational management
will tend always to neutralize or reject organizational entrepreneurs and therefore that the two groups should be in different
organizations. Taken to its logical conclusion, this might imply,
as one approach suggests, three separate companies or divisions:
one for new business development (for entrepreneurs specializing in innovation); another for new business start-up (for organ-
izational-builders whose job is to exploit potential innovations);
and a third for current business operations (for the operational
management team).

Management systems and practices also need to be revised to
give more weight to strategic considerations. More attention
should be paid to the identification and selection of managers
with skills for developing and implementing plans for radical
change. Staff-appraisal schemes may need to be changed to give
recognition to efforts directed towards the survival and growth
of the total enterprise in the long-term; at present managerial
performance tends to be measured, and promotion and salary
based on, productivity, sales or return on investment last year.
Training and development programmes are required to train a
whole generation of managers in the techniques of formulating
and implementing strategic plans. Information systems need to
incorporate better techniques for monitoring and forecasting the
enterprise's environment nationally and internationally. Operational management will need to participate in the strategic
planning process to ensure the necessary motivation to carry out
the plans.

Growth and diversification usually rest on an assumption that,
given the right opportunities, men, money, buildings, equipment
and supplies will be available. Until recently the risk of scarcity
of these resources had generally not been thought of as a potential
limiting factor on growth, or alternatively it had been assumed
that acceptable substitutes would be available in time. Quite
suddenly a widespread concern has developed that unlimited
resources may not be available and that substitutes may not be
found in time. Clearly, a resource strategy should now be a key

part of strategic management.

Many large companies are now facing major challenges not in the traditional field of competition for products and markets but through conflict with Government bodies and strong pressure groups in society. Well-known examples are conservation, pollution, safety, pricing and worker unrest. Strategic management, of itself, cannot solve the problem posed by political and social threats of this kind, but it seems likely that in the immediate future high priority will be given to the generation of systems and procedures that will assist in the preparation and implementation of strategies and plans designed to cope with social and political change. What is required is a substantial improvement in the approaches used for the:

1 Setting social objectives and defining corporate responsibilities
2 Monitoring and forecasting social and political change
3 Appraising organizational performance
4 Developing strategies and policies designed to achieve social acceptance
5 The preparation of operational plans and programmes and the measurement of the effectiveness of these programmes in gaining social acceptance and support.

IMPLICATIONS

The task falling on senior management in all types of enterprise, public and private, is to try to change the orientation of management to ensure that increased attention is paid to the strategic problem of adapting the organization to its environment. This implies not only the formulation of explicit objectives, strategies and plans but also, possibly, a number of fundamental changes in the system of organization and management, for example:

1 The retirement of some of the present management and their replacement by others who are more entrepreneurial
2 A change in leadership style and organizational culture, using modern behavioural science approaches in order to make the organization more adaptive and responsive to change in the environment
3 A change in the organizational structure, possibly the formation of divisions or operational units with considerable

autonomy, and the creation of a larger capability for
enterprise development, e.g. setting up new ventures,
introducing new products and opening up new markets
at home and abroad

4 The adoption of operational planning, programming and
budgeting systems that emphasize both efficiency in the
operation and effectiveness in implementing the objectives
and strategies of the total enterprise in relation to its
environment

5 The introduction of motivation and incentive schemes that
encourage staff not only to maximize the return on investment in the short run, but to invest in longer-term development and in projects that will increase the acceptance
of the enterprise in society

6 Staff development and training programmes that equip
managers to monitor and forecast changes in the commercial and social environment; to produce explicit objectives, strategies and plans for their part of the organization;
and to organize and implement programmes for long-
range development

7 Wider information and control systems, which keep managers
aware of environmental changes and keep a check on internal projects that are likely to affect the long-term
success of the enterprise.

A major problem with strategic planning is how to get the
process started in an enterprise that is doing well. Strategic planning is frequently the last resort of enterprises in a crisis. It is
more difficult to secure management attention for a thorough
reappraisal of the enterprise and its environment in a prosperous
organization, yet many currently successful firms have within
themselves the seeds of their own decline.

The ideal procedure is for top management to see the need
for 'self-renewal' in the organization and to set up a regular
strategic review, planning and control system to ensure that the
enterprise continues to adapt to its environment. Alternatively,
it often falls to a consultant to provide the impetus that results
in the establishment of a strategic management process. Fundamentally, however, the initiative must come from the senior
management of the enterprise.

REFERENCES

1 Taylor, Bernard and Irving, Peter. 'Organised Planning in Major U.K. Companies', *Long Range Planning,* June 1971.

2 Thune, S. S. and House, R. J. 'Where Long Range Planning Pays Off', *Business Horizons,* August 1970; Ansoff, H. Igor. 'Does Planning Pay?', *Long Range Planning,* March 1969.

3 Ansoff, H. Igor, et al, *From Strategic Planning to Strategic Management,* Wiley, London, 1976.

2 The Changing Role of Business in Society

Bryan Lowes

Recent years have witnessed the beginnings of a revolution in the attitudes of industrialized Western nations towards the role of business in society. The restricted economic motive assigned to businesses – of producing goods and services in order to earn profits – is being broadened, so that the business sector is perceived as having a range of responsibilities befitting a major institution in society. This changing philosophy is frequently characterized as a move from a 'shareholder' view of the firm to a 'stakeholder' view. The former views the company as being in business solely to make profits for its shareholders, with the claims of other interested parties – customers, employees, the community and the managers themselves – operating as constraints upon this profit goal. By contrast, the latter view acknowledges that the company owes a responsibility to all the above stakeholder groups, not just shareholders.

Businesses do not operate in a social vacuum, and if they are to ensure their long-term survival, they need to respond to the growing public criticism of their activities, and to be seen to be making a positive contribution towards meeting society's goals. This radical new philosophy is as yet in its infancy. It represents a marked departure from the profit-orientated *laissez-faire* philosophy that has held sway over the past two centuries.

ORIGINS OF THE PHILOSOPHY OF PRIVATE ENTERPRISE[1]

The system of values, goals and beliefs prevalent in western industrial society has its origins in various religious, philosophical and intellectual developments that occurred in the eighteenth and nineteenth centuries, paralleling the technological changes associated with the Industrial Revolution. These changes provided a value base to the private-enterprise market-exchange economic system we have today.

The system of values inherited from the Middle Ages had two major themes: first, religious, stressing the virtue of poverty, acceptance of one's lot in life and ultimate reward in Heaven, rather than the accumulation of treasures on Earth; second, communal, man in the Middle Ages generally seeing himself as part of a family, a village group or a craft guild, rather than as an individual.

This value system changed rapidly from the late eighteenth century onwards. On the religious front the rise of the Protestant faith brought a re-ordering of social values. Protestant groups such as the Calvinists emphasized individualism and independence, encouraging man to see himself as an entity apart from his associates. At the same time Protestantism set a seal of approval upon the accumulation of personal wealth, regarding such wealth not as means to greater pleasures on earth, but as a sign of God's favour. These various Protestant beliefs eventually developed into a coherent religious philosophy nowadays described as the Protestant Ethic, stressing the sacred nature of property, the virtue of hard work, and the significance of thrift, the accumulation of wealth and independence. Such beliefs provided fertile ground for the development of capitalism. In so far as capitalism implies conflict and competition rather than cooperation between individuals, the new concern with individualism provided it with moral justification, while the Church's sanctioning of the accumulation of wealth conferred respectability upon the pursuit of individual gain and the use of wealth to finance the further growth of businesses.

Religious developments in value systems were paralleled by developments on the philosophical and intellectual front. In the late eighteenth century the English philosopher Jeremy Bentham preached the significance of self-interest as a basis for society, while similar ideas were taken up and developed into a comprehensive and unified economic model of society in the work of Adam Smith.

Adam Smith's book *The Wealth of Nations*, published in 1776, was significant not only as an intellectual analysis of the market mechanism but also as an exposition of Smith's moral philosophy. Smith saw human conduct as motivated by such forces as self-love, a desire to be free, the habit of labour and a propensity to barter or exchange. However, in Smith's world, the pursuit of self-interest resulted not in conflict but in co-operation, because he believed in the existence of a natural order in society that prevented the benefit of any one person from conflicting with the good of others. In Smith's hands this natural order was spelled out in terms of the market mechanism, which, given competition, would lead men pursuing their own self-interest to further the common good as if guided by some 'invisible hand'. This reconciliation of individual and community interests was effected though the process of exchange in so far as profit-seeking businessmen had to produce goods other people wanted to buy if they were to be able to exchange them in com-petitive markets. Thus entrepreneurs striving in their own self-interest for larger profit had to produce goods consumers wanted, and could not overcharge for them or underpay their workers, otherwise they would lose customers to competitors or be unable to attract sufficient labour to produce the goods.

This mechanism was also capable of responding automatically to changes in society's needs, increased demand for a product leading initially to an increase in its price and the profits of manufacturers, which in turn would attract new profit-seeking producers into the industry, thus ensuring a matching expansion in supply and in the resources devoted to making the product. Given this superior dynamic 'invisible hand' of the market, any human interference by Government was felt to be undesirable, and Smith's belief in a natural order made him a strong suppor-ter of *laissez-faire*.

Smith's analysis of the market mechanism has not only pro-vided the foundation for economic theories over the past two centuries, it has also formed an essential part of the business ethic. As Kempner[2] points out: 'In time the descriptions became a justification and acquired the position of morality.' But the philosophy derived from the Protestant Ethic and its pragmatic market-model manifestations have come under increasing fire in recent decades, first on the grounds that it fails to reflect the structure of modern industrial economies, and second on the grounds that the value system on which it was based has changed.

STRUCTURAL CHANGE AND THE PATTERN OF CURRENT CORPORATE CAPITALISM

In Adam Smith's market model businessmen selfishly pursuing profits end up producing an adequate supply of the goods and services required by society in the most efficient manner and at the lowest possible price because they are subject to the discipline of the market. The discipline is assured in an economy comprised of numerous small-scale competitive firms, where, to survive, a company must be as adaptable to changing demand and as efficient as its competitors. However representative this industrial structure might have been of the economic scene at the time Smith and his successors were writing, the structure of industry is clearly different today.

The modern industrial environment is not characterized by numerous small owner-managed firms operating in rigorously competitive markets. Over the past two centuries business units have grown appreciably in size, often reducing their unit production and marketing costs as they have grown by securing economies of scale, a possibility first pointed out, paradoxically, by Smith himself. The result of this growth has been the appearance of large diversified conglomerate companies as an important feature of the modern industrial scene.

Continued growth, mergers and takeovers have produced some very large companies indeed. General Motors, for example, has larger sales than the Gross National Product of all but the dozen largest nation states.[3] The American Telephone and Telegraph Company in 1964 employed almost 1 per cent of the total U.S. labour force, produced nearly 2 per cent of the American G.N.P., and accounted for 7·5 per cent of total business spending on plant and equipment, and for 4 per cent of the total stock of capital assets of American business.[4] Clearly such corporate giants can have a significant impact upon our national life, for although few in number they hold a dominant position in industry. For example, at the end of 1963 the largest ninety-six U.K. manufacturing companies with shares quoted on the Stock Exchange controlled 65 per cent of aggregate net assets in manufacturing, though they represented less than 7 per cent of the total number of quoted companies.[5]

At the same time, increased market concentration in many industries has served to insulate firms from competitive pressures.

In many markets dominant firms possess a degree of monopoly
power that partially protects them from competitive forces,
while in other markets interdependence between a few large
sellers produces a degree of caution about price or product
changes that lessens the penalties for sub-optimal performance.
For example, in 1951 Evely and Little found that in almost a
quarter of the 220 industries they investigated the largest three
firms controlled between them 67 per cent or more of the
industrial output.[6] Clearly in such markets 'we can no longer
depend, as classical market theory held, on consumer response
alone to encourage efficiency and competition that will result
in higher quality'.[7]

The increased size and market power of the large corporations
that now dominate national economies disturbs the balance of
power inherent in Smith's market system. Such large firms
are not merely automata responding to market forces unleashed
by sovereign consumers. They have power to influence the allocation of resources, for changes in resource deployments are
no longer brought about by the growth and decline of numerous
small firms but rather by internal management decisions about
diversification, divestment, divisional transfer pricing and plant
closure in large companies whose continued existence is rarely
placed in jeopardy. Such large firms can also have an impact
upon general living standards in so far as their individual investment decisions can have a significant impact upon total investment and thus upon the level of general economic activity, and
upon rates of economic growth.

These large conglomerate companies often operate in many
markets, so that they are not tied too closely to the fortunes of
any one. In addition they generally have the resources to with-
stand temporary market setbacks. This means that they are now
less affected by sudden changes in market conditions. The resulting degree of financial security may well enable them to adopt
a longer-term planning horizon, reducing concern with day-to-
day tactical issues and allowing more time to be devoted to
strategic planning. At the same time, the divorce of ownership
from control associated with the growth of large business units
has left most big firms in the control of salaried professional
managers who do not own large numbers of shares themselves.
Such managers are likely to take a broader perspective than
would an owner-manager, and to be more concerned with long-
run company survival and growth than short-run profits.

CHANGING SOCIAL VALUES

Some businessmen continue to think about the business system in the terms first used by Adam Smith, as can be detected from their fervent pronouncements about free enterprise and their fierce opposition to Government intervention in industry. Yet the values of individualism, competition and wealth accumulation on which the free-enterprise system is based are beginning to change. We can trace various strands in this changing value system.

As standards of living in the industrialized nations rise well above the subsistence level and the majority of people become wealthier and better educated, their priorities begin to change. Specifically, we might expect them to become less materialist and less orientated towards further economic growth. Other aspects of the quality of life, such as job satisfaction, job security, a 'clean' environment and adequate leisure facilities, become important as people's needs for consumer goods are satisfied. As Votaw[8] put it: 'In a land of scarcity, economics is king; in a land of plenty, economics is just another member of the court.' This reduced concentration on economic growth in the industrialized nations and concern with pollution and other costs associated with growth may well have an ultimate effect on growth aspirations of business firms.

Individualism in society has waned as belief in the harmonization of self-interest and social well-being has come under increasing attack. Critics have pointed to the inadequacy of the 'invisible hand' in dealing with problems of pollution where normal market forces do not apply, with the result that companies have pursued self-interest at the expense of the community at large. At the same time, urbanization associated with the growth of industry has served to heighten the sense of interdependence between people, and to highlight the need for cooperative rather than individual action to tackle economic and social problems.

Finally society shows signs of rejecting the Darwinian doctrine of survival of the fittest implied by the competitive philosophy. We are no longer content to allow a harsh competitive system to benefit the strong and weed out the weak and unsuccessful. There is an increasing concern for the problems of the old, the sick and the underprivileged. One way in which this concern has manifested itself has been an increasing tendency

to judge questions of income distribution in terms of fairness
and equity rather than supply and demand.

These changing social trends have created a new, questioning
mood in society about the role of business, and have led to the
emergence of various pressure groups concerned with particular
aspects of the business/society interface:

1   Recognizing that consumer sovereignty cannot be ensured
    in a situation where productive resources in many indus-
    tries are concentrated in the hands of a few large com-
    panies, and where products are becoming more technically
    complex, various consumerist groups have grown up; the
    most notable is that led by Ralph Nader in the United
    States. These groups have concerned themselves with such
    issues as the safety and quality of products, the effects
    of persuasive advertising in stimulating demand, better
    information to allow consumers to make more informed
    choices between brands, etc.
2   Large-scale plants and improvements in technology have
    increased the capability of business to affect the physical
    environment. In response to this threat environmentalist
    groups such as the Friends of the Earth have emerged.
    These have concerned themselves with such general
    themes as depletion of world resources and pollution
    problems, as well as with such more specific issues as
    non-biodegradable packaging and non-returnable con-
    tainers.
3   As Graham Turner[9] points out: 'Shareholders put money
    into a business; workers often invest their lives.' The con-
    sequent concern with issues of job security and job satis-
    faction, and the pressure for a greater say in how firms
    are run through industrial democracy movements, is
    hardly surprising. These trends could well be interpreted
    as a reaction to the growth of large, relatively impersonal
    organizations in which decision-takers are remote from
    employees.

In addition to these three major interest groups one can also
identify various smaller groups, such as those pressing for equal
employment and promotion prospects for women, immigrant
workers, ex-prisoners and other disadvantaged people.

The importance of these interest groups is that they serve to focus public opinion on the activities of particular companies and to publicize their failings in these various respects: for example, the safety of certain General Motors models, the use of non-returnable bottles by Schweppes, etc. This pressure of public opinion makes itself felt in two major ways. It has a direct effect over time on the ethical and moral standards of the managers running companies. As Anthony[10] points out: 'A businessman is a human being and it is completely unrealistic to assume that he should act in an ethical vacuum.' Thus we see managers themselves becoming more aware and concerned about problems like pollution. In addition, public opinion has an indirect effect in so far as it generates political pressures and can lead to changes in legislation affecting business.

THE RESPECTIVE ROLES OF GOVERNMENT AND BUSINESS

As deficiencies in the market mechanism's role of automatic regulator of economic activity have become more and more apparent, the policy of *laissez-faire* has crumbled and Government intervention in industry has grown. Though from the earliest days Governments intervened to regulate the worst excesses of unrestrained business with child labour and factory safety legislation, at first they were hesitant about regulating business. But from the 1940s onwards Governments have adopted more positive approaches. A major increase in Government intervention followed the 1930s' depression, when the inability of the market system to ensure full employment was exposed and Government accepted responsibility for demand management policies to regulate the level of total output and the price level. Since then Government regulation has grown rapidly, with monopolies and restrictive practices legislation to curb the exercise of market power by large firms; legislation to veto mergers that might create business units with excessive market power; regional policies to influence the geographic location of new plants; air and water pollution control legislation; prices and incomes controls; employment legislation to provide minimum redundancy payments and detailed contracts of employment; and consumer protection legislation concerned with the honest description of products, correct labelling and product safety.

As well as such direct Government regulations as prices and incomes controls, Government's growing concern with business gives it further influence over businesses' ethical standards. As a major customer Government can exert influence through the incorporation of such devices as fair wages clauses in its purchasing contracts. In its role as a provider of capital for various joint projects, and as a major shareholder in certain companies, Government can give an ethical lead to companies. As ultimate controller of the nationalized industries the Government can create a favourable environment for pioneering social policies, such as the introduction of worker directors within the British Steel Corporation, and landscaping efforts by the National Coal Board. Finally, within the forum of joint industry-government planning institutions such as the National Economic Development Office and the various 'little Neddies' for specific industries, Government can ensure that such issues as the social implications of growth policies receive adequate attention.

The governments of all industrial nations are now to a greater or lesser degree concerned with regulating business, and one cannot foresee them reducing their level of intervention even if businesses voluntarily curb the anti-social side-effects of their activities and commit themselves to various socially beneficial programmes — for as Steiner[11] reminds us, 'Business is a predominant instrument of society in dealing with social problems, but not the institution of sole or last responsibility'. Only Government has the ultimate responsibility, and it is increasingly accepting this responsibility.

Some critics of social responsibility in business argue that Government should be responsible for social policies and that business should stick to its economic role of making profits. These critics stress the nature of companies as economic institutions whose obligations to society stop at the creation of goods and services, provision of jobs and payment of taxes. Michael Beesley in a recent Stockton lecture[12] endorses this view, suggesting that 'If the common aims of securing growth and desirable social ends are to be sensibly maintained, a rigorous . . . framework is essential. The prime responsibility for setting this out is government's'. Such a framework would establish legal controls to limit company profit-seeking behaviour in areas like factory safety and consumer protection and might also provide subsidies to companies bearing the costs of such socially desirable but unprofitable programmes as manpower retraining. However, within this framework companies would continue to operate in a profit-seeking manner.

Yet if businesses confine themselves to their traditional economic role, curbing their profit-seeking behaviour only to the extent that they are required by law, then they will always appear to the public to be exercising their great power irresponsibly. Business is only tolerated by society as long as it is a net contributor to community welfare, and if businesses are continually seen to be resisting attempts to control the more anti-social side-effects of their behaviour and only grudgingly curbing such behaviour when forced by legislation, then the clamour for even tighter control by Government over business and pressure for the taking of larger firms into public ownership will undoubtedly grow. To pre-empt excessively harsh controls it is in the interests of large companies to go at least part of the way to meeting the legitimate objections of their critics.

IMPLICATIONS OF SOCIAL CHANGE FOR MODERN BUSINESS

In the future large companies will need to pursue certain minimum social objectives over and above the legal minima, if they are to achieve a degree of public tolerance necessary to ensure their long-run survival. And although ' . . . there might be serious questions of equity involved in asking corporate executives to tackle social problems with money belonging to other people (i.e. their stockholders)',[13] the long-term view should convince them that they must come to regard the costs of meeting social responsibilities as part of the normal costs of doing business.

This has implications for planning procedures in the large company. In setting company objectives as a basis for planning, companies will have to give due weight to non-profit goals, integrating them along with economic targets into the formal corporate planning process. Of course, company objectives will still attach a high priority to profit goals, for without profits companies cannot survive in the short run or grow in the longer term. A minimum level of profits is necessary to provide internal finance for investment programmes and to pay adequate dividends to facilitate the raising of further external capital and

avoid possible takeover bids. Therefore the company cannot
bear all the costs of social programmes out of profits and may
have to pass some of them on in higher prices to consumers.
On the other hand, any enterprise following a course that conflicts with society's values will not be tolerated in the long term,
however commercially successful it may be. To ensure long-term
survival the large company must attach due weight to non-
profit goals, foregoing some short-term profits in the interests
of harmony with society.

Formulation of social goals immediately leads managers into
largely unknown territory. As Adams[14] elegantly puts it: 'The
situation is one where new power and responsibility has been
acquired, where decisions have to be taken where there are no
precedents and where there is no world-wide acceptance of
what constitutes a just or good society'. Senior company managers have responded to this problem in two main ways.

First, increasing efforts have been devoted to formulating
ethical codes to guide businessmen in their planning and
decision-making. The Watkinson Report represents one attempt
to develop 'A set of principles . . . which we believe should
guide corporate conduct'.[15] Such codes can help managers in
making decisions in the grey area lying between the minimum
standard required by law and the usually higher standards demanded by current public opinion, for by its very nature legislation tends to lag behind changing social attitudes, so that:
'The law sets minimum standards of conduct. But it does not,
and cannot, embody the whole duty of man; and mere compli-
ance with the law does not necessarily make a good citizen or
a good company'.[16]

Second, initial attempts are being made to monitor social
attitudes towards such issues as pollution, product safety, urban
decay and minority hiring. This is necessary because attitudes
now change rapidly, so that, as Bauer and Fenn[17] point out,
'Social responsibility is a moving target'. By using survey techniques companies may be able to derive information about
community attitudes and expectations as a guide to formulating appropriate responses.[18]

To ensure that information about the company's environment is properly analysed and its implications promptly considered, certain changes in the organizational structure of the
company may be required. One possibility is the establishment

of an external affairs or social responsibility department to
act as the principal interface between the company and the
community. Such a department could report direct to senior
managers, briefing them on relevant social trends and focusing
attention on the social implications of company decisions.
It could also serve as a major information channel for publiciz-
ing the company's social contributions and as a major instigator
of long-run social plans. The large number of companies that
have created such departments in recent years[19] testifies to their
potential value.

As well as attempting to assess what is currently expected of
them by society, managers also need to be able to gauge the
current social contribution being made by their company if
they are to plan appropriate programmes to help fill any gap
between the two. Interest in evaluating current social performance has led to the development of social responsibility audits.
Few companies have, to date, undertaken such audits, so it is
difficult to talk in terms of a standard method for measuring
social contribution. However, a start has been made by researchers
such as Bauer and Fenn,[20] and no doubt the technique will increasingly be used and refined in future years.

Having gauged what society expects of them and assessed
their current contribution, managers can then plan to undertake social programmes in those areas where their company's
particular resources and skills allow them to make the best
contribution. This, though, is not the end of the problem, for
senior managers may well encounter difficulties in implementing
such programmes. If social objectives are to be achieved, long-
and short-term social plans need to be formulated and appropriate control information collected to monitor performance
in relation to these plans. Without expansion of the traditional
profit-orientated budgeting system to report on-going social
performance and offer rewards for the achievement of social
goals, managers will not be suitably motivated to strive for
such goals with the enthusiasm devoted to profit targets. To ensure that social programmes are given sufficient weight alongside profit goals might well entail additions to the company's
budgeting and accounting systems.[21]

The assumption of social commitments by senior company
managers will not be an easy task, but certainly it is a necessary
and inevitable one. Looking to the future, we may well find

some truth in Neil Jacoby's prediction that 'Corporate managers in the 1990 s will be deeply involved in the measurement of social attitudes and expectations and in designing corporate responses to them . . . Although profit optimization will continue to be the central goal of business and the master criterion for judging managerial performance, stockholders will expect managers to act with enlightenment in a long-term framework'.[22]

REFERENCES

1 For a fuller exposition of the ideas presented in this section, see McGuire, J. W. *Business and Society* (McGraw-Hill, 1963), ch. 2 and 4.

2 Kempner, T. 'The Changing Role of Business in Society', *Journal of General Management,* Autumn 1973, vol. 1, no. 1, p. 68.

3 Monsen, R. J. *Business and the Changing Environment* (McGraw-Hill, 1973), p. 108.

4 Kuhn, J. W. and Berg, I. *Values in a Business Society* (Harcourt Brace & World, 1968), p. 59.

5 Utton, M. A. *Industrial Concentration* (Penguin, 1970), p. 65.

6 For a review of this and other concentration studies, see George, K. D. *Industrial Organisation* (George Allen & Unwin, 1971).

7 Nader, R. (ed.). *The Consumer and Corporate Accountability* (Harcourt Brace Jovanovich Inc., 1973), p. 5.

8 Votaw, D. 'Genius Becomes Rare: A Comment on the Doctrine of Social Responsibility', *California Management Review,* Winter 1972, vol. 15, no. 2, p. 30.

9 Turner, G. *Towards a New Philosophy for Industry and Society,* Ashridge Papers in Management Studies, p. 10.

10 Anthony, R. N. 'The Trouble with Profit Maximisation', *Harvard Business Review,* November 1960, vol. 38, p. 132.

11 Steiner, G. A. *Business and Society* (New York: Random House, 1971), p. 152.

12 Beesley, M. Second Stockton Lecture, reported in the *Sunday Times,* 15 February, 1973.

13 Burck, G. 'The Hazards of Corporate Responsibility', *Fortune,* June 1973, p. 115.

14 Adams, K. 'The Impact of Business on Changing Social Values', *Journal of Business Policy*, Summer 1973, vol. 3, no. 4, p. 52.
15 *The Responsibilities of the British Public Company*, Final Report of C.B.I. Company Affairs Committee, 1973, p. 4.
16 Ibid., p. 8.
17 Bauer, R. A. and Fenn, D. H. 'What is a Corporate Social Audit?', *Harvard Business Review*, January—February 1973, vol. 5, no. 1, p. 41.
18 See Worcester, R. M. 'Monitoring Public Attitudes to Business', *Journal of General Management*, Autumn 1973, vol. 1, no. 1.
19 See Eilbert, H. and Parket, I. R. 'The Corporate Responsibility Officer: A New Position in the Organisation Chart', *Business Horizons*, February 1973, vol. XVI, no. 1.
20 Bauer, R. A. and Fenn, D. H. *The Corporate Social Audit* (New York: Russell Sage Foundation, 1973).
21 See Lowes, B. and Sparkes, J. R. 'Social Responsibility Accounting', *Journal of Business Policy*, Summer 1973, vol. 3, no. 4.
22 Jacoby, N. H. *Corporate Power and Social Responsibility: A Blueprint for the Future* (New York: Macmillan, 1973), p. 260.

3 Strategic Planning for Social and Political Change

Bernard Taylor

INTRODUCTION

Formalized planning at the moment is applied to planning for operations and capital investment, planning for products and markets, and occasionally for manpower. However, there is little evidence that companies are producing formal plans and programmes to deal with social and political change. Public opinion is moving against business, action groups inside and outside companies are challenging the authority of management, and public officials and politicians are already framing laws and regulations. Unless managers begin to take more interest in the framing of these controls, they are likely to find laws enacted and enforced by people who have little knowledge or sympathy with business. In this chapter it is suggested that senior managers and their staff advisors should assess the social and political challenge to their business, and formulate and implement social and political strategies and plans aimed at ensuring the survival and prosperity of their organizations.

THE SIZE OF THE PROBLEM

To put the strength of the social and political challenge to business in perspective, it is only necessary to recall some well-known examples of companies that have recently faced major crisis because of social and political pressures. For example, the General Electric Company was fined by the U.S. Government and was sued by customers for price-fixing. General Motors' management have had to revise their product designs, largely through the efforts of Nader's Raiders. ITT management have come under federal investigation for their political activities at home and in Chile. BP and some other oil companies have for many years been barred from extracting Alaskan oil because of the likely destruction of the tundra. The Distillers Company has been forced by public demand and by pressure from institutional shareholders to pay £20 million in compensation to Thalidomide victims. Albright and Wilson, a large British chemical company, had to close down a plant in Newfoundland to avoid damaging the fisheries. The workers at Upper Clyde Shipbuilders refused to have their shipyard closed down, organized a 'sit-in' and helped to arrange a merger with an American company. Automobile workers in the U.S.A. and in various parts of Europe appear to be rebelling against the mass-production system by strikes, non-cooperation and even sabotage, and are demanding a say in the redesign of their working environment.

There is also an impressive list of legal measures affecting business in many parts of the Western world. There is legislation concerned with the public interest in terms of monopoly and takeover, consumer protection, price control, pollution control and environmental protection. There are laws to protect the employee, and to ensure safety and good working conditions; and laws establishing new systems of industrial relations, retirement and sickness benefits, industrial training, and equal job opportunities for women, ethnic and national minorities. Finally, there are laws concerning industrial democracy and various forms of public ownership.

Recent public-opinion polls in the U.S.A. and Britain emphasize that business and businessmen have never fallen lower in the public esteem. The opinion polls also suggest that a majority of the public (and a majority of workers in major companies) believe that private companies have a responsibility to help solve important social problems and should do *more* than is legally required to improve the quality of the environment.[1]

DEFINING OBJECTIVES AND SOCIAL RESPONSIBILITIES

In response to this challenge from society leading businessmen in Europe and in the U.S.A. are re-examining and redefining their social responsibilities. In the U.S.A., for example, the Committee for Economic Development has outlined ten areas where business can help in solving social problems (Figure 3.1),[2] and in Britain the Confederation of British Industry has prepared a Code of Behaviour for business.[3]

In the public debate about the social responsibilities of business, economists, politicians and businessmen are expressing a wide spectrum of opinions. At one extreme there are traditionalists who agree with Milton Friedman that 'the one and only social responsibility of business is to increase its profits',[4] and at the other extreme there are the liberals who say, like Michel Crozier, that 'profit has become a measure . . . but it is no more the end'.[5] In fact, of course, to survive and prosper

1. *Economic growth and efficiency*
   — employment, innovation, price control, etc.

2. *Education*
   — management and financing of colleges and schools.

3. *Employment and training*
   — helping disadvantaged groups, women, aged, and sick.

4. *Civil rights and equal opportunity*
   — help to ethnic and racial groups.

5. *Urban renewal and development*
   — low-cost housing, shopping centres, transportation.

6. *Pollution abatement*
   — improving facilities, recycling materials, cooperating locally.

7. *Conservation and recreation*
   — preserving recreation areas, trees and animals.

8. *Culture and the arts*
   — giving support and advice.

9. *Medical care*
   — improvement of community health services.

10. *Government*
    — support reform and help to improve management.

    Source: Social Responsibility of Business Corporations (Committee for Economic Development 1972).

Figure 3.1   Defining social responsibilities: Ten areas where business can help.

a business needs to make a profit, *and* it must be acceptable in the eyes of society. There is also, however, a moral issue, and that is how far businessmen *should* go in trying to solve the problems of society. Businessmen in every firm need to face this issue and to define for their own organization what they believe are their moral and social obligations to the local community in which they operate, to society at large, to their workers, their customers, their shareholders, and to distributors and suppliers, many of whom depend on them for their livelihood.

The implications of this debate are well illustrated by the view currently being propagated in General Electric, which was the pioneer of the marketing concept. The management of General Electric still see their business as a process for converting resources such as labour, money and raw materials into profits through providing efficient customer service. Now, however, they see the whole process wrapped round by pressures from society and Government (see Figure 3.2).[6] The original marketing idea that a business exists to satisfy a customer need is being challenged just as strongly as the financial or legal view that management should aim to make the maximum return to the shareholders.

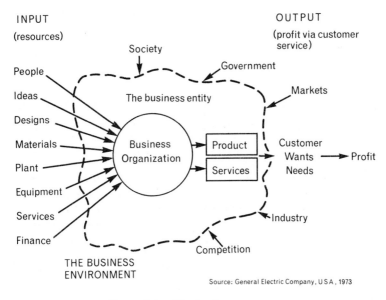

Figure 3.2   The business process.

DEVELOPING SOCIAL POLICIES AND PROGRAMMES

The following are three approaches businessmen may find use-ful in assessing the social priorities for their businesses:

Attitude Studies

It is clearly important to monitor and, if possible, forecast changes in the attitudes of the firm's employees, customers, shareholders, Government officials and various opinion leaders in society. Figures 3.3 and 3.4 show how attitude studies were used to monitor the demand for Government control of prices and public concern about pollution.[7]

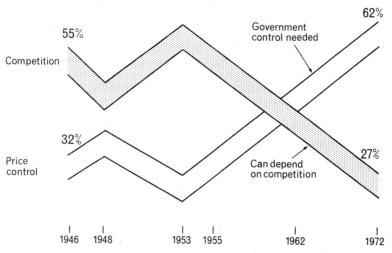

Figure 3.3   Monitoring public opinion about business: need for price control (U.S.A.). Source: Opinion Research Corporation.

Figure 3.3 shows how, in the face of growing inflation, the public in the U.S.A. has become more and more convinced of the need for Government control of prices. It was possible for businessmen to monitor this trend and to foresee the present price control regulations. Figure 3.4 shows the way that, first in the U.S.A. and then in Britain, the public has become increas-ingly worried about water and air pollution. The graph shows how management in the United Kingdom might have forecast the trend in Britain by examining the results for the United

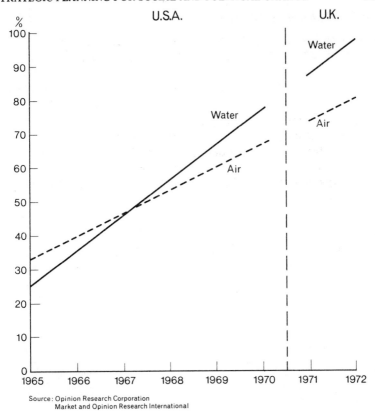

Source: Opinion Research Corporation
Market and Opinion Research International

Figure 3.4   Public opinion surveys (U.S. and U.K.): 'the problem of water/air pollution is serious'.

States. In these days of instant communications public opinion in Europe often follows a movement in the U.S.A.

The Social Responsibility Audit

Management may also wish to carry out a corporate appraisal — what John Humble and others have called a social responsibility audit — asking, for a whole range of topics concerned with the internal and external environment of the firm, 'In my organization what are the Strengths? Weaknesses? Opportunities? Threats? And what action should we take?'[8]

The Social Priority Analysis

Managers may also find useful a technique that has been used at
General Electric for the analysis of social priorities. First they
listed the major demands of various pressure groups in society.
Next they rated these according to 'intensity', i.e. the emphasis
which they were given by each pressure group (see Figure 3.5a).
Finally they listed what they regarded as the most important
long-term social trends, asked whether these changes would be
likely to strengthen or reduce the demands of the pressure
groups, and weighted each demand accordingly for 'convergence'
(see Figure 3.5b). The results of the General Electric analysis are
given in Figure 3.6.[9]

Major demands	Consumer	Conserv-ation	Racial	Women	Etc.
Marketing					
Production					
Personnel					
International					
Etc.					Rank intensity 1-4

Source: Virgil B. Day, General Electric Company

Figure 3.5(a)   Analysis of social priorities: pressure groups.

Major demands	Affluence	Education	Quality of life	Urban-ization	Etc.
Marketing					
Production					
Personnel					
International					
Etc.					Rank convergence 1-10

Source: Virgil B. Day, General Electric Company

Figure 3.5(b)   Analysis of social priorities: social trends.

1. *Constraints on company growth*
   — control of mergers, diversification, prices, taxation.

2. *Public control*
   — control of pollution, product safety, advertising, ownership.

3. *Constraints on industrial relations*
   — legislation on benefits, etc., stronger unions.

4. *Managing the 'new work force'*
   — participation, job enrichment, minorities, women.

5. *Power within the company*
   — wider board representation, disclosure.

6. *Partnership with public bodies*
   — pollution, urban development, social problems.

Source: Virgil B. Day, Vice-President, General Electric Company, 1972.

Figure 3.6   Key public issues for business.

DEVELOPING POLITICAL POLICIES AND PROGRAMMES

In the face of the current social and political attack on business, businessmen must take more part in local and national politics. Business pressure groups do exist, and they compete with others for political influence, but a recent study by the Conference Board suggests that in America businessmen tend to be passive or negative in their approach. In their survey 63 per cent of respondents said that they reviewed legislative issues continuously or frequently, and 50 per cent said that they made frequent representations to government, mostly protesting against legislation. But only 5 per cent of managements said they were making positive proposals for introducing new legislation.[10]

Managers in the Western countries might learn from the developing countries, where businessmen have had long experience in influencing Government legislation on business affairs. In the developing world managers are forced to make their policies and plans in collaboration with Government officials, who produce the national five-year plan and grant production licences and permission to use scarce local currency for the import of know-how, machinery and raw materials. Liaison with Government officials and with politicians is a professional job requiring the recruitment of former senior civil servants and other specialists to act as company representatives to Government. The process necessitates the preparation of positive proposals for legislation and the mustering of social and political support for the measures proposed.[11]

ORGANIZATION AND IMPLEMENTATION

As regards the organization of political programmes, four main points emerge:

1 In most large companies there appears to be a need for a central policy or coordinating department. Currently 12 per cent of major U.S. companies have departments of urban of community affairs. General Motors has a committee of external directors called the Public Policy Committee, and General Electric has a Business Environment Department. In Europe, too, large companies are now forming departments of public and social affairs: the British Steel Corporation has a Social and Regional Policy Department and IBM (U.K.) has an External Affairs Department.

2 Secondly, there is the problem of motivating operating managers to give priority to social programmes. Managers typically concentrate on matters where they are criticized or rewarded. The manager is likely to ask himself who is likely to get promotion: Manager A who develops social programmes and builds social acceptance for the company, or Manager B who gets 10 per cent over his annual profit or productivity target?

     A related question for management is how will these social policies affect profits? Are line managers liable to over-react or to embrace social responsibility as an alibi for poor performance?

3 The new social challenge to business also has important implications for project planning. Managers who have long been working in socially sensitive areas — for example, in open-cast mining and the siting of electric power stations — find it necessary to plan well in advance, to have a variety of possible sites available and to include social and political aspects as important considerations in their project plans. Increasingly, for most projects, social and

political considerations must appear as a matter of routine on project plans.

4   Finally we must look at risk. It must be remembered that planning can only reduce uncertainty. It cannot eliminate risk entirely. In the current challenging social and political climate the political risk to business is substantially increased. The planner therefore needs to make his contingency plans, so that the company will not suffer serious losses if a particular project fails because of social or political opposition. This argues for diversifying the business interest geographically and in terms of types of business, and keeping fixed inflexible investments at a minimum. It also suggests the need for Government participation in risky ventures.

Managers must be made aware that they have two sets of obligations: 'operational', i.e. achieving productivity or profitability for their particular department or division in the short term, and 'strategic', i.e. looking after the survival and profitability of the total enterprise in the long term. This strategic responsibility (which includes a duty to promote the acceptance of the firm in society) needs to be emphasized by management, and it also should be reinforced by the management system. In General Electric headquarters there is a specialist employed to review their management system (i.e. selection, training, payment, appraisal, promotion and other procedures) to ensure that they achieve the right balance between these two sets of priorities.

THE ROLE OF THE PLANNER

What, then, should the corporate planner do to initiate and co-ordinate this process of strategic planning for social and political change?

1   *From past experience with strategic problems we know that the planner's first task will usually be to convince top management that there is a problem — that the company is facing, or may in the future meet, an important social and political challenge.*

Most managers see their critics inside and outside the company as a vociferous and untypical minority. It takes a major crisis for them to realize that social values have changed and the criticisms being raised may be widely felt to be valid.

When a company management is out of step with its workers and with society generally, then we may expect that the last group of people to realize this will be the present top management. The recent history of General Motors, General Electric, Distillers and other leading companies amply illustrates this point. Occasionally the times throw up a leader with unusual breadth of vision who is able to perceive the social trends even when they imply criticism of his own organization, but this is not very common.

Management blindness has caused a number of academics and researchers to see an important role for the planner as a 'licensed revolutionary', one of Shakespeare's fools who 'speaks the unspeakable' and tells top management what they are doing wrong. To some extent planners and consultants are always holding a mirror up to management, so that they can appraise themselves and their organizations more clearly. However, there are precise limits to the criticism top management will accept even from a respected member of senior staff, and the history of planning is filled with stories of planners who left their organizations because they gave advice that was honest but unacceptable.

2   *The second problem of the planner in the social and political area is to help top managers to define their attitudes to social responsibilities.*

This is another difficult area. These attitudes will be a function of the top managers' personal values, and the research that has been done into the setting of objectives and policies among boards of directors suggests that there is a great deal of conflict and confusion in this area. However, the corporate planner needs to know what is the position of the chief executive or the ruling caucus in relation to social issues, e.g. whether they wish to take a lead in the business community and so achieve more social acceptance and visibility for their firm; whether

they would prefer to wait for others to take the lead;
or whether they would like to fight new legislation and
pay the cost, e.g. of pollution control, only when they
are legally forced to do so.

3   *The third task is to formulate a strategy, e.g. guidelines for
divisions, and to set up programmes designed to ensure
that the firm achieves social acceptance, with profitability in the long term.*

In developing a strategy it is worthwhile examining
three approaches which are currently being used and
were discussed earlier. The first is the use of attitude
research on employees, the public, shareholders and
Government officials. The second is John Humble's suggestion that we need a corporate appraisal – a kind of
check-list approach, which he calls a social responsibility
audit. The third is a system for analysing social and political priorities by listing the demands being made, ranking
them according to the emphasis they are given by powerful pressure groups, and forecasting whether they are likely
to become more or less important in the future in the light
of identifiable social trends.

4   *Just as war may be seen as an extension of political action,
so politics can be viewed as a development of social action.
And corporate strategies for coping with social and political change should logically include political policies and
programmes.*

This is something that most businessmen learn out of
sheer necessity. But the pattern of corporation politics
is already established in areas where Government influence
is strongly felt, e.g. in developing countries and in quasi-
public enterprises such as electric utilities and telephone
companies. Once the political arena has been identified
as a major area for competition, political strategies and
programmes tend to be evolved in familiar ways – by the
analysis of resources (finance, organization, regional influence, etc.), the assessment of competition, the formation of alliances (e.g. in trade associations) and the development of positive political programmes.

5   *Next, the planner faces the long-term problem of how to
make the management more socially and politically sensitive.*

This will mean selling the social policies and programmes inside and outside the organization, and training management in implementing these programmes at various levels and in different contexts. It will also probably mean establishing a group of specialist staff at headquarters to monitor social trends and keep management informed, and help to develop new policies and programmes as they are required.

It will be necessary, too, to reflect these new management priorities in the appraisal and reward system, so that staff will know that if they do not implement the new social programmes, their salary level and promotion prospects may suffer.

The company should also review its systems and procedures for planning and controlling the development of major projects. Product plans and plans for new facilities need to take account of social and political aspects, as a matter of routine. It is also likely that project plans will have to build in longer lead times and a larger number of alternatives to provide for delays and failures resulting from social and political protests.

6   *Finally the planner must ask in what other ways he may minimize the social and political risk to the company.*

It may be necessary to reduce the company's investment in areas of the world that are politically unstable, to withdraw from socially sensitive projects or to enter joint ventures where Government or other companies will share the risk.

REFERENCES

1 See Worcester, R. 'Monitoring and Forecasting Public Opinion about Business', *Journal of General Management,* Autumn 1973, vol. 1, no. 1.
2 Research and Policy Committee of the Committee for Economic Development. *Social Responsibility of Business Corporations* (New York: Committee for Economic Development, 1971), p. 37.
3 'Bernard Taylor Interviews Lord Watkinson', *Journal of General Management,* Autumn 1973, vol. 1, no. 1.

4 Friedman, Milton. *Capitalism and Freedom* (University of Chicago Press, 1962), p. 133.

5 Crozier, Michel. 'A New Rationale for American Business', from Goldstein, Eli, *et al. The American Business Corporation* (MIT Press, 1973).

6 Michel, Kenneth O. 'Design of an Intrafirm Management Development Programme for Strategic Management', International Conference on Strategic Management (Vanderbilt University, May 1973).

7 Worcester, R. op. cit.

8 See Humble, John. *Social Responsibility in a Changing Environment* (London: Foundation for Business Responsibility, 1973), pp. 23—57.

9 See Day, Virgil. 'Business Priorities in a Changing Environment', *Journal of General Management,* Autumn 1973, vol. 1, no. 1.

10 *The Role of Business in Public Affairs,* Studies in Public Affairs, no. 2 (New York: National Industrial Conference Board, 1968), pp. 8—10.

11 Moddie, A. 'Corporate Planning and Public Policy in India', *Journal of Business Policy,* Autumn 1972, vol. 3, no. 1.

Part II
Monitoring and Forecasting
the Business Environment

4 The Role of Forecasting and the Problem of Uncertainty

John R. Sparkes

FORECASTING AND PLANNING

Forecasting is concerned with predicting the future, and business planning with making decisions that are based upon some assessment of the future. Forecasting is then a means of helping business to cope with the uncertainty of the future. The more accurate the forecast made for planning, the more useful it will be. But precision in forecasting is not always the most important thing. Accurate forecasts of sales, for example, are very important in the short run so far as production scheduling is concerned, but forecasting sales, say ten years ahead, does not need the same kind of precision. The more important feature in the long run is the trend and probable range of sales; the purpose of such forecasting is to put the business in a better position to anticipate the future. In this way forecasting, while not a means of avoiding uncertainty, serves to *lessen* uncertainty about the future.

Although it is difficult to generalize, companies' planning procedures are usually built around three different planning horizons. The *short term* generally covers a period of one or two years ahead, the first year often being the annual budget against which management performance is assessed. The *medium term* is concerned with a period of between two and five years ahead and requires forecasts for each sector in which a company is (or is likely to be) engaged during the planning period. The *long term* plan is more a 'broad-brush' strategic appraisal, looking ahead over ten or more years and seeking to identify those sectors where major opportunities or threats may lie.

How short-term, medium-term and long-term plans fit into the planning cycle is clearly a matter for the individual company, but there must invariably be overlap between the different planning horizons. Short-term and medium-term plans may be combined so that the first year or first two years of the medium-term plan becomes the forecast for the short-term. The long-term plan may be combined with the medium-term plan, which in any event will normally incorporate both strategic (long-term) and tactical (short-term) planning characteristics. Even for short-term planning a check with long-term trends is often useful. While we need to remember, therefore, that there are different planning horizons, we equally need to realize the links between them. Our discussion of the role of forecasting in corporate planning should be seen against this interdependence of the various planning horizons.

The Need for Forecasting

Everybody makes forecasts, because forecasting derives from the economic problem that confronts every individual. The problem is that an individual's wants are unlimited while his means are limited. This problem of scarcity, if only that of allocating time between competing alternative uses, gives rise to the need for choice, and this decision-taking process is based on some assessment of likely results. Even if we do not make explicit forecasts, we at least make assumptions about the future in connection with our current actions.

Similarly the businessman has no choice but to forecast. The production manager needs sales forecasts in order to plan future production; the financial manager has to budget for cash needs; the personnel manager needs forecasts of the availability of labour for purposes of manpower planning, etc. Whatever a company's objectives, its efforts to achieve them inevitably call for the formulation of expectations about the future. All such forecasting is directed at reducing the uncertainty surrounding the future. But in the context of business planning the need for some *explicit* forecasting procedure emerges. Among all the possible forces that can affect a business, those significant to the individual business need to be identified. Only by systematic analysis of the future can a company isolate those variables that are important to itself; and it can do this only if it first evaluates the accuracy of past estimates as a basis for correcting forecasting procedure. In this respect the company needs not only to record what is happening at the present but also to have some means of judging what has happened in the past.

Limitations of Business Forecasting

Experience of the past is the best guide we have to the future. The adequacy and reliability of recorded data is therefore a particularly important problem, and one of the major limitations on business forecasting. But its very existence alerts us to the importance of judgement in forecasting, especially in interpreting data, in selecting methods of analysis and in applying them to specific problems.

There is a very wide range of methods of forecasting, from the completely intuitive type to the highly mathematical. But whatever the method employed all forecasters face three major problems:

1   *Identification.* For almost any important forecast the causal factors entering into the forecast are too numerous for them all to be taken into account in any systematic fashion. The identification problem is therefore one of isolating the key strategic variables causing change.
2   *Measurement.* Measurement is complicated by the fact that relations that have been observed to hold in the past cannot be assumed to hold precisely in the future.
3   *Sequence.* The sequence of cause and effect between relations is subject to variation with changes in the environment within which they operate.

Corporate long-range planning requires that the company continuously seek to identify, first, those industries and markets in which, as future changes take place, major opportunities or threats may lie; and, second, those areas of its business that are potential sources of strength or weakness. In which of its existing areas of business does a company want to increase its commitment? From which does it want to break away? What *new* areas of business are likely to offer opportunites? How do these fit in with existing activities? In seeking to answer such questions managers will find no simple formula to tell them which variables to forecast. It is for each company to determine systematically in the light of its own strategic objectives which factors have a high probability of significant impact on the company.

The limitations of business forecasting mentioned above require that forecasts presented in a way suggesting great precision should be treated with caution. It is impossible to describe future events precisely, since one can never eliminate the uncertainty that attaches to the future. Single-figure forecasts, which attach only one value to the forecast variable, are very rarely realized, and if they are, it will be as much by good luck as by good forecasting. Under the conditions of uncertainty surrounding forecasts the single-figure prediction inevitably becomes hedged round with qualifications, and even hopelessly blurred. Uncertainty, if it is to be properly handled, requires that the forecaster defines different possibilities and evaluates the likelihood of their occurring. To be of value in corporate planning, the forecast must be susceptible to checking after the event. Given the margin of error that surrounds such a forecast, a single-figure forecast should therefore have some form of probability attached to it, if only in order to give it the capability of verification. Furthermore, by thinking in terms of probabilities, the business forecaster is adopting a systematic approach to the problem of reducing uncertainty.

SENSITIVITY AND RISK ANALYSIS

By using past data the forecaster can analyse the effects of making alternative assumptions about what is now known. He will be able to assess the sensitivity of forecasts of some dependent variable such as sales, say, to variations in the forecasts of numbers of such independent variables as incomes, credit terms, etc.[1] (See Model building, p. 57.) The purpose of such an analysis is to identify the *significant* variables in the forecast (sometimes referred to as 'key factor analysis') as well as to show the extent to which the forecast of the dependent variable is sensitive to variations in the forecast values of the independent variable.

The fact that the values of the independent variables have themselves to be forecast means that although the critical factors have been isolated, alterations in these key determining forces will cause a range of possible values of the dependent variable. For example, a 7 per cent growth in sales may be the most likely forecast, but variations in the independent variables may result in growths of 5 or 10 per cent. What is the probability that each of these forecasts will materialize? It could be argued that the very uncertainty of future events makes it impossible to attach probabilities. But whilst probability assessments are highly subjective, judgement nevertheless plays an important role in any assessment of likely future alternatives. Without some idea of likely alternatives, a business will lose its flexibility to deal with the future. Systematic forecasting is a means by which a business can assess the probabilities of future events. Because of the impossibility of forecasting the actual *single* value that will be achieved, the kind of approach suggested above implies that the forecaster is already making some estimate of the probability distribution of future values of the dependent variable. Therefore, although he may produce a single most probable forecast, it is important to realize in interpreting it that the forecaster is in effect summarizing the probability distribution of future values of the dependent variable.

The single-figure forecast can be misleading for the reasons suggested above. Furthermore, given the range of possible outcomes, it is conceivable that the most likely forecast will have a probability little higher than other quite different forecasts. Equally the probability distribution may be skew, so that while the most likely forecast, for example, has a higher probability than any other outcome, there is nevertheless a much greater chance that the actual outcome will be less rather than more than the most likely forecast. These possibilities are important, and it is better if the forecaster points them out.

It has, of course, been suggested that the person using the forecast is no less likely to be misled by a whole range of possible outcomes than he is by a single figure that gives a false air of certainty to the future. But because the business needs to retain flexibility in dealing with the future, and because nothing it does can eliminate the uncertainty of the future, techniques that will help it to reduce that uncertainty are potentially valuable. The fact that they are not precise simply underlines the danger in placing too much emphasis on techniques. Judgement, based upon a full awareness of general economic and industrial conditions, has an equally valuable role to perform.

If the future were known with certainty, businessmen could always make correct decisions. But because the future is uncertain, decisions can be made only on the basis of 'most likely' outcomes. Whenever managers take decisions about the likelihood of future events, they are either implicitly or explicitly assigning subjective probabilities. But how are probabilities formulated? H. A. Simon[2] mentions three simple models:

1   Assuming that the future will be the same as the present
2   Assuming that the rate of change between past and present periods will operate on the present to determine the change in the future
3   Assuming that the future is a weighted average of past and present periods (e.g. exponential smoothing in which the present is more heavily weighted that the past in estimating the future).

Uncertainty in Investment Decisions

Probability forecasts are particularly important in the area of investment decisions;[3] one example is the effect on estimated rates of return of variations in the estimates of future sales, prices, costs, etc. A single figure for each of a project's cash flows and a single figure for return generated by discounting procedures tend to give a false illusion of accuracy and precision to an investment appraisal. The essential feature of any proposed investment is that the costs and revenues associated with it arise in the future, and thus cannot be known with certainty now. Single figures for cash flows are no more than estimates, not infallible predictions, so that the returns from an investment may be very different from those anticipated at the time the project was undertaken. Each item of cost or revenue associated with a project can take a range of possible values, and when managers select a single value for each item, they are in effect choosing what they consider to be the most likely value for that item. When the most likely values are combined in a project assessment, they show only the most likely return, and give no indication of the range of possible returns.

What is needed is a whole range of estimates for each cost

and revenue item collected, in the form of probability distributions. These distributions would reflect the subjective judgements of various management personnel: in the case of a new machine the sales manager might estimate the distributions for market size, market share, selling price, etc., for the good produced by the machine; the production engineer would indicate

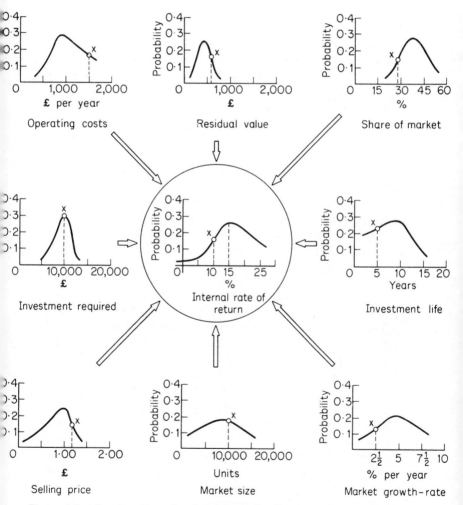

Figure 4.1   Construction of an investment distribution. Adapted from 'Risk Analysis in Capital Investment' by D. B. Hertz, *Harvard Business Review,* Jan.–Feb. 1964, p. 95.

the likely distributions for operating costs and machine life; and
the purchasing manager might estimate the possible cost of the
machine and its residual value. A typical set of distributions is
shown in Figure 4.1. They can take many different forms —
some narrow and symmetrical, some relatively broad, and others
perhaps skew. But if we take just the single most likely value
for each distribution and combine them in a discounted cash
flow calculation, they would yield a return of 15 per cent as
shown in the central circled distribution. This is the figure that
would be generated were managers to work with only single-
figure estimates for each relevant cost or revenue item.

Rather than a single-figure estimate for project return, what
is needed is a complete probability distribution of likely returns.[4]
A single value for each cost or revenue item can be selected at
random from each distribution, and values thus selected can be
combined in a discounted cash flow calculation to yield a rate
of return for that combination of outcomes. For example, if
the values marked 'x' on each distribution are combined, they
will yield a return of 10 per cent. This process of random selection and calculation of return must be repeated a large number
of times, values for cost and revenue items being selected with
a frequency dictated by the probability distributions. In this
way a probability distribution for the project as a whole can be
obtained.

Such probability distributions for project returns are much
more informative than single-figure estimates of returns, for
they allow managers to take risk into account when selecting
and ranking projects. Managers with a strong aversion to risk
will prefer projects offering a lower return with little variance
from the mean, while managers who are less averse to risk will
choose projects with high average returns and a wider range
of possible outcomes. In addition to the relative 'broadness' of
the probability distribution, managers will also consider the
skew of distributions. In Figure 4.2 the probability distributions
for two projects, A and B, are shown. The most likely return
for project A is 10 per cent and for B 15 per cent; and if
managers were to consider only single-figure returns for the
two projects, they would prefer B. The probability distributions
give an entirely different picture, however, for although project
A has a relatively low 'most likely return', there is only a small
probability of returns being less than 10 per cent and quite a

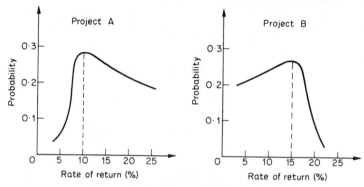

Figure 4.2   Return on investment distributions.

good chance that returns will exceed 10 per cent. By contrast, project B has a higher most likely return, but there is little likelihood of returns exceeding this figure and quite a high probability that returns will be below 15 per cent. A final choice between the two will depend upon managers' attitudes towards risks.

Sensitivity analysis and risk analysis complement one another in their approach to the problem of reducing the uncertainty that attaches to the evaluation of strategy and tactics for the future. In subsequent chapters we discuss the changing economic, technological, social and political environments of business. The remainder of this chapter is therefore devoted to a brief description of some of the techniques of forecasting used in these various contexts.

TIME SERIES ANALYSIS

Time series analysis is a technique for grouping factors causing fluctuations into four basic categories: those attributable (1) to long-term or 'secular' trends, (2) to the business cycle, (3) to seasonal variations, and (4) to irregular or random changes (see Figure 4.3). It is therefore appropriate to long-term and short-term forecasting, although we shall here concern ourselves only with the secular trend as an aid to long-term forecasting. Statistical analysis of past movements of a time series can provide an indication of the likely future pattern of movement of the series.

Before discussing some of the techniques of time series

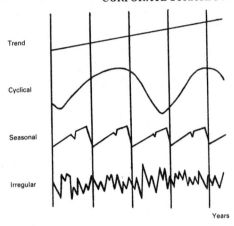

Figure 4.3   Types of economic fluctuations.

analysis, we must add a qualifying note relating to our earlier discussion. Examination of the past as a guide to the future is relevant given that the causal conditions which held in the past continue to hold in the future. This is seldom the case in economic and business activity. Thus, in what might otherwise appear a mechanical exercise, subjective judgement is often necessary, even when a suitable probability approach to the analysis of time series is available.

Long-term Trend Projection

The concept of a secular trend is useful in forecasting because many time series display long-term tendencies related to forces operating in the environment over long periods of time — for example, population growth and technological development. The long-term tendency of a series of data is represented by a trend curve such as that in Figure 4.4(b). (The word 'curve' incorporates any continuous functional relation, including a straight line.) The smoothness of the curve corresponds to the notion that 'trend' represents the continuous and gradual change caused by the workings of long-term factors.

Growth Curves

Long-term trend patterns for many companies, industries, products, markets and so on have shown a period of rapid

growth after the companies, etc., are established. But as size increases, the *rate* of growth slows down until eventually a saturation point is approached. Trend patterns of this life-cycle type
are described mathematically by *growth curves*. In trend analysis of business and economic time-series data two such curves
often used are the *Gompertz* curve and the *Logistic* curve, sometimes referred to as S-curves (the shape they take on an arithmetic scale), as shown in Figure 4.4(a). The S-shape indicates
that as growth takes place, absolute changes become larger up

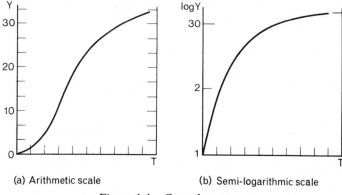

(a) Arithmetic scale   (b) Semi-logarithmic scale

Figure 4.4   Growth curves.

to a point, beyond which they decline. The *rate* of change constantly declines. The Logistic curve has a more pronounced
S-shape than the Gompertz curve, so that the latter applies when
the 'launch' or initial growth period (when absolute increments
of growth are small) is relatively short, followed by a gradual
approach to saturation.

Growth curves imply, because of their mathematical properties, an upper limit to growth. While many activities show a
declining rate of growth over time, they do not approach a
fixed ceiling. When such curves are fitted for purposes of projection, therefore, interpretation and revision in the light of changed
circumstances may be called for.

Straight-line Trends

Some business and economic time series display a constant
long-term rate of growth. Figure 4.5(a) illustrates a straight-

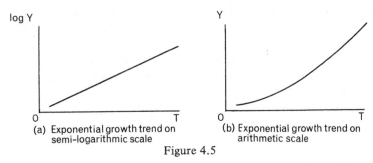

(a) Exponential growth trend on
    semi-logarithmic scale

(b) Exponential growth trend on
    arithmetic scale

Figure 4.5

line trend curve on a semi-logarithmic scale, indicating a constant *percentage* rate of growth. The same exponential trend on an arithmetic scale, Figure 4.5(b), illustrates that the *absolute* amounts of increase become larger over time as the level of the series becomes higher. A constant long-term rate of growth is more usually associated with movements in the economy as a whole than with movements in individual industries or companies, where the 'life-cycle' trend patterns of increase at a decreasing rate are more usual. Where this is the case, a semi-logarithmic straight-line trend is likely to be inappropriate unless a relatively limited period of time is being considered — say up to ten years ahead.

Some time series show a *constant* absolute increment of change from period to period. This is described by a straight line on an arithmetic scale similar to the semi-logarithmic straight-line trend in Figure 4.5(a).

The few time-series patterns discussed above are among those most frequently used in trend analysis. When using trend patterns for forecasting, it is necessary to project the trend curve to derive an estimate of its level at some future date. This first requires 'fitting' a given type of curve, which may be done freehand or, probably more accurately, mathematically, to determine the curve's equation. The latter at least has the advantage that a given mathematical method used to fit a particular type of trend curve to a time series produces one definite projection. This may then be the basis for the exercise of judgement that might otherwise go into the freehand projection of a visual fitting.

Such a projection can only be a starting point because, as we noted at the outset, the secular trend related only to the smooth, continuous and gradual change. To forecast a definite point in the future requires an awareness not simply of the trend aspect of a series but of the fluctuations around the trend. Forecasting cyclical turning points more than a short time ahead with any degree of accuracy is extremely difficult. But, while this is a limiting factor, it is not a serious constraint on long-term forecasting, whose importance is in helping management decision-making about long-range plans, such as plant expansion. In this context the trend level of sales five to ten years ahead is generally more significant than a sales forecast for a specific year.

Short-term Forecasts

Short-term forecasts, used in planning and controlling more immediate business operations, need to be more precise than long-term forecasts. Trend projections are rarely adequate for the purposes of making short-term forecasts because of the cyclical, seasonal and irregular components in a time series, illustrated in Figure 4.3. The major problem in the short-term is to predict cyclical turning points. In this situation analysis of conditions within the industry and in the economy as a whole is essential to the individual company's forecast, as we shall see in Chapter 5. But statistical business indicators, i.e. time-series data on key activities in the economy, are an important part of such an analysis.

MODEL-BUILDING

Trend projection as a method of forecasting is of limited use if the key variables that have influenced a series in the past are likely to change with time. In this event we need to be able to isolate and measure *relations* between variables. Here we are still dependent upon the study of changes in past events as a basis for forecasting the future, but the advantage of a model-building approach is that it helps to identify, in relation, for example, to fluctuations in demand, the changes in the major *determinants* of demand.

The model-building approach is concerned with piecing together, in the form of a set of mathematical equations, aspects of business or economic behaviour, by looking for quantitative estimates of relations generated historically and *then* projecting past behaviour into the future. Compared with trend projection of time series, the model-building approach puts historical data to a different use by identifying causal relations such that the variable to be forecast is specifically related to other variables that have determined the dependent variable in the past. By estimating the *extent* to which the independent variables have influenced the dependent variable, and by forecasting the independent variables, a forecast for the dependent variable may be derived.

This implies, of course, that one can make accurate forecasts of the independent variables. More usefully, one can make several estimates to show what the value of the dependent variable will be according to a variety of different assumptions. Certainly a model-building approach offers no guarantee of accuracy. No model, however complicated, can contain all the factors likely to influence a given situation. Thus it becomes important in making a forecast to estimate the likely error in such relations to be expected on the basis of past experience. But divergence between forecast and outcome may be more than is accounted for by expected error. It is therefore important to appreciate why the divergence occurs; and here the model-building approach has certain advantages.

It may be that the divergence is due to a wrong forecast of the independent variables. More significantly, the structure of the model may be wrong. In an extreme case a relation whose forecast values are widely different from actual values may have to be rejected and some alternative explanation examined. In a less extreme case it may be that some new factor is influencing a relation, causing the relation between the dependent and independent variables to change; or indeed some crucial independent variable may have been omitted from the relation. The model can be tested for these kinds of deficiencies by feeding in *actual* values of exogenous variables (i.e. variables determined outside the model). By doing this we see whether the model produces values for the endogenous variables (i.e. variables determined within the model) which closely approximate those variables' actual (and now known) values. This gives us no measure of the model's ability to forecast; but it does give us a measure of the model's ability to forecast the dependent variable given accurate predictions of the exogenous variables.

If, therefore, there is divergence between forecast values and actual values, a mathematical model enables us to set about tracing the source of forecasting failure. It may arise from an error in forecasting exogenous variables, or from the faulty structure of the model.

A final advantage of the model-building approach is that it is, unlike trend projection, likely to identify changes in trends. The quantitative estimates of economic relations that make up a model mean that it should be possible to identify the *causes* of trend changes. If, therefore, the growth of sales of a particular product is forecast to decline, the company can relate the cause of the change in trend to the necessary corrective action. By strategic and tactical planning the company can take steps to accommodate or combat the change in trend in a manner consistent with its policy objectives.

SOME GUIDELINES FOR FORECASTING

1   In times of increasing uncertainty it is worth recalling, in the light of what has been said in this chapter, that *major* trends change only gradually. There will, for example, undoubtedly have to be an adjustment during the next few years from cheap and plentiful energy to dearer and scarcer energy. But the adjustment should be seen in the context that over that period the value of world consumption of energy might as a consequence have to rise from 2 per cent at the beginning of the 1970s to about 5 per cent of world output – still a comparatively small figure.[5] Such shocks to the system, while producing discontinuities, are unlikely to be significantly disruptive to long-established trends.

2   The future is fraught with uncertainty. But on the premise that it is better to be vaguely right than precisely wrong, the uncertainties of the future are easier to handle if we grasp the certainties first.

3   A forecast is no better than the assumptions on which it is based, and the more explicit and specific the assumptions, the better for forecasting purposes.

4   Judgement will always play an important role in forecasting. However sophisticated a forecasting model may be, inadequate data will always yield inadequate results. The adequacy of recorded data should therefore always be

questioned in the light of the forecaster's knowledge and understanding of the market in which he operates.

FUTURES-FORECASTING TECHNIQUES

In Chapter 6, Gordon Wills discusses in detail, with illustrative examples, morphological analysis, the Delphi technique, and scenarios. Further reference to Delphi studies and scenarios, as well as to cross-impact analysis, is to be found in Chapter 7, where Ian Wilson also discusses the use of probability-diffusion indices, values profiles and priority analysis.

REFERENCES

1 See Robinson, Colin. *Business Forecasting* (Nelson, 1971), especially ch. 9.
2 Simon, H. A. 'Theories of Decision-making in Economics and Behavioural Science', *American Economic Review,* June 1959, vol. 49, no. 3, pp. 253–93.
3 I am grateful to my colleague Bryan Lowes for allowing me to use this illustration from Lowes, B. and Sparkes, J. R. *Modern Managerial Economics* (London: Heinemann, 1974). For a fuller discussion of uncertainty and investment decisions the reader is referred to chs 3 and 13 in that book.
4 This can be derived by means of simulation techniques. See Battersby, A. *Mathematics in Management* (Penguin, 1966).
5 See Connelly, P. and Perlman, R. *The Politics of Scarcity* (Oxford University Press, 1974).

5 Monitoring the Economic Environment

John R. Sparkes

It is something of a truism to say that business planning is inevitably based upon forecasts of the changing economic environment within which business operates. Clearly any advance warning of changes to come in the economic environment will be valuable to firms in their day-to-day decision-making. It is therefore necessary for the firm to have some appreciation of how the economy works, how the workings of the economy are influenced by government policy, and of the time lags between changes in policy and their impact upon the economic environment.

Forecasting the economic environment is relevant to corporate-planning procedures in respect both of planning assumptions and as a background to such corporate-development decisions as acquisition planning and capital-expenditure projects. But the 'economic environment' means different things to different firms, so that, while it is useful for businesses to have forecasts of such broad aggregates of the economic system as gross domestic product (G.D.P.) and consumers' expenditure, these need to be considerably refined before they can be used for corporate-planning purposes.

For planning purposes the firm's operating environment will generally be seen in terms no broader than the particular industrial or consumer sector to which it belongs. Often the problems of defining market boundaries (see Chapter 8, p. 121) which result from widespread diversification beyond conventionally catalogued industrial groupings mean that the firm is forced to regard its operating environment on an individual rather than an industrial basis. It is appropriate, therefore, to qualify what we

say about the economic environment by realizing that as well
as the broad aggregates of economic behaviour, the sectors of
industrial or consumer demand such as housing, machine tools,
motor-vehicle production and so on are potentially useful indicators of change.

DEFINING THE TIME HORIZON

It is difficult to isolate the business outlook over the short run
from the outlook over the medium or long run. In considering
the time horizon of the planning and forecasting period it is
useful to begin with the economist's definition of what constitutes the short run. It is the period in which there is time, in
response to a movement in demand, for a company to vary the
rate of output from its existing plant, but not time to alter the
scale of the plant itself or for new firms to build new plants. It
is therefore a fluid concept in the sense that some elements of
the plant (buildings, machinery and organization structure) can
be expanded or contracted more quickly than others, and dif-
ferently for different areas of business.

Dennis Robertson once observed that 'the short period is not,
so to speak, the same length at both ends'.[1] The significance of
this remark is that the length of time it takes to create physical
equipment is generally shorter than that equipment's length of
life when created. This leads to the important fact that an increase in demand will react more quickly on the scale of plant
than a fall in demand. The implications of this for the time horizon of forecasting and planning is that it embraces not only the
inception of an investment project until its commissioning but
also the prospects for sales during the lifetime of the investment.
The time periods in planning inevitably merge with each other,
and while we talk conventionally about the short term, the
medium term and the long term as a basis for building planning
procedures, the appropriate strategy will aim to give flexibility
at all stages of the process.

TRENDS IN THE BUSINESS ENVIRONMENT

The majority of firms find difficulty in tracing any strict relation between movements in the economy as a whole and their
own individual experience. For most businesses G.D.P. appears

to have little immediate relevance. Yet it is possible to trace significant links between the economy and the individual business, provided the firm can identify some causal relation between the two. An examination of companies' accounts over time clearly reveals the impact of the cycle in the general level of business activity through the pronounced cyclical profit pattern that emerges. The peaks and troughs in company profits, are, as Figure 5.1 illustrates, separated by intervals corresponding to those in the cycle for the whole economy. In monitoring the economic environment the company needs, therefore, to forecast the pattern of the business cycle and also to assess its own position within the cycle in the economy as a whole.

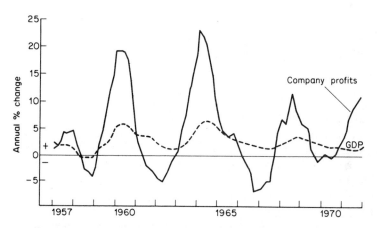

Figure 5.1   Annual percentage changes in company profits
and in G.D.P.

Figure 5.1 shows the relation between annual percentage changes in G.D.P. and company profits between 1957 and 1971. In order to eliminate erratic movements in the series, annual percentage change of a four-quarterly moving average of the two series is plotted. As is well known, when output is rising, profits expand at a faster pace than gross domestic product, and they decline more rapidly when the rate of growth of output falls. But it is striking how large the swings in the rate of increase in profits are, particularly when output is growing fast, as during 1959–60, 1962–4, 1967–8, and 1971–3.

Accounting for the Profit Cycle

These fluctuations in company profits are easily accounted for. Quite small changes in sales revenue on the one hand and costs on the other can combine to produce sharp swings in profits. When the causes of fluctuations in sales and costs are examined, changes in the economic environment can generally be seen to have a significant influence. If we assume a period of general business expansion, then the longer the expansion phase, the greater the number of firms operating at or near the lowest unit cost consistent with their capital structure. In reaching this point unit costs will generally have fallen because output increases more than in proportion to operating expenses. But as productive capacity becomes fully utilized, and labour and raw-materials shortages occur, so increased costs per unit will characterize the latter stages of expansion.

This stems from a number of possible sources: the use of less efficient labour and consequent decline in productivity; increases in wages and salaries that outstrip any rise in productivity, due perhaps to rises in the cost of living; the more intense utilization of capital, resulting in increased maintenance costs; increased costs of borrowing short-term operating funds, resulting from greater competition for loans and the greater selectivity of banks in deciding on new loans and investments; and increasing costs of raw materials, whose shortages may be made good by imports, with all the implications that implies for the balance of international payments.

In an expansionary phase, therefore, increasing costs represent a threat to profit margins. These, together with the institutional and other limitations on price increases in the face of this threat, place considerable stress on company profits, to the point at which they decline. The squeeze on profits forces companies to decide whether to continue with present production plans and employment levels or to take steps to reduce unit cost pressures. An initial reaction can be expected to be a reduction in overtime working and the length of the working week, rather than a reduction in the labour force — thereby reducing the costs that were first incurred in the expansion phase. Laying off workers will be avoided if it is thought that the slowdown is temporary and the level of production will again need to be increased; that avoids the delays of rehiring labour, particularly skilled labour, which might be lost to other firms and difficult to replace.

A reduction in the size of the labour force normally follows later only if it is a necessary adjustment to a more lasting change in demand. Conversely, when sales begin to recover as activity rises from the trough of the cycle, an increase in hours worked will precede an increase in the demand for labour. The same number of machines and employees produce more as the utilization of capacity increases and short-time working falls. As labour productivity increases, unit labour costs fall in the manner described earlier, but because of the importance of labour costs (about 50 per cent of total costs), this will have a multiplied effect upon profits. Profits do not, of course, continue to accelerate indefinitely, even when output continues to expand rapidly. Eventually additional labour is recruited, labour costs rise through wage increases, and these, together with increasing non-labour costs, reduce profit margins. If the annual percentage change in unit labour costs were superimposed on the chart in Figure 5.1, it would be found that the largest percentage changes immediately preceded the downturns in company profits.

THE BUSINESS CYCLE AS A CONSENSUS

We have seen how the profit cycle is related to and leads the business cycle. In fact cyclical movements take place within the economy for different industries at different times. The investment cycle, for example, is also led by the profit cycle. Capital-goods industries are dependent for orders upon the profitability of business, and the rise in profits is generated by general consumer spending, the cycle in which is preceded by the rise in consumer durable spending. In general, so far as the private sector is concerned, an upturn in company cash flow will lead to an increase in investment spending after a lag of about one year. So it follows that the business cycle of capital-goods producers lags behind other cycles within the economy. Although not as rigid as Figure 5.2 suggests, the sequence of events in the cycle is generally as illustrated.

When the cycle in consumer spending on durable goods reaches a peak, the investment-goods industries are generally just beginning to expand. It is therefore possible to trace out a pattern in the various industrial cycles and, provided the individual firm is sufficiently aware of its identity within the

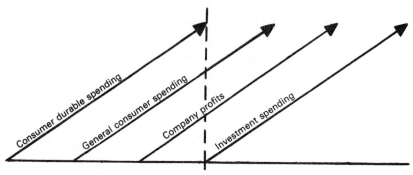

Figure 5.2   Sequence of events in the cycle.

industrial structure, it will be able to find its place in the sequence of the general economic cycle and use it as a leading indicator.

The usefulness of this approach is perhaps better appreciated if we realize that the business cycle is in fact a consensus of specific cycles. There are vast numbers of time series within an economic system, all of which convey *some* information about the direction of economic activity, but many of them move in conflicting directions. As we saw above, not all economic activities are sensitive to expansion or contraction simultaneously. Yet the sum of individual activities obviously does have a net effect in the aggregate expansion or contraction of the economy. While conflicting in direction, these various economic processes do tend to move consistently, although in different time sequences. A. F. Burns has clearly stated this point:

> A continual transformation of the economic situation occurs beneath the surface phenomena of aggregate expansion and contraction. A business cycle expansion does not mean that nearly everything within the economy is moving upwards, nor does a business cycle contraction mean that nearly everything is shrinking. There are two cycles in economic activity, not one. First there is the cycle of sustained expansions and contractions within the aggregate. The first cycle is seen, since we are accustomed to following comprehensive records of business conditions. The second cycle is unseen, since few of us subject the components of comprehensive aggregates to close examination.[2]

Thus there should be particular occurrences during one phase of the cycle that indicate the arrival of conditions favourable to another phase, so that one set of business conditions transforms itself into another. The leading indicator approach to monitoring the economic environment is therefore to make some assessment of the cyclical fluctuation by its effect on the behaviour of various time series, and the way these series interact with each other.

The Problem for the Company

The individual firm faces the problem of deciding where it expects the expansions, the levelling out and the contractions in the business cycle to occur as a framework within which to assess the precise periods in which its business is likely to go through these phases. The machine-tool industry, for example, is a laggard in the business cycle, whereas the motor industry is a leader, and the peaks in their respective cycles are probably separated by some two years.

Owen Davies[3] has well illustrated for the chemical industry the importance of analysing the 'market place' in which the industry operates. He relates the investment cycle in the U.K. chemical industry to profits and prices in the way shown in Figure 5.3. Davies's concern is with the build-up of a purchasing information base for strategic long- and mid-term purchasing planning, analysing and interpreting such factors as the investment cycle. In order to forecast adequately Davies suggests that the purchasing organization needs to take planning account of periods up to ten years ahead. Figure 5.4 is his projection of

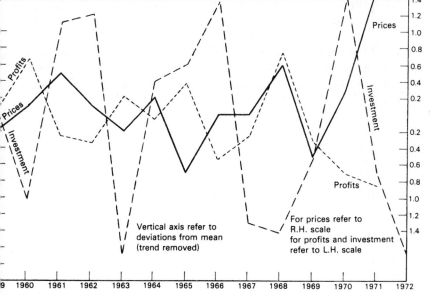

Figure 5.3   Profits, investments and prices in U.K. chemical industry.

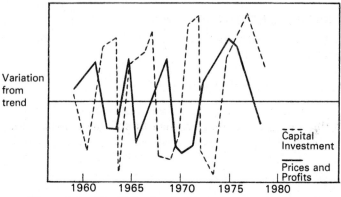

Figure 5.4   The U.K. chemical industry investment cycle.

the investment cycle, taking the historical data on which Figure 5.3 is based and extrapolating the data to forecast trends by means of exponential smoothing techniques.

The object of forecasting is different for the firm than for the Government. The Treasury (and the National Institute of Economic and Social Research, whose forecasts are published quarterly) forecasts on the basis of existing Government policies — so-called 'conditional' forecasting. The purpose of assuming that Government policy remains in its currently known form is in part to give guidance to the changes in policy that may be required. The business planner is much more concerned with the 'unconditional' forecast, which incorporates the changes in policy the government may be likely to introduce. Gauging the timing of changes in Government policy so as to anticipate the development of the business cycle is perhaps the most difficult aspect of the whole task. The desired level of stocks, staffing, sales strategy, etc., must all be determined in the light of the likely development of the business cycle.

Cyclical developments are, of course, very much influenced by changes in Government policy. The questions facing the business at that point are whether the Government will act, and in what direction, and what measures it will adopt. Before considering these questions we need to examine in slightly more detail the way in which the economy works.

HOW THE ECONOMY WORKS

When we talk of the 'macro-economic' structure of the economy, we are dealing with the broad 'aggregates' of the system —

consumption, investment, exports and so on — which relate to
the economy as a whole rather than to individual sectors. Each
of these aggregates represents a demand on economic resources,
and the total demand (the sum of all the aggregates) is met from
home production (which mainly determines the level of employment) plus imported goods and services.

The economy's capacity to produce goods and services increases through time as technological and managerial development increases the productivity of resources, and as the supply
of resources — particularly labour and the capital stock — increases. The pressure of demand in the economy (output in relation to the level that would ensure full employment of resources)
affects such key policy objectives as unemployment, the rate of
inflation and the balance of payments, which have prompted
most of the major changes in postwar macro-economic management. Home or domestic production is therefore central to any
analysis of the economy, and Table 5.1 shows expenditure, subdivided by broad aggregates, on the gross domestic product in
1975.

It will be noted that consumers' expenditure accounts for
almost one-half of total final expenditure. The importance of
stocks within the economy should not be underestimated. Total
stocks are estimated to be equal to some three-quarters of gross
domestic product, so that there are about nine months' stocks
in the economy at any time. While stock-building is therefore
a very small proportion of total final expenditure, annual
changes in stock levels are an important source of variations in
the rate of growth of total expenditure. The other significant
features to emerge from Table 5.1 are that domestic product
is less than three-quarters of total final expenditure and 21.5
per cent of final expenditure is met from imports.

Given the importance of the pressure of demand for maintaining both internal and external balance in the economy, it
can be appreciated that the largest single item in total demand —
consumers' spending — will be the one Governments will be
likely to seek to influence in controlling the economy. This influence will be gained through fiscal and monetary policy
changes, and while it is often difficult to anticipate the timing
of such policy changes, the timing of the impact of the changes
is more predictable. The impact of any change in Government
policy instruments is likely to lag behind the particular discre-

Table 5.1   Expenditure on the U.K. gross domestic product in 1975

	Value £m	Proportion of total final expenditure %
Consumers' expenditure	63,373	48·2
Public authorities current expenditure	22,907	17·4
Gross fixed investment	20,510	15·6
Exports of goods and services	26,093	19·8
equals: Total final sales	132,883	101·0
plus Stockbuilding	− 1,349	1·0
equals: Total final expenditure	131,534	100·0
less Imports of goods and services	−28,248	21·5
Adjustment to factor cost[1]	−10,140	7·7
equals: Gross domestic product (at factor cost)	93,146	70·8

Source: C.S.O. National Income and Expenditure, 1975, HMSO, 1976.

[1] When goods and services are valued at the prices actually paid on the market, the price includes indirect taxes (less subsidies), and the value of products is at 'market prices'. Net indirect taxes go to the government, so that factors of production receive the value of product after deducting indirect taxes and adding subsidies. The resulting value is at 'factor cost'.

pancy between potential output and aggregate demand that it was intended to offset. This does carry the implication that Government stabilization policy may in fact be destabilizing in its effects. By the time the impact of the policy change is felt, the pressure of demand may have changed of its own accord, owing to built-in stabilizing influences. This could, of course, be crucial to any attempt at forecasting, so the best way to appreciate its implications is to consider the likely lags in the impact of government policy changes.

LAGS IN THE IMPACT OF GOVERNMENT POLICY

The total lag may be subdivided into three parts, as follows:

1 The recognition lag is that between the emergence of the discrepancy and the recognition of the need to offset it. This lag will, of course, be the same regardless of the particular measure the Government adopts to counter the discrepancy. On the basis of evidence from the United States that would seem valid in the United Kingdom context it is estimated to average four months.

2 The implementation lag is the lag between the recognition of the need for a change in the policy instrument and its implementation. As regards monetary instruments this lag is very short for the *cost* of finance, which may be effected through a change in the minimum lending rate. Hire-purchase finance controls can also speedily affect the *availability* of finance. But the lag may be as much as six to nine months if the availability of finance is effected through the supply of bank credit (particularly in the case of a reduction, because of the difficulty of curtailing existing overdraft facilities). This applies equally to the stock of liquid assets, which is mainly manipulated by operating on the supply of bank credit.

   Turning to fiscal instruments, the implementation lag for changes in the tax and transfer payment structure is short, as little as one or two months. (Changes in transfer payments have not generally been used for stabilization purposes.) Government expenditure is quite a different matter. The implementation lag will vary considerably dependent on (a) whether the change is an increase or a decrease, and (b) on the way in which the change is implemented. For an increase in Government spending, the implementation lag will be relatively short — between one and three months — and achieved by rescheduling the start of central Government works programmes, speeding up existing programmes, increasing *current* spending, or increasing the funds available to local Government to finance capital spending. These same methods work in reverse for a decrease in Government spending, but are invariably slower, varying from up to just one month for rescheduling, three to four months for curtailing existing projects, three to seven months for funds available to local government, and up to eighteen months for a reduction in central Government current spending.

3   The impact lag is the lag between the change in the policy instrument and its impact upon aggregate demand. Monetary instruments influence aggregate demand via two components of demand — consumption spending and investment spending. The impact lag for the cost and availability instruments is of the order of three months, taking a weighted average of consumption and investment expenditure. The impact upon consumption will in fact be immediate, while for most investment spending it is appreciably longer than three months; but this figure again reflects the importance of consumption expenditure as a proportion of total private spending in the economy.

      The impact lag for fiscal instruments varies considerably with the instrument used. For Government spending the impact lag is zero, because we see from Table 5.1 that Government spending is a component of aggregate demand, so that its impact will be immediate. Changes in the personal or business income-tax structure or the transfer payments structure will affect disposable income, which will affect consumers' spending. A change in the indirect-tax structure will directly affect consumers' spending. But the effects of different types of tax changes on consumer spending vary. J. C. R. Dow[4] made 'guesstimates' of the incidence of tax changes on the volume of consumer spending, as shown in Table 5.2. It is assumed from the table that an increase in taxes on income of £1 million will lead to an equal reduction in consumer demand if the increase is concentrated upon the lower ranges of income. Such an increase in taxes on personal expenditure will lead to a reduction of £800,000 in consumption demand. Employment income and expenditure taxes are clearly the most significant in terms of their impact on consumer spending. As far as the timing of the impact is concerned, major policy changes to influence personal consumption have actually affected spending with a lag of about three months. Less severe measures

Table 5.2   Incidence of tax changes on consumer spending

Type of tax change	% share spent on consumption
Tax on income from employment:	
lower ranges	100
upper ranges	67
Tax on dividends, interest and trading income	50
Tax on personal expenditure	80
Tax on personal capital	10

will have their full impact on consumption expenditure over a much longer period.

Examination of fluctuations in the level of business activity, therefore, suggests primary importance for changes in Government policy directed at increasing (generally in response to rises in unemployment) or reducing (in response to a deteriorating balance of payments) the pressure of domestic demand. The result has been shorter and less severe cycles than prewar, displaying *mainly* variations in annual rates of growth. But the most significant postwar development has been the sequence in which cycles occur in the various components of total expenditure. Consumption has clearly led in the cycle, suggesting that Government policies operating on consumption – particularly changes in tax rates and hire-purchase finance controls, and to a lesser extent monetary controls – have instigated business fluctuations.

The individual firm has a real interest in reaching an understanding of the cyclical factors affecting its operations, and in constructing its forecasts of sales, selling prices, costs, profits, etc., in the light of the identified cyclical relations. But in order to do this, it is necessary first to analyse the major components of total demand and the interaction of changes between the different sectors of the economy.

REFERENCES

1 Robertson, Sir Dennis. *Lectures on Economic Principles,* vol. I (Staples Press, 1957), p. 142.

2 Burns, A. F. *The Frontiers of Economic Knowledge* (New Jersey: Princeton University Press, 1954), p. 114.
3 Davies, Owen. 'The Marketing Approach to Purchasing', *Long Range Planning,* June 1974.
4 Dow, J. C. R. *The Management of the British Economy, 1945–60* (Cambridge University Press, 1964).

6 Forecasting Technological Innovation

Gordon S. C. Wills

The application of forecasting procedures to patterns of technological change is not a new phenomenon either in Britain
or North America. Managements have traditionally, though
perhaps intuitively, kept a cautious eye on the pace of technological change in those sectors they thought likely to impinge
on their business interests. But, as is so frequently the case in
management, it was a defensive eye more often than a purposeful one. The problem was often construed as lying in the danger
of being overtaken by new technologies before an adequate
return had been obtained on a particular investment.

Technology was often viewed as a by-product of basic research
work. That this view is changed, and in many industrial sectors
is now mere history, is reflected in a series of international,
national and corporate events that characterized industrial technology in the 1960s. The issues have been pinpointed by the
journalistic presentation of Servan-Schreiber with his catch-
phrase 'Le défi americain',[1] in the more sober thoughts of John
Duckworth, managing director of the expanded National Research Development Corporation[2] and through countless political and ministerial pronouncements. The movement forward,
and 'la sensibilisation' of senior management to a positive role
for technology in British industrial prosperity, was institutional-
ized not just in a Ministry of Technology, but in the educational
system through the eleven new technological universities and
the enhanced status of the polytechnics.

This positive deployment of national resources, as the basis
for the British industrial structure, has entailed the abandonment of intuitive thoughts about technological futures. A new

technology for the mastery of technology has been spawned, not based solely on the extrapolation of existing trends in functional capabilities but on normative demands about the sort of future we wish to create. As a vitally important corollary to that, a realistic understanding of the sort of role Britain can play in the totality of world technology, either from the British industrial base or the wider industrial base of the European Economic Community, has emerged.

The normative approaches inherent in much of the new field of technological forecasting are equally exhilarating from the individual, social and commercial viewpoints. They provide a rigorous framework for the exploration of alternative futures and the opportunity for all to participate more meaningfully in the development of the environment in which we and our heirs shall need to live.

Within Britain already the purposeful structuring of our technological initiatives is beginning to pay off, although there are as many instances where the failure to take the initiative in technological change has led to catastrophic decay, both commercially and socially. The pattern of our trade with other nations, however, emphasizes some of the success we have achieved. Fred Catherwood, former Director General of the N.E.D.C., has pointed to the transformation of the structure of our exports.[3] In 1959 39 per cent of our exports went to the sterling area, but the comparable proportion in 1968 had fallen to 28 per cent. The shifting balance has been occasioned by the growth in British trade with the major advanced industrial economies in the world. We are moving towards a situation where we must increasingly 'live and cope with the rigorous competition of advanced high-technology, high-wage, capital-intensive economies rather than the closed-trading system inherited from the Empire'. Britain can no longer afford to cover the whole industrial waterfront. We must concentrate further in those areas of our greatest expertise. When this is done, we can be seen to be succeeding, for example, in aerospace, computers, electronics and chemicals.[4] In each of these industries the techniques of technological forecasting are in action. The Programmes Analysis Unit, jointly established by the United Kingdom Atomic Energy Authority and the Ministry of Technology at Didcot, played an important role in promoting their use both in strategic Government planning and more widely throughout British industry.

TECHNOLOGICAL FORECASTING IN THE CORPORATE CONTEXT

The integration of the technological forecast into the framework of corporate long-range planning is fundamental to its effective use. It is directly analogous with the place of the sales forecast in the planning of operational activities for the company in the shorter term. While the latter is now virtually universally accepted as the starting point for operational planning procedures, this is scarcely yet the case for technological forecasting in the long-range plan — mainly because of the ascendancy the marketing function of the business has obtained during the past two decades. While few would deny that the viewpoint of the customer had gone by default in the era of production and sales orientation that preceded marketing's ascent, the grip it simultaneously took on production strategy in many companies has led to increasing difficulties, particularly in areas of rapidly advancing technology. Corporate planning demands the effective collusion of the technologist and the marketeers if costly errors are to be avoided from both ends of the corporate process.[5] The relegation of marketing to a realistic perspective is, however, a vital early stage in the development of effective corporate long-range planning. This relegation covers its usurpation of the strategic-planning role in the company, not the process by which marketing's tentacles have reached out to collaborate in the process of new product introduction and control through a variety of such organizational patterns as task forces or new enterprise divisions.[6] Without the process of strategic collusion between the technologist and the marketeers the company is doomed to rely on the often conflicting views of one or the other, probably a recipe for less success in forecasting corporate futures now than in the past.[7] There is an equally urgent requirement for the separation of operational marketing activity from its concern with the strategic planning of the corporate future. These two strands are apparent in several emergent forms of organizational structure in British industry, such as are illustrated in Figure 6.1.

Nowhere is the need for technology/marketing collusion more clearly demonstrated than in the recognition of the need for balance at any given time between the creating and satisfying of customer needs. No aggregated technological sector can

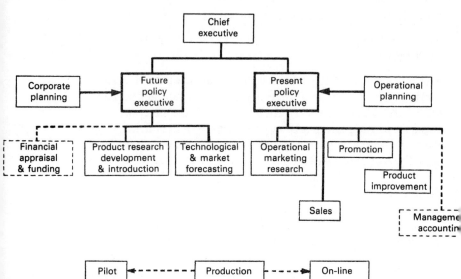

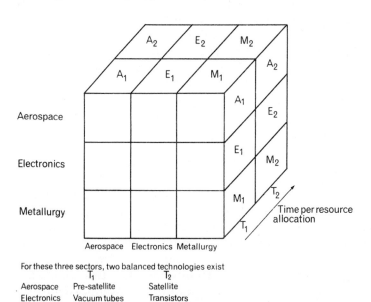

Figure 6.1   Future/present dichotomous structure.

For these three sectors, two balanced technologies exist

	T_1	T_2
Aerospace	Pre-satellite	Satellite
Electronics	Vacuum tubes	Transistors
Metallurgy	99·99% metals	99·999% metals

Figure 6.2   Technological capability/market requirement balance. Source: James C. Hetrick, 'The Impact of Technological Forecasting on Long Range Planning', *Technological Forecasting and Corporate Strategy,* Ed. Wills, Ashton, and Taylor, University of Bradford Press, 1969.

exist unless its input technological sectors exist; equally none should exist unless its output satisfies a need either directly or as an input to another coexistent technological sector. Hetrick develops this concept fully into a model of technological planning,[8] illustrating it with a technology composed of three sectors — aerospace, electronics and metallurgy (Figure 6.2).

He assumes that each exists at two levels — aerospace at pre-satellite and satellite levels, electronics as based on vacuum tubes and solid state physics, and metallurgy as capable of producing 99.99 per cent pure and 99.999 per cent pure metals. Figure 6.2. shows two balanced technologies to exist. Time is not, of course, used as an absolute here; rather it is relative to resource allocation.

Where new technologies are postulated for development, of course, such analysis indicates the sequence for the development of component technologies. The analogy with networking is readily apparent. It has not been appropriate in these remarks on the corporate context of technological forecasting to comment on more than a few of the implications of technological change on company policy formulation. The full gamut has been exhaustively dealt with elsewhere and with particular reference to technological forecasting by Quinn,[9,10] Ansoff and Stewart,[11] Jantsch[12] and Wills.[13] The two key issues raised here, however, have frequently been overlooked and have accordingly been emphasized. They will be of particular concern for the marketeer.

Introducing Technological Forecasting into the Business

While a considerable body of knowledge has already been accumulated[14] and reviewed[13] on the various techniques available for technological forecasting, little attention has been given to the problem of preparing forecasts within a business. The author has been associated with a number of U.K. organizations as they have endeavoured to introduce such forecasts for the first time. The comments and suggestions made below, and the examples, are drawn from a considerable range of British technological forecasting activities. Where the companies concerned are not named, this is in accord with their wish to remain anonymous. (Sincere thanks are due to all concerned for willingness to make such data available, and frequent forbearance in explication, particularly H. Jones and Dr J. Grigor.)

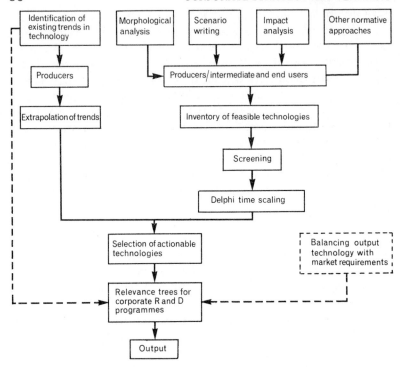

Figure 6.3   Sequence for the introduction of technological forecasting in a business.

Figure 6.3 identifies the main strands in the sequence of introduction observed and found to be operationally effective. It is an aggregated flow rather than illustrative of all organizations or any particular one considered. Few organizations consciously use the full range of approaches available. Most use only the extrapolation of technological trends, and even those employing normative approaches seldom use more than one in any particular circumstance. The *avant-garde* expert in technological forecasting is wont to be severely critical of extrapolative forecasting. Frequently the identification of envelope curves of functional capability within a technology and of exponential growth for technologies generally are dismissed as beautiful but worthless. From a managerial viewpoint such harshness is unwarranted. These two fundamental relations act both as a fillip to technological research and as a warning to be constantly on the lookout for technology switch-over points. The importance for R. and D. programming and project cut-off decisions cannot be ignored. Hall[15] has cited the importance of such an approach in the development of computers to indicate what speed capabilities must be reached. The envelope curve he produced at ICL is given as Figure 6.4. There are now numerous instances of envelope curves and 'S' curves in the literature, and most managements I have discussed the phenomenon with are able to instance their own. Marketing's own concept of the product life cycle is often of this type. The major hazard lies in identifying the correct functional capability with which to concern oneself. There can be no doubt in the reader's mind that arithmetical speed is not the only important functional variable of a computer, even though it may have the best relation with commercial success or some other criterion of effectiveness. This problem came into sharp focus recently in attempts to identify the best parameters for a technological

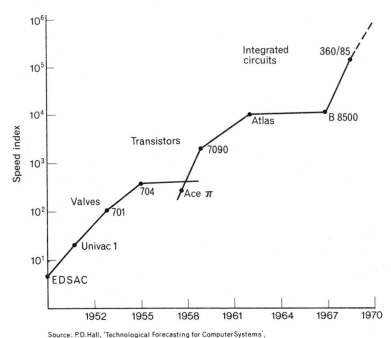

Source: P.D.Hall, 'Technological Forecasting for Computer Systems', in Technological Forecasting and Corporate Strategy .

Figure 6.4   Computer technologies (arithmetic speeds).

forecast in the area of agricultural chemicals. The germane
functional capability has in the space of little more than two
decades been perceived as needing to:

1   Kill weeds
2   Increase crop yield +1
3   Decrease labour content of crop +1 and 2
4   Avoid the need for mechanical ploughing +1, 2, and 3.

Morphological analysis, an approach to the exploration of
technological opportunities first described by Zwicky,[16] is also
extensively used. It is a systematic analysis of a technology into
its basic parameters, and such an analysis frequently reveals a

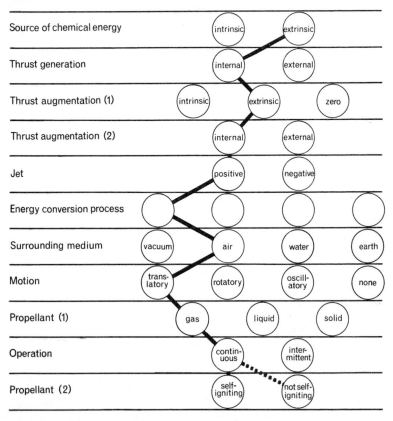

Source: E. Jantsch, 'Forecasting the Future', Science Journal, and
'Morphology of Propulsive Power' by F. Zwicky.

Figure 6.5   Morphological analysis of a jet engine.

	1	2	3	4	5	6	7	8	9	Notes
A Effect	Renders flexible	Reduces friction	Energy transfer Mech Heat Elect Sound/Light	Adhesion	Absorption	Dispersion	Protection anti-rust	—	—	Dispersion here is the ultimate effect, not the means as in line E
B Interfaces (macro- or molecular levels)	Metal Metal	Plastics Plastics	Fibres Fibres	Inorganics Inorganics	Elastomerics Elastomerics	Other solids Other solids	Liquid Liquid	Gas Gas	—	Those are the ultimate interfaces between which the functional permanently resides and achieves the effect on line A
C Initial interfacial phase	Solid	Liquid	Gas	—	—	—	—	—	—	This is *the* functional fluid
D Ultimate interfacial phase	Solid	Liquid	Gas	—	—	—	—	—	—	ditto
E Process used	Temperature change	Pressure change	Reaction	Precipitation	Diffusion	Direct application	Electrostatic	Dispersion	Solution	Means of locating interfacial phase dispersion here is the *means* not the effects as in line A

Known technologies are:

A1 – B2/B2 – C2 – D2 – E1   Plasticization of PVC
A2 – B1/B1 – C2 – D2 – E6   Liquid lubrication of metal faces
A3 – B1/B1 – C3 – D3 – E3   Internal combustion engine
A1 – B1/B1 – C2 – D3 – E1 – E2   Steam engine
A4 – B4/B4 – C2 – D1 – E8 – E3   Cementing bricks
A3 – B1/B1 – C2 – D2 – E2   Hydraulic fluid system
A7 – B1/B8 – C2 – D1 – E9 – E6   Solvent applied rust preventative
A6 – B2/B2 – C2 – D2 – E8   PVC Rigisol Plasticizer is only a processing aid
A5 – (B4 or – C2 – D2 – E5   Air filter medium
      B6)/B8

A suggestion is:

A1 – B4/B4 – C2 – D2 – E1   Plasticized (non-crystalline) inorganic material

*Prepared by H. Jones and Dr. J. Grigor.

Figure 6.6(a) Morphological analysis of functional fluids.

Figure 6.6(b) Morphological analysis of building bricks.

	1	2	3	4	5	
A Material	Natural clay	Metal	Plastic	Waste materials	Figures	
B Forming process	Extrude	Mould	Press	—	—	
C Bonding process	Heat	Chemical	Molecular	—	—	
D Properties	Opacity	Thermal insulation	Elasticity	Aesthetic	—	
E Form	Rectangular	Spherical	Interlocking	Cube	—	

e.g. Known technology: A1, B1, C1, D2, E1 Thermal insulation brick
    A suggestion is: A3 B2 C2 D1 E2 Opaque spherical plastic brick

wide variety of novel devices. Zwicky's morphological analysis
of the jet engine, which resulted, *inter alia,* in the identification
of a ramjet deriving its energy entirely from the surrounding
medium, is shown in Figure 6.5. The rigorous analysis and fresh
orientation on customary technologies that a morphological
analysis demands is a most valuable instrument, acclaimed by
R. and D. managers and scientists. It provides, they report, a
fruitful basis for brainstorming and allied creative activities.

Figures 6.6(a) and (b) show hypothetical examples prepared
by British companies of morphological analyses of some of
their product range. They identify not only known technologies but feasible technologies worthy of screening, along with
opportunities derived by other approaches. The two illustrations examine functional fluids and building bricks. Figure
6.7 demonstrates a further instance of morphological analysis,

Figure 6.7   Morphological analysis for marine communications:
communications-master morphological matrix.

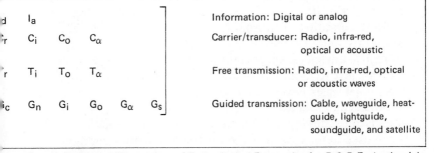

d	I_a					Information: Digital or analog
r	C_i	C_o	C_α			Carrier/transducer: Radio, infra-red, optical or acoustic
r	T_i	T_o	T_α			Free transmission: Radio, infra-red, optical or acoustic waves
c	G_n	G_i	G_o	G_α	G_s	Guided transmission: Cable, waveguide, heat-guide, lightguide, soundguide, and satellite

Source: T. Garrett, 'Illustrations of Technological Forecasting for R & D Evaluations', in
Technological Forecasting and Corporate Strategy.

this time in marine technology, cited by Garrett.[17] It relates
specifically to the marine communications matrix, and yields,
for instance in (Ia; Cr; Gs), a satellite communication system.
The method gave twenty-two distinct systems of marine communication, and it was possible to proceed to time scaling on
the basis of what was thought to be technologically feasible in
1985.

The preparation of scenarios demands less apparent rigour
than the morphological analysis of existing technologies for
new insights. Nonetheless creative stimulation and imagination

are vital. A tight statement of possible technological futures is required if any meaningful consensus of expert opinion concerning time scales for introduction is to be prepared. The problems of adequate definition in scenarios can best be illustrated with some examples from the textile industry:

1   Non-flammable fibres of inorganic types
2   Controlled release perfume finish
3   100 per cent mass-coloration of synthetic fibres
4   Commercial introduction of single class of dye with equal affinity and fastness for all fibres
5   50 per cent of all outer garments moulded.

Each of these scenarios seems meaningful enough, but in submitting them to a wide range of experts, unable to classify the meaning of particular situations, confusion is bound to arise. What are outer garments, and for whom? Are we concerned with the sheer invention of the necessary technologies or their commercial introduction? What do we mean in any event by commercial introduction? The importance of absolute precision is paramount if time-scale estimates are to be of any real value.

In the conduct of morphological analysis, in the writing of scenarios, and in the evaluation of the impact of given technological advances, there is no reason to limit the corporate canvass just to members of an R. and D. department. Marketing personnel, sales personnel, and intermediate and end-users of products and technologies can all be included. A range of standard psychological and group-dynamics techniques have been used here, as well as the unstructured and structured questionnaire approaches. All these approaches are searching for creative insights, the technological opportunity, and none should worry from whence it comes. The preparation of an inventory of feasible technologies, their screening in terms of corporate objectives and finally the ascription of time scales for their development – these call for a much finer judgement.

In the field of time-scaling the Delphi technique has become widely used. It seeks to take a consensus view of as wide a body of experts as possible about the most likely date of the event described either in scenario, postulated from an impact analysis, or morphologically derived. ICL's experience in this area is as strong as any in Britain, and has been described by Hall.[15] He reports, in particular, the vital importance in gaining

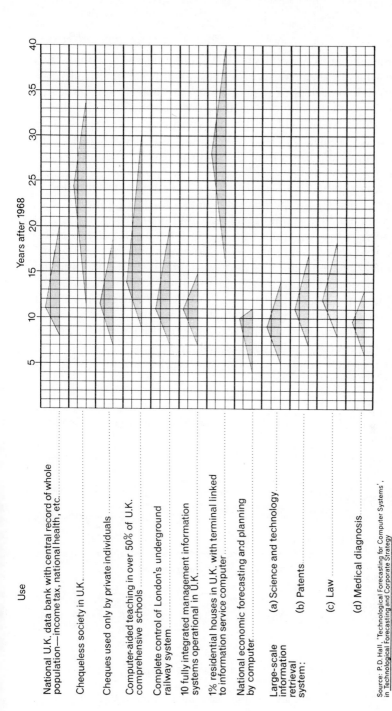

Use

National U.K. data bank with central record of whole population—income tax, national health, etc.

Chequeless society in U.K.

Cheques used only by private individuals

Computer-aided teaching in over 50% of U.K. comprehensive schools

Complete control of London's underground railway system

10 fully integrated management information systems operational in U.K.

1% residential houses in U.K. with terminal linked to information service computer

National economic forecasting and planning by computer.

Large-scale information retrieval system:

(a) Science and technology

(b) Patents

(c) Law

(d) Medical diagnosis

Years after 1968

Figure 6.8   Delphi timescale for computer applications.

Source: P. D. Hall, 'Technological Forecasting for Computer Systems', in Technological Forecasting and Corporate Strategy

time estimates of specifying the event envisaged as precisely as possible. In the analysis of replies it is normal practice to go through a number of sequential stages, each feeding back to the experts the outcome of the previous stage in order that revisions can be made if thought appropriate. The results from Hall are tabulated in the conventional way, each bar excluding the upper and lower quartiles and the peak representing the median value (Figure 6.8).

An example of a form of structured first-round questionnaire, used by the Hercules Powder Company Limited, for a Delphi exercise within the chemical industry early in 1969, is shown as the Appendix to this chapter. The Delphi forecast went to three rounds. A private communication from the organizer has indicated the extreme value of the re-presentation of earlier outcomes to participants. Figure 6.9 shows the outcome after Round III for questions C6, C7 and C8, relating to Foodstuffs in the Hercules study. There was a slight hardening of opinion since Round II as regards the long-term market share for 'synthetic' proteins as defined, and a notable decline in long-term market percentage rating for 'synthetic' edible oils.

	% of total defined market served for each year							
	0% or negl.	1—4	5—9	10—14	15—19	20—24	25—29	Othe
C6. 'Synthetic' protein								
1980	6	7	1	0	0	0	0	0
1985	1	7	5	1	0	0	0	0
1990	1	4	3	4	2	0	0	0
C7. 'Synthetic' nutritive carbohydrates	'Not in prospect' — no dissentients							
C8. 'Synthetic' edible oils								
1980	12	0	0	0	0	0	0	0
1985	7	4	1	0	0	0	0	0
1990	2	9	0	0	0	1	0	0

*Reproduced by permission of the Hercules Powder Company.

Figure 6.9   Delphi outcome for foodstuffs.*

Most probable sources of 'synthetic' proteins were cited as follows:

1   Directly or indirectly from petroleum and/or natural gas —
    fifteen positive replies. This included two who expected
    the feedstock to be petrochemicals rather than raw pe-
    troleum (probabilities 8, 5, dates 1980, 1978 respectively).
    Another member specified microbial processes (a) on
    petroleum hydrocarbons (8, 1975+) and (b) on natural
    gas (3, 1980) — treated as two entries. One respondent
    ascribed probability 4, but qualified 'unlikely'. A further
    member predicted use of n-alkanes (1978), methane
    (1980) and naphtha (1985) — all probability 9. General
    average probability rating was 7, and average year of U.K.
    commercialization 1976.

2   Three members cited as sources vegetation, including the
    development of special vegetable growths. Two assigned
    probability 8, year 1980; the third 2 and 1975, mention-
    ing 'low commercial barriers' as compared with oil and
    natural gas sources.

3   Two respondents envisaged marine sources, including fish,
    by 1980, with probability ratings 8 and 9.

4   Micro-organisms were cited by two members (excluding the
    entry citing microbial action on petroleum, etc., already
    mentioned), one working on oil residues base, 'available
    via animal feeding' (8, 1975), and the other on cellulose
    (5, 1985).

5   Another respondent cited cellulose waste as source, route
    unspecified (2, 1980), qualifying with 'very limited accep-
    tance'.

6   One other respondent cited photo-synthesis (8, 1980).

Most probable sources of 'synthetic' edible oils commanded
very few entries. Four respondents cited petroleum and/or
natural gas with probability ratings 7—9, placing the year of
commercialization most probably in the late 1980s. Of these,
one asserted that the sources would be important by 1990
(predicting market share 20 per cent). Another, who pointed
to the rising costs of natural products such as whale oil, specified microbiological action on selected hydrocarbon feedstocks,
with probability ratings 3, 6 and 9 for 1980, 1985 and 1990
respectively.

Marine sources, fish and seaweed had one mention (7, un-
dated); and cellulose sources two, one specifying enzyme processes (2, 1980) and the other unqualified (1, 1990). Enzyme
action on carbon dioxide was cited once without ratings. One
member mentioned soya as a source 'already developed'.

SELECTION OF ACTIONABLE TECHNOLOGIES

The exhaustive search for technological opportunities through
extrapolative, morphological, and normative approaches, and
the allied time-scaling, merely provide the managerial input for
the selection of actionable technologies. This is scarcely the
place to discuss the full range of appraisal procedures available.
It is important to recall that once the directions for action have
been set, they should be kept under constant review in the light
of change in technology and competitive initiatives. The process
of technological mapping and monitoring of the business environment has been described in detail by Quinn.[9] The balancing of the eventual output technology with its input requirements and the creation and fostering of market needs must also
be an ever-present management concern. The precise details of
project management in order that the output technology will
be most effectively obtained are also outside the scope of this
chapter but are well documented. In essence they demand the
close scrutiny of existing technology and the appraisal of patterns of technology transfer to the normative requirements.
In most circumstances a variety of possible routes exist for such
transfer as indicated in Figure 6.10; the search for the optimum
route is of key concern in R. & D. planning. It poses the range
of alternatives and clarifies, for instance, through sensitivity
analysis, how critical any particular phase of activity might be.

These comments on the preparation and deployment of technological forecasts will have indicated quite clearly the still tentative state of much of the art. The major catalyst in bringing
forward the development of skills in this area has undoubtedly
been the voracious appetite of the corporate planner, and he
can be expected to continue to make increasing demands in
the future. Successful corporate deployment, however, undoubtedly rests on effective collaboration between the technologist and the marketeer, and will always demand an intelli-

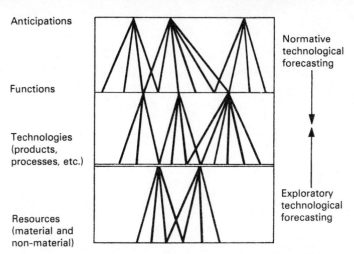

Anticipations

Functions

Technologies
(products,
processes, etc.)

Resources
(material and
non-material)

Normative
technological
forecasting

Exploratory
technological
forecasting

Figure 6.10   Alternative routes for technology transfer. Source:
E. Jantsch, 'Technological Forecasting in Corporate Planning',
Technological Forecasting and Corporate Strategy.

gent, and at times a cautious, treatment of the forecasts prepared. *The immediate pay-offs can be expected to emerge from
a greatly enhanced coherence for the planning of research and
development activities and the formulation of priorities within
the range of opportunities presented.* In the longer term the
normative approach, by orienting more and more senior-
management thinking to the identification of opportunities
rather than the more myopic task of problem solution, promises
a great deal besides.

APPENDIX
QUESTIONNAIRE USED BY THE HERCULES POWDER COMPANY, 1969

Notes

In answering numerical questions, please give *single figures* only
in the appropriate boxes, not ranges. The figure should be your
own 'most probable' judgement at the time of responding.
(Reports will show the range embraced by the replies from all
the panel, and thus indicate any areas of wide disagreement.) It
is expected that your quantified replies may well be amended
during rounds II and III in the light of fresh thinking stimulated
by the intervening panel reports fed back to you.

It will be assumed throughout that your quantified predictions
take account of the technological developments you consider
most likely, including those which come to your notice during
the course of the exercise.

Answers to numerical questions should relate to U.K. industry only (but take account of new developments elsewhere in the world).

Answers to 'speculation' questions should relate to new developments regardless of where in the world you think they may start.

Definitions

'Manufactured organic chemicals'. Include all organics, regardless of raw material source, which differ in a material chemical

First round 'Delphi' exercise
(Future pattern of U.K. industrial-chemical industry)

Respondents are asked to give their own considered opinions on the issues listed below
Very important The scope of the questionnaire is broad. It is suggested that respondents omit entries on issues where they hold no views. The value of the exercise would be undermined if respondents merely 'thought of a number' to complete an entry where they were on unfamiliar ground. However, considered views in areas outside a respondent's direct experience are valid for inclusion.

	Enter your forecast production index (1967=100) for each year				% of total market served for each year		
	1980	1985	1990		1980	1985	1990
A1 All manufactured organic chemicals				C1 Transport (a) New sources of automotive energy (e.g. fuel cells) versus petrol and oil			
A2 Primary organic chemicals obtained from petroleum				(b) New energy source(s) envisaged			
A3 Manufactured organics from non-petroleum sources				(c) Date(s) of first commercialization			
A4 Manufactured inorganic chemicals (incl. minerals chemically refined)				C2 Transport (a) New mobile loadbearing devices (e.g. air cushions) versus rubber tyres			
	1000 tonne units			(b) New device(s) envisaged			
	1980	1985	1990				
B1 (a) Organic chemicals from any major source(s) other than petroleum (e.g. air/water)				C3 Construction alternative metals versus iron and steel			
(b) New source(s) envisaged				C4 Construction alternative non-metals (e.g. plastics) versus iron and steel			
(c) Date(s) of first commercialization				C5 Construction alternative organics (e.g. plastics) versus mineral products (bricks, concrete, slate, etc.)			
B2 (a) Novel inorganic chemicals from new fundamental technology(ies)(e.g. inorganic polymers)				C6 Foodstuffs (a) synthetic edible proteins versus natural			
(b) New technology (ies) envisaged				(b) Synthetic protein source(s)			
(c) Date(s) of first commercialization							

Reprinted by permission of the Hercules Powder Company

Figure 6.11   Questionnaire for a 'Delphi' exercise.

sense from the raw material. Commercially pure chemicals fractionated from natural chemical mixtures qualify, but refined raw materials, still substantially the same mixtures, do not.

'Transport'. Transport which is itself mobile qualifies. Conveyance via static structures, e.g. pipe lines, does not.

'Proteins'. Include all proteins made by synthetic industry. Allow in 'total market' for proteins recovered from natural sources not commercially exploited at present. Identification of source will help.

'Petroleum'. Includes other current natural sources of organics, e.g. shale oil and natural gas, but excludes coal.

'Manufactured organics from non-petroleum sources'. Sources include established raw materials such as molasses, cellulose,

	1980	1985	1990
C7 Foodstuffs (a) synthetic nutritive carbohydrates versus natural			
(b) Synthetic carbohydrate source(s)...............			
C8 Foodstuffs (a) synthetic edible oils versus natural			
(b) Synthetic oil source(s)............................			
C9 Textiles (a) man-made fibres of kinds not so far commercialized			
(b) General nature of the new fibres.....................			
C10 Agricultural chemicals (a) new agricultural chemicals not so far commercialized			
(b) Sources of new chemicals..........			
(c) Purposes for which developed............................			

Section D Broad speculation

D1 Advances of broad chemical interest not included above, with anticipated dates of commercialization.............................
....

D2 (a) Will fresh fundamental chemical principles capable of commercialization be discovered between now and 1990? Yes/No

(b) In what fields of study, if any, do you think such discoveries will be made?
....

(c) When?............... ....

Section E Personal

E1 Current duties include (a) long-range planning/ technological forecasting
(b) full-time/part-time/not at all

E2 Technical qualifications are in pure chemistry/ applied chemistry/chemical engineering/ mathematics/statistics/economics
Other...

Figure 6.11 cont. Questionnaire for a 'Delphi' exercise

coal and coal tar, rosin and turpentine, vegetable matter generally.

'Construction'. Is meant to include all housing, office, factory, bridges, tunnels and the like, but excludes roadmaking, process plant, fabrication, transportation, machinery, etc. If mobile housing is expected to become significant, it should be included.

' "Synthetic" edible proteins'. Covers proteins for human consumption, from any purely synthetic process or by enzyme/bacteriological/biological processes or others, applied to non-protein starting materials. It excludes proteins 'won' by new methods from protein-bearing sources not exploited today.

'Textiles'. Includes all synthetic fibres plus any non-woven synthetic fabrics, films, etc., used as alternatives to traditional textiles.

REFERENCES

1 Servan-Schreiber, J. J. *The American Challenge* (London: Hamish Hamilton, 1968).

2 Beer, S. and Wills, G. S. C. 'Government Money for the Inventor', *Management Decision,* Summer 1969, 3, 2.

3 Catherwood, F. 'The Planning Dialogue', *National Westminster Bank Review,* May 1969, pp. 2—9.

4 'Special Survey: Technology in Britain: a Test of Strength', *British Industry Week,* 3 May 1968, 2, 33.

5 Hayhurst, R., Mann, J., Saddik, S. and Wills, G. S. C. *Organisational Design for Marketing Futures,* Part A (Nelson, 1970).

6 Lorsch, J. W. *Product Innovation and Organisation* (Columbia University Press, 1965).

7 Wills, G. S. C. 'Educating Marketing Men for the Task of Long Range Planning', in *The Role of Marketing in Corporate Planning,* Annual Conference of the Marketing Society, April 1967, pp. 32—48.

8 Hetrick, J. C. 'The Impact of Technological Forecasting on Long Range Planning', *Proceedings of National Conference on Technological Forecasting* (University of Bradford Management Centre, July 1968), pp. 256—71.

9 Quinn, J. B. 'Technological Forecasting', *Harvard Business Review,* March—April 1967, 45, 2.

10 Quinn, J. B. 'Technological Strategies for Industrial Companies', *Management Decision,* September 1968, 2, 3.
11 Ansoff, H. I. and Stewart. J. M. 'Strategies for a Technology-based Business', *Harvard Business Review,* November–December 1967, 45, 6.
12 Jantsch, E. 'Technological Forecasting in Corporate Planning', *Journal of Long Range Planning,* September 1968, 1, 1, pp. 40–50.
13 Wills, G. S. C. 'Technological Forecasting: the Art and Its Management', *Commentary,* April 1968, 10, 2, pp. 87–101.
14 Jantsch, E. *Technological Forecasting in Perspective* (O.E.C.D., 1967).
15 Hall, P. D. 'Technological Forecasting for Computer Systems', in Wills, G. S. C., Ashton, D. and Taylor, B. (eds). *Technological Forecasting and Corporate Strategy* (Crosby Lockwood for Bradford University Press, 1969).
16 Zwicky, F. *Monographs on Morphological Research* (Pasadena, Cal.: Society for Morphological Research, 1962).
17 Garrett, T. 'Illustrations of Technological Forecasting for R. & D. Evaluations', in Wills, Ashton and Taylor, op. cit.

7 Forecasting Social and Political Trends

Ian H. Wilson

The paradox of forecasting in an era of 'radical change' is that it becomes at once more necessary and more difficult. In a relatively stable society, in which today is much like yesterday and tomorrow will predictably be much like today, forecasting is relatively easy; but, by the same token, it is scarcely necessary, since today's way of doing things will still be valid tomorrow. The more rapid, complex and pervasive change becomes, the more essential it is to try to 'make sense of change', to 'get a fix on the future', to gain the lead time needed to develop business responses adequate to meet the change. But, of course, the difficulties of forecasting increase geometrically with the number of sources of change.

It is scarcely surprising, therefore, that most attempts to monitor the business environment have drawn the line at economic and technological forecasting. Such a limitation does, after all, appear to have the merit of making the problem manageable; it accords with most managers' perception of what the business *really* needs; it has (for them) the persuasive fact of dealing with what they would term 'hard-data'. It is also wrong. It is wrong because, in an increasingly interdependent world, these 'hard' trends are influenced by the 'soft' factors of the social and political arena. It is wrong because it presents an unbalanced and highly unrealistic view of the environment in which business operates. It is, finally and dangerously, wrong because it blinds managers to many of the major challenges with which business will be confronted, and so tends to generate or reinforce an attitude of fatal complacency.

THE NEED FOR NEW DIMENSIONS TO PLANNING

This complacency is typified by the assumption, too often made
in corporate planning, of 'other things being equal'. 'Other
things' in this case are taken to be events and trends that lie
outside what managers have thought of as the normal concern
of business. Corporate planning today, that is, typically bases
its strategies on inputs derived from economic forecasting
(predictions about G.N.P. consumer and Government spending,
savings and investment, etc.) and technological forecasting
(assessments of 'state of the art' developments, expected outputs from one's own and competitors' laboratories, and so on).
The planning parameters of the present can, therefore, be concep-
tually represented by the model in Figure 7.1. Certainly these

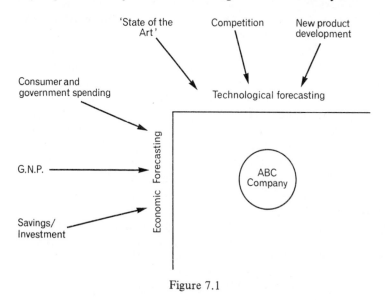

Figure 7.1

inputs have been, and will continue to be, vital to the planning
process; change — and, therefore, forecasting — in these fields
is becoming a more complex and needed process. However,
these inputs alone can no longer suffice, as the 'exposed flanks'
in this model might lead one to guess.

  The typical business now finds itself the focal point for a
bewildering array of external forces that have an impact on it
from every angle. The larger the company, the more likely is

this to be true. There is virtually no major trend in the social, political and economic arena, at home and abroad, that does not affect the operations or future growth of the large corporation in some way. To create an 'early warning system' on only two fronts — economic and technological — is therefore apt to leave a company highly vulnerable to attack from an unexpected quarter. Managers have been too ready to pretend that other factors were adequately covered by generalized assessments of the conventional and obvious political events — war, an election, or international trade agreements — or to rely on the caveat 'other things being equal', which in the circumstances of today is a highly unsatisfactory (and unbusinesslike) treatment of vital factors.

If we have learned one lesson from the disruptions of accelerating change in the past decade, we should by now have recognized that 'other things' have an uncomfortable habit of *not* being 'equal'. To look no further than the outbursts in our cities and on our campuses, at the surge of a heightened ecological consciousness, at the proliferation of legislation on product safety, equal-employment opportunity and occupational health, it should be obvious that social moods, personal attitudes, and political action have become dynamic and determinative forces for business.

It is vital to future business success, therefore, that managers recognize the need for two further dimensions to the planning process — social and political trend analysis. If this social and political forecasting is done comprehensively and successfully, on both a short- and long-term basis, a business is not so likely to be taken by surprise by shifting public moods, the changing aspirations of customers or employees, or the legislative or administrative actions of Government. The model for the future will be more nearly represented by the four-sided planning framework illustrated in Figure 7.2.

When all is said and done, of course, the element of chance or surprise will always remain. Indeed, one certain prediction is that managers will have to learn how to live with, and manage, uncertainty. However, within a framework of these four parameters (social, political, economic, technological) business plans can be formulated with greater assurance that the major predictable environmental factors have been taken into consideration. With anything less an otherwise sound

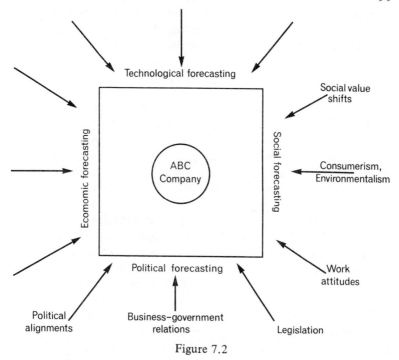

Figure 7.2

strategy will remain vulnerable to the new discontinuities of our age.

At the very least such a broadened planning perspective will serve to make *explicit* the whole range of managerial assumptions about the future. Any plan is, of course, predicated on the planner's model of the future. The present trouble in this regard is that the assumptions underlying this model are normally left *implicit*: indeed, often they are so subtle and so unexamined that even the planner himself is only half aware of them. If, then, trends and events in the future fail to accord with these implicit assumptions, there is no automatic warning signal to alert the business to question whether the plan that was based on these assumptions continues to be valid. A process that insists on making these assumptions explicit has, at a minimum, two advantages over earlier planning:

1 It sets out all the assumptions for critical examination by all those concerned in, or affected by, the planning process

2 It establishes a number of checkpoints at which explicit
   predictions can be monitored against events, and the
   plan can, if necessary, be revised.

SOCIAL CHANGE AND BUSINESS PLANNING

The question might reasonably be asked, 'What makes social
and political forecasting so critical to business planning at
this time?' The answer is to be found in the character of the
change that is taking place around us. First, however, it must
be stated that we are talking here about something more than
dealing with the passage of a particular bill affecting, say,
business taxes, or the question of community relations during
a labour-management dispute. These are essentially matters of
tactical significance, for which business has developed more or
less adequate programmes and procedures. The changes in question now are of a long-term nature and vastly greater sweep, and
so should give rise to *strategic* questions in the corporate-planning process

   This is not the place to engage in a detailed attempt at
socio-political forecasting, but some indication of likely social
change is required to point up its importance and the need for
strategic decisions by business. Some idea of the magnitude of
this change can be gained from a recognition that (1) its like
has occurred only three or four times before in human history,
and (2) it is starting to have profound effects on our individual
and social value systems.

   Taking the first proposition, we can find comparable transi-
tions in human history when man the hunter and nomad became
man the settled farmer, when agriculture was invented; again,
when life in cities — civilization, in its literal sense — emerged as
a new form of society; and again, very recently in terms of
human history, a 100 years ago when the agricultural society
gave way to the industrial society. Now the United States — and,
soon after her, much of Western Europe and Japan — is on the
brink of becoming something different, a form of society that
the world has not seen before.

   Exactly what this new society will become is still hard to
say, though we can begin to perceive some of its outlines. Some
futurists have already labelled it the 'post-industrial society';
others refer to it as the 'technetronic age'; still others as the

'learning society'. Whatever term future generations may give it, we can scarcely doubt that it will be a new world, quite radically different from our present world, not only in its physical properties but also in its attitudes, its values and its perceptions. Small wonder, then, that we are experiencing, in this period of transition, such agonies of uncertainty, unrest and turmoil, such questioning of our social, political and economic institutions — including, of course, business.

Secondly, perhaps as a result of this transition, we are facing a change in our value systems. In many ways the years 1965–70 were a watershed period; since then the streams of our social thinking have started to flow in quite different directions. One can cite, for example, our thinking about such key relations as those between man and woman, the individual and institutions, the majority and minorities, business and society, the economy and ecology. The full institutional impact of these changing values has only begun to be felt (which may account for the relative ease with which they have so far been absorbed into our social systems), but it takes little imagination to recognize that institutions that fully reflect these changed relations will be vastly different from those that we operate today.

Among the consequences of these values shifts will be a rewriting of the public's 'charter of expectations' of corporate performance, and a shaking of the 'seven pillars of business', those basic values that we have up to now considered to be eternal verities undergirding our business system — growth, technology, profit, managerial authority, technical efficiency, 'hard work', and company loyalty:

1 The concept of economic *growth* as an unqualified good is being seriously modified, both in our thinking and in public policy decisions, by considerations of quality and balance.

2 *Technology,* which certainly is a major dynamic of our economic growth, is being subject to challenge on the grounds of our need for environmental control, safety and social stability. This is not to imply a total public revulsion from growth and technology. Such an extreme reaction would form a highly improbable scenario in the foreseeable future. However, there *is* likely to be some redrawing of the policy lines within which growth

and technology will be allowed to develop. And that,
in itself, would represent a major discontinuity in 'traditional' public thinking on the subject.

3   *Profit* is being rejected as an unsatisfactory statement of
the *purpose* of business, and debates will continue to
rage about the extent to which the profit motive can be
squared with the need for business to assume some additional measures of 'social responsibility'. It is highly
probable that profit will remain as a means, a motivator
and a measure; but business in general, and individual
companies in particular, will have to search for some
more socially acceptable statement of their purpose and
mission.

4   The legitimacy of *managerial authority* is being called into
question, with demands for greater participation by
employees (and other corporate constituencies) in the
decision-making process.

5   *Technical efficiency* in job structure, production methods
and systems/products operation is being balanced with
considerations of the human factor and human scale.

6   The notion that '*hard work*' (in the sense of being done 'in
the sweat of thy face' — or, one might add, in the numb-
ness of thy mind) is being put aside in favour of developing meaningful work responsive to an individual's interests
and self-development.

7   And, finally, the concept of *company loyalty* is being
narrowed more and more both by the realities of career
mobility and by the 'whistle-blowing' belief that the public interest must be an overriding factor.

BROADENING THE STRATEGIC PLANNING PROCESS

It should be obvious, even from this cursory examination of
prospective future change, that business planning must be
concerned with a much broader spectrum of strategic decisions
than in the past. We can see this perhaps more clearly in the current debate over that changing concept called 'social responsibility'. This concept is now being broadened and deepened
considerably. Up until recently it was defined almost exclusively
in quantitative, material terms (i.e. improving the material standard of living for the majority of people), with lesser degrees

of emphasis on certain 'peripheral' areas of corporate performance (e.g. educational and cultural support, community activities). Now, however, the corporation's social charter is being redefined to include a range of qualitative expectations concerning the scope and objectives of a company's business, its style of operations, its governance, and its support for social objectives.

As a result, questions of social responsibility are no longer peripheral, but central to decisions about corporate planning and performance. This is *not* to say that the corporation has, or should, become a non-profit charitable institution. Indeed, to argue — pro or con — in those terms would be to misconstrue the new social charter as being merely an extension of the old peripheral 'do-good' concept. Rather this proposition asserts that social responsibility and business needs are now so intertwined that they cannot logically be separated, and that both factors must be weighed simultaneously at the primary level of corporate planning — that is, in the formulation of strategies and in the process of resource allocation. To put the matter another way — on the one hand, virtually all business decisions are now infused with considerations of broad social significance; and, on the other hand, matters of social responsibility are now of such importance and concern to management that they must be handled in a businesslike manner. If, as has been said, 'social responsibility is too important to be left to the public relations staff', it is equally true that strategic business decisions are too important (to the corporation) to be made without reference to the potential impact of changing social conditions.

It is not merely that we must have a more distant time horizon for our strategies — ten years is now about the minimum horizon for strategic decisions — or that we should have the 'four-sided framework' for our planning, as discussed above. The new complexities that are demanded of us are even greater. We must also broaden our concept, and evaluation, of what we mean by 'strategy'.

In our approach to strategy we currently suffer from the same sort of limitation that afflicts our planning framework: we are prepared to acknowledge the necessity for strategy as it applies to investment, technology, production and marketing; but for the other aspects of a business we seem content to rely on tactics and improvization. However, if predictions about the

pace and nature of the change in public expectations of corporate performance are anywhere near right, such an approach
(or lack of an approach) is almost precisely designed to maximize the amount of reaction in corporate policy-making, and
minimize the number of corporate initiatives; to maximize the
constraints and added costs on the business, and minimize
the opportunities for creating new markets, utilizing new resources, winning new vitality and new public acceptance.

In General Electric strategy is defined as 'that activity which
specifies for a business a course of action that is designed to
achieve desired long-term objectives in the light of all major
external and internal factors, present and future'. In such a
definition there is no restriction on the scope of objectives
and courses of action, limiting them only to, say, financial
goals, technological objectives and marketing strategies. It implies, indeed encourages, the notion that we need strategies
for the *totality* of a business, including, importantly, strategies
for manpower development, for business-Government relations,
for community-action programmes, and for dealing with the
developing issues of corporate governance.

This broader definition of strategy is underscored when one
considers that the first element of strategy must be a definition
of 'mission'. The mission of a business determines its long-term
goals and objectives; it at once raises questions about the scope
and nature of a company's activities, about the 'style' of its
operations, about the proper 'mix' of objectives. Add to this
the fact that an important end-result of strategic planning is
the allocation of corporate resources, and it becomes even
clearer that *all* elements of strategic alternatives must be considered, simultaneously and on an equal footing, if we are to
arrive at a balanced and admissible set of corporate objectives.
In developing a course of strategic action it is necessary to discuss the allocation of manpower resources as well as financial
and facilities resources, to determine what is appropriate social
action as well as adequate market penetration, and to assess
management style as well as the styling of products. These are
all matters of strategic importance to the corporation, and the
strategic planning process must, therefore, be made to embrace
them all.

A further necessary enlargement of scope concerns the criteria used for strategy evaluation. In assessing the relative merits

of alternative strategies we are used to considering their impact on corporate growth, market position, return on investment, cash flow, and earnings per share. However, in view of the new dimensions to risk in this period of accelerating change, we need to add to these criteria an assessment of each strategy's social responsiveness, political acceptability and employment attractiveness.

To understand the significance of these new criteria, consider some of the questions that might be asked under each of these headings:

1   *Social responsiveness.* To what extent will the strategy increase the company's ability to contribute toward the attainment of national goals and the serving of 'social needs' markets? Will the strategy increase or decrease commitment to products and manufacturing facilities that are inherently more polluting? What impact will the strategy have on the company's 'social legitimacy', i.e. its recognition and public acceptance as a major social asset.

2   *Political acceptability.* Will prospective expansion of government regulations and controls tend to raise the level of risk, and so impair the attractiveness of the strategy? Will the strategy raise or lower the level of exposure to antitrust action? How will the policies and programmes needed to implement the strategy affect the acceptability of corporate objectives by government leaders?

3   *Employment attractiveness.* Will the strategy tend to enhance the company's public and campus image as a good place to work? Will the strategy tend to enhance the company's ability to attract needed talents and skills? Will the challenge and excitement of the corporate mission and objectives tend to increase employee morale, and therefore the level of commitment and productivity?

If society is going to evaluate corporate performance against a broader set of criteria, it surely makes good business sense for management to ward off future problems — or to seize anticipated opportunities — by building these criteria into its own strategy-evaluation process. The fact that there are no simple quantifiable answers to such questions certainly complicates the task, but in no way diminishes the need for it.

STEPS TOWARD IMPLEMENTATION

It should be clear from these illustrative examples that forecasting social and political trends is more than a challenging
intellectual exercise for the corporate planner. He must use
the results of this forecasting to change his frame of reference,
broaden his definition of strategy and make his evaluation of
alternatives a more complete and sophisticated process.

The basic determination to broaden the perspectives of business planning is, of course, one that only top management can
make, or make effective. If they are unaware of, or unpersuaded
by, the importance of socio-political forecasting, then business
planning will remain essentially a two-dimensional affair. This is
not to say that planning specialists should be cast in a merely
passive role in this regard. The burden of proof is on them, after
all, to demonstrate the feasibility of this type of forecasting and
its specific relevance to their company's business needs. However, it is only top management that can *require* this forecasting
to be part of the planning process, that can assign responsibility
and resources for this work, and that can probe to ensure the
environmental soundness of any plan that is to be reviewed and
approved.

The second need — for *systematic* monitoring of the environment — can, of course, be met in many ways; trend projections,
Delphi forecasting, scenarios, 'cross-impact analysis' and so on
are among the more available methodologies. Whatever approach
is chosen, however, it cannot be undertaken on a 'one-shot'
basis, for *continuity* of monitoring is absolutely essential if the
early warning system is to operate effectively. Continuity and
in-depth analysis of specific developments are needed to ensure
the full relevance and comprehensiveness of study findings. And,
since there is a limit to the comprehensiveness of even the most
sophisticated system, we should try to identify the most probable discontinuities, or breaks in trend lines, to which our monitoring should give priority. If we cannot monitor all fronts at
all times, we must concentrate on the most critical points. For,
clearly, it is the sudden departure from a projection of past
trends — the break point from which trends move off in a new
direction — that would disrupt our planning more than even
quite major deviations between forecasting and events along the
same trend line.

The third stage may prove to be the most difficult of all — bringing the generalized forecast down to specific implications for each particular business, function or role. We are all most apt to be blind in matters that closely affect us, but, however difficult the exercise may be, we must each make a thorough-going and conscientious effort to answer, in precise terms, the question 'What does this trend mean for me? For my work? For my business?' This exercise may be particularly difficult for managers because many of the implications will seem to challenge, and even undermine, some basic business values. These implications are therefore most apt to be set aside as mistaken interpretations, as 'unthinkable', or as inconsistent with past experience and future forecasts along 'traditional' lines. Yet it is precisely these seeming 'wild cards' that our future research must seek to uncover and evaluate.

Only when this rigorous analysis of implications has been completed is it possible to move to the fourth phase — integrating the socio-political forecasts into the business plan. There are many difficulties along this path, one being that of relating the 'soft' data derived from socio-political analysis to the relatively 'hard' data of economic and technological forecasting. One possible way to bridge this gap is to reduce both sets of data to their basic assumptions and then to examine the two sets of assumptions for consistency. Another would be to develop a business plan, as at present, on the basis of economic and technological inputs, and then to determine whether the social and political projections tend to confirm or deny the feasibility of this plan. A third, and perhaps preferable, approach is to deduce from the various data four sets of parameters (opportunities and constraints) within which the business plan must be evolved.

In the reforming of General Electric's strategic-planning process, which took place in 1970, the first step in the planning cycle was the development of a long-term (ten to fifteen years) environmental forecast. The philosophy underlying this requirement is made apparent in the very definition of strategic planning offered by Hershner Cross, one of the four senior vice-presidents in the Corporate Executive Staff: *'Strategic Planning might be termed the process of sensitizing a business to the opportunities and threats in the external environment, of determining what objectives are desirable and possible, and of*

deploying resources to match these objectives.' It is the comprehensive analysis of societal as well as competitive forces
that provides the starting point, and sets the tone, for the
whole of the planning process.

Let us look a little more closely at this critical first element
in the process as it emerged in the first (1971) planning cycle.
In developing this required long-term forecast, we first produced
at General Electric nine separate views of aspects of the future
business environment — 'tunnel visions' of the future, if you
will — dealing with probable developments in international,
defence, social, political, legal, economic, technological, manpower and financial affairs. In each of these segments we tried
(1) to give a brief historical review (1960—70) as a jumping-off
point for our analysis of the future; (2) analyse the major future
forces for change — a benchmark forecast for 1970—80; (3)
identify the potential discontinuities, i.e. those events which
might have low probability but high significance for General
Electric; and (4) raise the first-order questions and policy implications suggested by these forecasts.

These were, by definition, *segmented* views of the future,
and inadequate, therefore, as a final product. So we proceeded
to a 'cross-impact analysis', selecting out of the hundreds of
trends/events in those nine environmental 'slices' the seventy-
five or so that had the highest combined rating of probability
and importance. (Some events that were quite probable had
little significance for General Electric, while others of low probability would have critical importance for the Company, should
they occur.) On these seventy-five trends/events we performed
the sort of cross-impact analysis developed by Theodore J.
Gordon, asking 'If event A occurs, what will be the impact on
the other seventy-four? Will the probability of their occurrence
increase, decrease, or remain the same?' In effect, this process
enabled us to build sets of 'domino chains', with one event
triggering another, and then to construct a small number of
consistent configurations of the future.

The final step in the environmental-forecasting process was
the development of scenarios as an integrative mechanism for
our work, pulling together the separate forecasts of the nine
'slices', and blending quantitative and qualitative data.

We developed multiple scenarios; we did *not* take a single
view of the future. In fact, we ended up with four possibili-

ties — a benchmark forecast, which combined the 'most probable' developments from the nine environmental 'slices'; and three variants that, in effect, were derived from varying combinations of discontinuities.

Significantly, I think, we rated even the benchmark forecast no more than a 50 per cent probability. That, at least, is a measure of our own uncertainty about the future. Two of the scenarios — a 'greater consensus' world and society; and a 'greater disarray' world and society — were drawn up mainly as polar extremes to demonstrate the wide spread of possible results from the occurrence of divergent discontinuities at home and abroad.

SOME FORECASTING TOOLS

Socio-political forecasting is nothing if not an art. By any standard it is still far from being a science. Beginning methodologies, such as the Delphi studies, cross-impact analyses and scenarios already mentioned, are being developed, and the alert practitioner will use them whenever possible. But the magnitude of the problem, and the need to tailor studies and analyses to particular company situations, should be a constant challenge to him to develop his own tools and techniques.

In the remainder of this chapter we discuss three techniques that we have found useful in particular cases. They are offered here *not* as finely honed and scientific tools but simply as examples of ways in which it is possible to start bringing some sort of order out of the chaos of the diverse, and often conflicting, evidence that the soft data of social and political-trend analysis will often bring to light. These techniques should therefore be used with care, if at all; their principal purpose should be to stimulate the planner to improve on them, rather than to use them blindly.

Probability-diffusion Matrix

In predicting developments over a decade it is more meaningful to talk in terms of degrees of relative probability than of certainty or 'inevitability'. In the final analysis assigning probability to a trend or future event is a matter of judgement after weighing the known data and cross-checking with informed

opinion. A further cross-check can be run by plotting the
predictions along a probability axis so that their relative positions are made apparent.

It is also helpful to assess the probable 'diffusion' of a trend
or event — that is, the extent to which it is uniformly distributed over the population to which it applies (world, U.S.A.,
an industry, etc.) or relatively confined to a segment of that
population. Again, plotting the predictions along a diffusion
axis makes explicit, in a coordinated fashion, the relative
weightings assigned in separate judgements.

Combining these two axes into a probability-diffusion matrix,
as is done in Figure 7.3, serves as a check on the internal consistency of a relatively large number of predictions, from two
viewpoints. By itself such a matrix adds little to a scientific
approach to environmental forecasting, but it does provide a
way of looking at the future that may perhaps be helpful.

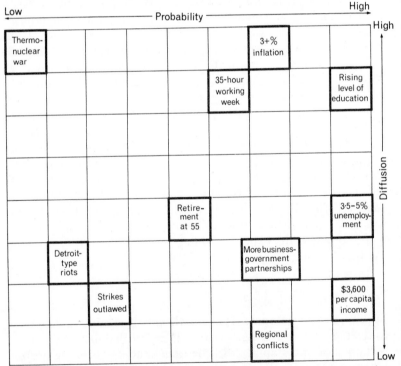

Figure 7.3   Probability/diffusion matrix for events and trends occurring
in U.S. and world by 1980.

The plottings made in this matrix are largely for purposes of illustration, and not to be taken as final judgements. To the extent that they provoke debate they will have at least demonstrated the value of making judgements clearly explicit so that planned action can more surely be taken. A few words of explanation about a sampling of the plottings may help to make clear the basis for them:

1 The probability of thermonuclear war is generally judged to be low, but it if did occur, its catastrophic impact would be felt worldwide. Hence it is assigned a low probability/high diffusion rating.
2 Regional or local wars in the developing nations, on the other hand, are much more likely to occur, but they will be confined to relatively limited areas. Consequently, they are assigned a high probability/low diffusion rating.
3 At the high end of the probability axis there are three developments with different plottings on the diffusion axis:

   (a) Levels of education should rise, in absolute terms, for virtually all segments of the U.S. population.
   (b) Unemployment rates should remain generally low, but the averages will cover a diversity of rates for various skill, age and racial groups.
   (c) Even more is diversity true of per capita disposable income, which, while increasing by an average of 50 per cent in fifteen years, will do so at different rates for different groups, possibly even increasing the gap between the 'new affluents' and the smaller, but more visible, poor.

Values Profile

As we have already noted, changes in value systems may be the major determinants of social and political trends in the future, and business planning would be well advised to try to get a fix on these changes as one essential element in its forecasting system. One way of systematizing analysis of value trends is to develop a 'values profile' (Figure 7.4). Like the probability-diffusion matrix, this chart should be viewed not as a precise scientific measurement but merely as a useful way of looking

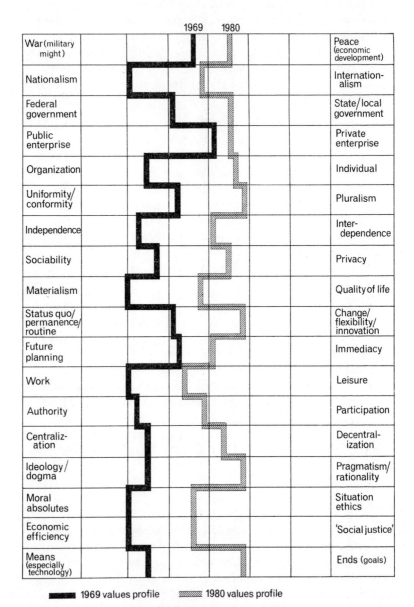

■■■ 1969 values profile   ▨▨▨ 1980 values profile

Figure 7.4   Profile of significant value-system changes: 1969–80 as seen by General Electric's Business Environment section.

at the future. Like the matrix, too, it contains plottings that are meant to be indicative — pointing the way to a more comprehensive study — rather than definitive.

To point up the possible attitude changes as dramatically as possible, the chart works as follows:

1   It has been made of up contrasting pairs of values (to a greater or less extent, that is: enhancement of one value implies a diminution of the other — e.g. war vs peace; conformity vs pluralism). Each society and generation has tended to seek its own new balance between these contrasting pairs, with the weight shifting from one side to the other as conditions and attitudes change.

2   It emphasizes the value changes likely to be most prevalent among the trend-setting segment of the population (young, well-educated, relatively affluent, 'committed'). These are the people among whom companies recruit the managerial and professional talent they require.

Plotted on the chart are two value profiles — one representing the approximate balance struck by these trend-setters in 1969 (when our initial study was undertaken) between each pair of values: the other indicating the hypothetical balance that might be struck in 1980. It is important to stress that the chart attempts to predict value changes, *not* necessarily events; even though trend-setters may value, say, arms-control agreements, events may lag behind their influence (e.g. owing to the political thinking of the electorate as a whole) or lie outside their control (e.g. regional wars among developing nations).

Social Pressures Priority Analysis

In a pluralistic society it is predictable that the criteria by which corporate performance is judged at any one time will be many and varied. The social pressures on the corporation will also shift over time. In the face of such variety and shifting it is essential that there should be, located in the strategic-planning process, some systematic means of assigning corporate priorities to these pressures. Almost certainly the demands that are made on the corporation at any one time will exceed its ability to respond, equally and effectively, to all; for it is doubtful if the corporation can ever be all things to all men. Furthermore there is a

legitimate question to be raised about the societal ranking of
these demands; not every demand is equally valid, or pressed
with equal vigour.

In an effort to meet this need for priority analysis we developed at General Electric a systematic screening and analysis
procedure whose main elements are charted in Figure 7.5.
Essentially this is an attempt to supply a rational systematic

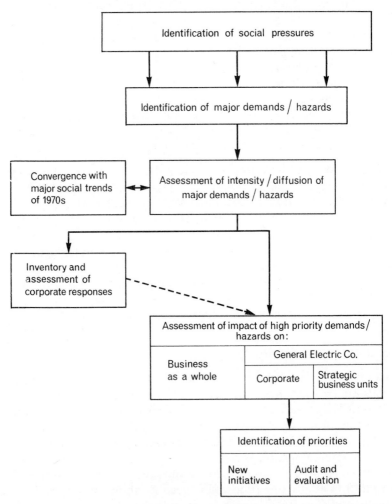

Figure 7.5   Social pressures on business: a systematic analysis for
corporate priorities.

and (as nearly as possible) objective evaluation of social pressures, with a view to determining priorities for corporate response in the development of strategy or making of policy.

The first step in the process is building up an inventory of social pressures as expressed in the major complaints commonly made about corporate performance. At this stage we have aimed to be as comprehensive and inclusive as possible, preferring not to omit any, and have grouped the pressures into eight principal categories: Marketing/Financial, Production Operations, Employee Relations/Working Conditions, Governance, Communications, Community and Government Relations, Defence Production, and International Operations.

Next comes the identification of the major demands and hazards associated with these complaints. In this context 'demands' are defined as the range of solutions advocated to remedy the defect that is complained about (e.g. federal chartering to curb 'market power', stringent emissions standards to control pollution, job enlargement to upgrade the challenge in 'boring, dehumanizing work'). 'Hazards', on the other hand, are the adverse consequences that might flow from inadequate corporate response to some of these demands: a good example would be the progressive alienation of employees, and lowering of productivity, that would flow from failure to meet the new and growing demands for 'meaningful, significant work assignments'.

The third step is a two-phase screening process that is performed on each one of these demands and hazards. In an effort to arrive at their relative societal validity and ranking, we have assessed each one in the following terms:

1   *Its 'convergence' with the major social trends of the 1970s.*
    To what extent are thirteen major trends likely to accelerate or impede the realization of each demand or hazard? These trends are increasing affluence; rising level of education; proliferating technology; emergence of 'post-industrial society' (including the services economy); growing interdependence of institutions (including business—Government partnerships); increasing emphasis on individualism; growing pluralism (groups, organizations) and diversity of life styles; the 'equality revolution'; growing emphasis on 'quality of life' (ecology, culture, education, Maslow's

Levels 4 and 5); redefinition of work/leisure patterns; continued increase in foreign competition; growing/changing role of Government; and continued urbanization. The impact of each trend on each demand is assigned a numerical score from 1 to 10, either positive or negative, depending on whether the impact is accelerating or impeding. An aggregate 'convergence' score is then computed for each demand/hazard.

2 *The intensity/diffusion of pressure behind it.* To what extent are fourteen major constituencies/pressure groups of the corporation likely to press for this demand? The fourteen comprise consumer groups, share owners, Government, unions, blue-collar workers, managers and professional workers, small business, minorities, women, college youth, environmental groups, 'populists', academic critics, and 'moralists' (i.e. pressure groups focused on moral issues). Each demand is ranked 4-3-2-1, according to whether it might be included in the top, second, third or bottom quartile of each group's demands and interests. An aggregate 'intensity/diffusion' score is then computed for each demand.

As a result of this third step it is possible to plot each demand on a scoring sheet, using the two aggregate scores for 'convergence' and 'intensity/diffusion'. The important point is *not* the precise score assigned to each demand but its final position *in relation to the median* score on both axes. In other words, our purpose is to identify, and focus on, those demands that fall in the 'high/high' quadrant of the chart, scoring high on both convergence with major trends and intensity/diffusion of pressure.

The fourth and fifth steps are then performed only on these high-priority demands. (This is not to say that we can wholly ignore demands falling in the other three quadrants, only that they would, on current assessment, appear to have a lower order of societal validity and ranking.) These two assessment steps deal with the following:

1 The impact of these demands on the business community as a whole, and on General Electric (both at the corporate level and on the Strategic Business Units, the operating components of the company)

2   An inventory and evaluation of corporate responses (to
      date) to these demands.

So far the impact analysis has been done only on a rudimentary
basis, assessing the high-priority demands on a low to high impact scale; and the evaluation of corporate responses is in process, and is, in a sense, a never-ending task.

The outcome of this whole process should be at least an
approximation to a set of corporate priorities on social pressures that should be factored into strategic planning and decision-making. Based on the evaluation of corporate responses
to date, it should also be possible to differentiate between
those areas in which new initiatives are clearly called for, and
those in which the main need is continuing audit and evaluation
of existing responses.

'GET ON THE LEARNING CURVE'

Professor Raymond Bauer of the Harvard Business School has
this advice for companies contemplating the social audit: 'Get
on the learning curve'. The same advice might well be given
to those considering the need for adding social and political
forecasting to their planning systems. It must be frankly recognized that one is asking a lot in the way of added complexity
by so doing, for it entails the following:

1   Going from two dimensions (economic, technological) to
      four (social, political, economic, technological).
2   Talking about 'alternative futures' (and, therefore con-
      tingency planning) rather than about certainty.
3   Broadening the concept and reach of strategy.
4   Enlarging the range of criteria used in strategy selection.

But nothing is to be gained, and much may be lost, by further
delay. Neither the 'softness' of the data that must be handled,
nor the lack of precise tools and tested methodologies, should
be counted sufficient excuse for not making corporate planning
meet this new test for relevance.

Part III
Formulating Key Strategies and Plans

8 Economic Analysis of Corporate Strengths and Weaknesses

John R. Sparkes

A company's objectives, together with the policies and strategies to achieve those objectives, must be seen in the light of its assessment of future opportunities and threats as related to its own strengths and weaknesses. This assessment comprises two parts. One is the assessment of all those factors affecting the company that are beyond its immediate control. These environmental factors include economic, political, social and technological changes of the kind discussed in Part II of the book. The other is an evaluation of the company's strengths and weaknesses, the purpose of which is to highlight its general competitive position relative to some desired performance level. In view of the importance of economic analysis as a foundation of effective corporate planning, this chapter will suggest how such analysis of company strengths and weaknesses might be developed.

Economic analysis in this context takes in two broad areas for examination. The first is a review of the total industry to which the company belongs, and the second is an examination of the company's competitive position within that industry. The role of economics is therefore one of diagnosis, which is essential in carrying out strategic planning.

DEFINING MARKET BOUNDARIES

Before looking in detail at the process of economic analysis, it is useful to consider the contribution economics makes to defining market boundaries, which is often a practical difficulty. In

answering the question, 'What business am I in?', potential as well
as actual competitors need to be included in the market boundary,
whether or not they are supplying products of the industry to
which one believes one's firm to belong. In the last resort, of
course, all commodities compete for consumers' income, which
means that one can never define the market boundary absolutely.
Nevertheless the problem cannot be evaded.

We would say that two products, one made by Firm A and one
made by Firm B, were competing in the same market if changes
in the price (or some other competitive variable) of one had a
'significant effect' on the sales of the other. In other words, we
can approach the question of defining market boundaries through
the economic concept of cross-elasticities of sales between firms.
For Firms A and B this is defined as

$$\frac{\text{Percentage change in sales volume of Firm B}}{\text{Percentage change in price of Firm A}}$$

But what constitutes a 'significant effect'? How high does the
cross-elasticity of sales need to be before Firm A regards Firm B
as selling in the same market as itself? It would be costly (even
assuming it were feasible) to seek precise answers to the question
of the significant value of cross-elasticities as a means of defining
market boundaries, but the *concept* of cross-elasticity is of value
because it does force us to think about the issue of defining
market boundary, even when this thinking stops short of being
translated into elaborate analysis.

The demand emphasis of cross-elasticity gets us away from the
traditional view, which regards an industry essentially from the
supply side; we traditionally group firms into industries by
Standard Industrial Classification because they produce physically similar products. While obviously essential for other purposes, this approach to the grouping of firms overlooks the wider
market in which the firm's products are substitutes for or complements to other products of firms not in the same supply
industry, and whose products, although competing or comple-
mentary so far as the consumer is concerned, are physically
different.

As instances of substitutability and complementarity one
may cite, for the former, the sale of plastics in existing markets
for steel products; and, for the latter, the demand for petrol
derived from the demand for cars. So from a demand point of

view goods with significant cross-elasticities (positive for substitutes, negative for complements) should be regarded as being in the same 'industry'. The traditional supply point of view may even be positively misleading in a corporate-planning context. If we take, for example, the metal manufacturing industry, the various products of that industry are likely to have very low cross-elasticities with each other. So the question 'What business am I in?' is better approached in terms of *market boundaries* based on those products that have (or in the future appear likely to have) significant *cross-effects* on one's own.

THE PROCESS OF ECONOMIC ANALYSIS

Having suggested a conceptual approach to the problem of establishing what business a company is in, we must consider the first stage in an economic analysis of corporate strengths and weaknesses, which requires a review of the industry to which the company belongs. This first broad area of examination can be subdivided as follows:

1   Analysis of the basic factors affecting industry supply and demand to determine the key factors for success in the industry
2   Identification of significant trends in these factors to highlight new problems or opportunities that may arise in the industry.

This subdivision illustrates the point that the review of a company's industry is not something static, but must take account of changes over time. Because this process of economic analysis is continuous, we shall treat these two aspects of the problem together.

REVIEW OF THE INDUSTRY

Analysis of the basic factors affecting industry supply and demand will generally cover four broad categories.

Market/Consumer Characteristics

These determine the forces that affect the demand for the products of the business as well as their growth outlook. The main considerations relevant in this context are as follows:

1 *Consumers.* It is important to know who buys the products,
   in what quantities, with what frequency, and (for seasonal
   goods in particular) when products are purchased.
2 *Distribution channels.* In defining channels of distribution
   it is necessary to know where consumers can buy the
   products, how the products reach the selling point, and
   what functions are performed at each stage in the channel
   of distribution. This latter point is necessary to any comparison of, for example, trade margins given by manufacturers on one industry's products, and margins given for
   other products handled by the same distribution channel.
3 *Product performance and end use.* In examining the product
   line, and in order to understand how the product is used,
   it is necessary to consider the specific applications of the
   product, whether other products could be substituted for
   it, whether the product is a necessity or a luxury, and its
   expected life cycle.
4 *Price.* How price is determined in the industry — for example,
   whether producers practise 'cost-plus' or 'going-rate'
   pricing — is relevant to any appreciation of why individual
   manufacturers may be able to achieve price differentials
   for essentially similar products. It is also important to discover how price trends compare with industry cost trends;
   and the pattern of price leadership in the industry.
5 *Basis of the buying decision.* Related to all the above considerations is the question of how consumers choose between
   essentially similar products being offered by different
   producers. What, for example, is the relative importance
   of price, quality, service, etc., and who influences the consumer's choice? This is such a complex issue that it should
   be analysed precisely for each particular kind of buying
   decision. For example, in considering retail-distribution
   strategy in the confectionery business it is important to
   know whether the consumer typically decides to buy
   sweets before entering a confectioner's shop, or whether
   the decision is made upon impulse on seeing the sweets in
   the shop. Is confectionary a planned purchase? Will the
   consumer seek a particular brand or take what is available
   in any shop?

Investigation of these market/consumer characteristics will provide an understanding of the factors affecting the demand for the industry's product. Trends in these characteristics will indicate the outlook for growth. To take one simple example, the changed buyer behaviour resulting from the growth of domestic deep-freeze capacity has provided considerable opportunities for expansion of the markets of frozen-food manufacturers.

Cost Characteristics

Cost characteristics significantly affect industry supply. An important area for analysis here is the variation of costs between the different functions of the business. In some industries the costs associated with the major functions — for example, manufacturing, wholesale distribution and retail distribution — may be easily identified by the individual company. In other industries, where an individual company may not take part in each of the major functions of the industry, the analysis of cost by function becomes more difficult. The problem of obtaining information is attributable to the company's difficulty in isolating the value added at each stage of the production process.

An appreciation of fixed and variable cost characteristics for the whole business and the way these vary between functions is also necessary if one is to understand how these costs vary with the *scale* of operations. The notion of economies of scale, while generally applied to the production process, also has relevance to such other related functions of business as physical distribution or the size of the retail outlet.

Changes in costs resulting from changes in the scale of operations — and possible consequent changes in the price and volume of output — are almost bound to have an effect on the return on investment. This impact will vary according to the type of business and the particular costs. For example, physical distribution costs are a significant proportion of total costs in the food business, so that a reduction in such costs would be likely to affect return on investment significantly, but in an industry with low distribution costs the effect might be negligible.

When one is thinking in terms of changes that will result in variations in cost, or indeed in price or volume, then the range over which the variation takes place should be meaningful in

terms of the company's current position in the market, and the
growth trends in the industry. One needs also to consider the
implications of such changes for the profitability of the business.
The *source* of industry profits, and consequently company
profits, is itself a specific question to be answered in looking at
cost characteristics. It is essential to know the main sources of
profits and how they vary between manufacturing units, product
groups or markets.

Technology

The degree to which supply of a product is flexible, and the extent to which new products can be made with existing resources,
are affected by technology. There are several considerations to
be taken into account in this regard:

1   *Relation between product and process.* The interrelation
    between the production process and the product itself may
    be such that a new or improved product can be introduced
    only after the development of a new process of production.
    This interrelation, therefore, affects the speed with which
    new products can be launched on the market, and even the
    speed with which production capacity responds to increased
    demand.
2   *Effect of changes in technology on the nature of the industry.*
    Changes in production or distribution technology can affect
    the nature of an industry. For example, by reducing the
    number of steps in the production cycle, and thereby re-
    ducing the investment outlay, a technological development
    may permit the entry of smaller manufacturers into an
    industry from which they were previously excluded. Such
    an effect can change the nature of competition within an
    industry, particularly where a few large firms had previously
    acted to maintain prices.
3   *Effects of rate of innovation on growth.* Technological innova-
    tions, particularly those resulting in the emergence of new
    products, can, as with synthetic fibres and the textile
    market, significantly affect the growth of the industry. It
    is necessary, therefore, to be aware of the rate of product
    innovation in the industry, and the way in which new pro-
    ducts or technological innovations have affected the growth
    of the industry.

The Structure of an Industry

The structure determines *inter alia* the extent and nature of competition in that industry, and specifically reflects the following characteristics:

1 *Concentration.* This refers to the number and size distribution of companies producing the particular type of output associated with the industry.
2 *Vertical integration.* The degree of vertical integration refers to the extent to which individual companies perform successive stages in the production of a particular product or service.
3 *Barriers to entry.* These are obstacles preventing new firms wishing to engage in the production of a particular product from entering the industry. Such barriers are largely dependent upon cost conditions associated with the product of the industry.
4 *Diversification.* This refers to the extent to which individual companies produce a variety of different products, with the accompanying advantage of product flexibility.

Having analysed the trends in these forces affecting supply and demand, we may try and identify the key factors for success in the industry or industries in which the company is operating. In most industries there are certain characteristics unique to that industry, which this type of analysis will highlight. It is also useful to identify the unique advantages of each company in the industry. This can lead to the specification of other key factors for the individual company's success — for example, the adoption of some sophisticated financial control system. The whole of this type of analysis should, of course, take place against the more general background of such economic and political trends as the reduction of tariff barriers to international trade or the introduction of more rigorous controls on mergers that impinge upon the industry.

The four broad categories dealt with above, reviewing those forces affecting *industry* supply and demand, constitute the first stage in an analysis of corporate strengths and weaknesses. The second stage in economic analysis identifies major problems and opportunities by assessing a *company's* competitive position within the industry.

COMPANY APPRAISAL

This appraisal takes place against the background of key factors isolated in the first stage of the analysis. The factors to be considered in an assessment of the company's competitive performance will therefore parallel those dealt with in the review of industry. The analysis at this stage requires the development of a basis for assessment of the individual company's performance in relation to these key factors. Of those areas covered in the review of the industry, the following are likely to be the main areas for quantitative evaluation.

Comparative Market Position

Comparison of individual items in the company's product line with those of competing companies in terms of price, promotional expenditure, product quality and other policy instruments affecting product performance is necessary to reveal strengths and weaknesses in the product. Changes in the company's marketing-policy variables are particularly likely to influence its share of the market. An assessment of the size of the *total* market is gained from the review of the industry in stage one. At the second stage it becomes necessary to estimate market *share* both at the present and, for sales-forecasting purposes, in the future. Without here dealing with methods of forecasting market share,[1] the company must analyse those factors that determine its share of the market. The economist's simple theory of consumer behaviour is a good starting point, taking price as the main determinant of quantity sold; but economists have long recognized that price is only one of the variables in market competition. The elasticity concept, which elementary economics has used to measure the responsiveness of quantity demanded to changes in price, has equal validity in the context of changes in non-price variables. Four variables have commonly been identified as major determinants of market share, and these provide a useful guideline to companies analysing comparative market positions:

1   The price of the company's products relative to the price of competing products
2   The company's advertising and promotional expenditure relative to that of competing companies
3   A quantitative assessment of the company's product quality relative to the quality of competing products

4   Some measure of the relative quality of the company's
     distribution channels.

Financial Comparisons

Financial analysis of the company compared with its competitors
is generally based on published financial statements. Although
these may not give precise data on the detailed cost characteristics of a company, they will generally serve to illustrate where
discrepancies between the performance of companies are evident
(see Chapter 9).

   The role of economic analysis in assessing corporate strengths
and weaknesses is therefore essentially one of identifying the
main opportunities and threats confronting the company. Having
identified them, the company should act in a way that will exploit opportunities and combat threats. Such action requires that
the company considers all the alternative courses open to it,
evaluating the costs and benefits of implementing specific action
programmes.

REFERENCE

1 See Lowes, B. and Sparkes, J. R. *Modern Managerial
   Economics* (London: Heinemann, 1974), chs 8 and 12.

9 Financial Aspects of Corporate Planning

Stanley Corlett

THE ROLE OF THE ACCOUNTANT IN THE PLANNING PROCESS

Accountants have for many years exerted a powerful influence at the centre of companies. They are responsible for measuring profits and for much of the interpretation of cost and profitability data, advising top management accordingly. In many cases they manage the company's finances. Thus it is inevitable that there should be a considerable overlap between corporate and financial planning. While the extent of this overlap varies from company to company, dependent upon organizational styles, the financial emphasis increases the closer one moves to the centre. Accordingly, the interaction of corporate and financial planning needs to be considered at both group and operating subsidiary levels.

FINANCIAL PLANNING

Financial planning has three distinct yet interrelated central themes — profitability, finance and capital investment. The general management of the operating subsidiaries is responsible for profitability, but the management of company finance — liquidity, solvency, fund-raising, gearing, dividend policy, taxation, currency management, etc. — is normally centralized. Cash is a highly flexible resource: it has a wide variety of potential uses, may be transferred easily and quickly, and is most economically obtained in large tranches. All of these point to centralized cash management, in which the finance department has a direct functional responsibility.

In between profit planning and financial management lies the field of investment decisions (defined to include acquisitions, diversification and divestment). This field has important implications for the profits, the cash flow and the funding of the company.

CORPORATE STYLES

A second set of parameters influencing the interrelation of financial and corporate planning relates to the specific features of the company and the environment in which it operates. What is its growth philosophy, its attitude to risk, its management style and its existing planning capability? Is it a manufacturing or a service company? Are its existing investments in growing, stable or contracting sectors of the economy and of the markets in which it operates? Is it strongly affected by cyclical and seasonal factors? How certain and favourable is the climate for business investment — or the reverse? Each affects the policies of the firm, and consequently the style of corporate planning.

FINANCIAL AND CORPORATE PLANNING IN OPERATING SUBSIDIARIES

Envisage a corporate planner, newly appointed to the operating subsidiary of a medium to large group, and anxious to get to grips with its financial planning activities. Where should he start? How should he proceed? The following four steps are suggested.

1 Determine How the Performance of the Subsidiary is Assessed and Review the Principal Financial Reports

Initially the objective should be one of range-finding rather than a detailed analysis, using the balance sheet, profit and loss statement and cash-flow analysis. Table 9.1 provides, for illustrative purposes, a simplified balance-sheet presentation.

QUESTION: Is the company, on the face of it, profitable?
TEST: Calculate the return on capital employed: operating profit or profit before tax divided by capital employed.
QUESTION: Does the company operate on high/low margins and a high/low asset turnover?

Table 9.1   Skeleton balance sheet

Item	£	Examples
Fixed Assets	80	Semi-permanent assets. Property, plant, vehicles.
+ Current Assets	40	Trading assets (stock and debtors) + cash and near cash.
− Current Liabilities	(20)	Trading liabilities (creditors), overdrafts, current tax.
CAPITAL EMPLOYED	100	
Shareholder Finance	75	Share capital, parent company loans, retained profits.
+ Long term liabilities	25	Medium and long term loans. Deferred taxation.
SOURCES OF FINANCE	100	

NOTES

1. This is a simplified presentation. Items such as trade investments and goodwill have been ignored.

2. In special cases, the nomenclature of assets may vary. For a garage, motor vehicles are a trading (current) asset.

3. This is the most commonly used measure of capital employed.

TEST: Calculate margins and asset turnover as follows:

$$\frac{Profit}{Capital\ employed} = \underset{(Margins)}{\frac{Profit}{Sales}} \times \underset{(Asset\ turnover)}{\frac{Sales}{Capital\ employed}}$$

An asset turnover of less than 1 indicates a heavily capital-intensive business, which ought to have high margins to compensate.

QUESTION: Which are the most important assets?

TEST: The balance sheet should show the order of magnitude.

QUESTION: Which are the most important sources of revenue and significant costs?

TEST: This should be disclosed by the profit and loss statement (management rather than financial accounts).

QUESTION: Does the subsidiary generate a trading cash surplus? Is this surplus/deficit increasing or declining? What happens to any spare cash? Here the corporate planner should consult his accounting colleagues.

It should be stressed that the above are 'quick and dirty' measures, needing some caution in their use. Remember that, firstly, all profit calculations and measures of return on capital employed are dependent upon how profits and asset values are measured. Secondly, where assets are leased rather than owned, both profits and capital employed are reduced, and this affects the calculation of ratios. Leasing can make a business appear to be less capital-intensive than it really is. Thirdly, as the balance sheet measures assets and liabilities at a point of time, whereas sales and profits are measured over a period of time, check that the balance sheet date is reasonably representative of the year as a whole. This is particularly important in a seasonal business where sharp variations in working capital and in bank overdrafts take place throughout the year.

2 Ascertain how Independent or Interdependent, in Economic Terms, are the Activities of the Division or Subsidiary relative to Other Divisions; and Check the Different Activities of the Division Itself

Table 9.2 provides a checklist that can be used in these investigations. The planner will almost certainly find that the higher the degree of interdependence, the more sophisticated the planning system needs to be, the plans of one division or product group continuously impinging upon another. The oil and chemical industry provides a particularly good example of a complex network of interlocking relations, stretching across exploration, production, transportation and refining, with end-products such as petrol, oil, lubricants, detergents and agricultural chemicals.

The independence and later interdependence of Unilever's food divisions show how initially independent activities may gradually coalesce. In 1950 Walls Ice Cream, Walls meat, Batchelors canned goods, and Mac-Fisheries were each well established subsidiaries with clearly defined, specialized products, and Birds Eye was a small but rapidly growing company, developing quick-frozen products (especially vegetables). Once frozen goods had taken off and Birds Eye had diversified into fish, meat and dessert products, these food lines started to become interdependent,

Table 9.2   Checklist to determine the degree of economic interdependence

(A) *Subsidiaries/Divisions*

1. Is the subsidiary or division an investment or profit centre?
2. Does the subsidiary both market and manufacture?
3. Are there similar subsidiaries elsewhere?
4. Does the subsidiary compete with other subsidiaries for the same markets?
5. Do inter-company sales feature strongly?
6. Does the subsidiary purchase raw materials or components from other subsidiaries?
7. If yes to 5 or 6, what basis of transfer-pricing is used?

(B) *Profit Centres/Products*

1. Is there more than one profit centre within the subsidiary?
2. Do the profit centres share the same production facilities?
3. Is production of the one item carried out at more than one location?
4. Are products grouped by markets or technological factors, and
5. Are such groupings homogeneous or conflicting?
6. Are product contributions assessed before or after the apportionment of overheads?
7. If overhead apportionments are used, how meaningful is the basis of apportionment?
8. Is profit responsibility measured, before interest and/or tax?

(C) *Technical Notes*

1. The words subsidiary (a legal entity) and division (a sphere of management responsibility) are frequently interchangeable.
2. An investment centre's performance is measured by return on investment. (Profit as a % of capital employed.) Profit volume may be used instead if the capital employed is small.
3. Profit centre implies responsibility for profit. In some divisions, several separately managed profit centres co-exist.
4. Direct overheads are specifically attributable to a product or process. Indirects cannot be so identified.
5. The bases of allocation vary from rent 'per square foot' to the arbitrary 'per sales £'.
6. Interest paid is normally deducted from operating profit in arriving at 'Profit before tax', rather than being charged against operating profits. Thus it is often ignored when assessing managerial performance.
   In the current inflationary era there is a strong case for treating this interest as an operating cost; particularly for those businesses which are working capital intensive.

particularly when the material specialists sought to add a quick-freezing arm to their material-processing techniques.

An understanding of the concept of economic interdependence is essential if the reader wishes to develop skills in interpreting profitability data and to understand the economic structure of a firm. Profit-reporting systems break the business down into small and apparently independent sections for the purpose of control. This independence is of course mythical, and the planner has to beware of reading too much into individual product, customer or profitability statements. His real concern must be with the aggregate result.

Whenever there is a marked degree of interdependence between his own and other subsidiaries, the planner will almost certainly need to set up close relations with his counterparts in those subsidiaries, and with the group personnel who have responsibility for the coordination of these activities. He should also study the theory of transfer pricing and its practical application within the company, for it will certainly remain a continuing bone of contention.

3 Can the Budget be Used Effectively for Planning Purposes?

Budgets are used for planning and control, particularly the latter. Figure 9.1 shows a typical control-orientated system, with some planning adjuncts. This system has the following features:

1 The budget preparation incorporates a comprehensive operational and financial review, in which market trends are matched with the availability of resources. Management plays a big part in formulating these plans.
2 Throughout the preparation period and the succeeding year middle management will be pressed to uplift their targets. Similar pressures are exerted on the top management by the parent company. Most managers recognize the name of the game and formulate their budgets accordingly.
3 The monthly and quarterly reviews focus on the achievement of the desired end result, rather than on the actuals to date.
4 The half-year assessment is nearly as comprehensive as the original budget.
5 The company has recently introduced five-year planning, based on market planning. The preparation of the five-year plan is undertaken separately from budget preparation.

Time	Event	1974	1975
September 1973	Budget preparation	A comprehensive budget	A provisional estimate
February 1974	Monthly review*	Confirm budget will be met	Not considered
April 1974	Quarterly review*	Review results and confirm budget will be met	
May 1974	Budget revision*	A comprehensive review	A revised estimate
*Monthly and quarterly reviews were held throughout the year.			

Figure 9.1   A typical financial control system.

The system may be assessed as follows for planning purposes:

1   The process was highly successful in integrating the activities of the company, up to the end of the forthcoming year. Both operational and financial criteria were met.

2   Beyond December 1974, the end of the financial year, there was a yawning void; 1975 was hardly considered at all until September 1974. Here a planning gap existed.

3   The system pressurized management towards short-term operating decisions, so that there was a tendency to assume that 1975 and beyond would be similar, though better than, 1974.

4   Financial analysts, when assessing alternative courses of action, almost invariably concentrated on the impact on the current year's profitability. In a number of cases a longer time horizon would have been preferable.

5   To some extent the planning defects were counterbalanced by the introduction of five-year planning. These five-year plans were kept separate from the annual budget. Projections as to market growth and market share were made for existing products and the resultant profits calculated, indicating as shown in Figure 9.2, that a profit gap existed. This gap was to be filled by new products, some of which

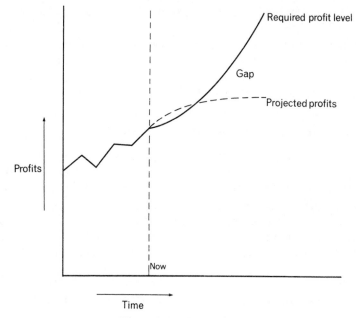

Figure 9.2   The profit gap.

were in the pipeline. The weakness of this long-range
planning system lay in the fact that it concentrated exclusively on the market. The methodology assumed that
resources could be easily obtained, and that the asset and
cost structures of the company would not be altered
significantly.

The example just quoted was taken from a growing non-
typical business, operating in a market in which growth was
reasonably predictable. In many ways the system used was highly
effective, though of limited use for longer-term planning. A
company whose principal activity is that of deep-water trawling,
say, faces an altogether different problem. If only it could predict the amount of fish its ships would catch and the price at
which the fish could be sold, it would be content. Nor can the
company be sure that poor catches would be accompanied by
high prices, for in-shore fishing could produce record catches
simultaneously. Here, as in any industry operating in highly
uncertain markets (demand or supply), planning activities have
to be largely divorced from budgeting, and concentrated on

strategic studies, as to the direction in which a business should go.

A different set of problems faces the business whose cash resources are strained. Here the questions becomes one of rationing cash as effectively as one can. Financial criteria rather than operational criteria dominate at such time.

4 Ascertain How Investment Decisions Are Made

Much of the recent literature surveying investment decisions has concentrated upon the use of discounted cash flow as a decision-making criterion (sometimes as the sole criterion). This is an oversimplified view. Discounting, which measures the time-value of money, is a project-appraisal technique that implicitly assumes the project is an entity in itself, whereas it is vital that the organization ensures that its investment policy presents a coherent whole.

Coherent investment decisions are normally achieved through undertaking strategic investment studies and using the capital

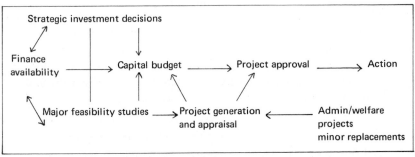

Figure 9.3   Capital investment decisions.

budget as a coordinating mechanism (Figure 9.3). Here an amalgam of proposals at different stages of completion — started, approved, analysed though unapproved, tentative — are considered jointly, being matched against the availability of financial and other resources. The ensuing decisions, though not sacrosanct, specify priorities and help to ensure that the necessary resources will be forthcoming. Capital intensive businesses that fail to plan or to integrate their investment and financial decisions through a capital budget frequently finish up with severe cash

problems or with a ragbag of investments, each promising a high
return but the whole failing through a lack of coherence.

PROJECT CATEGORIZATION

Over a number of years a business should strive to maintain a
balance between various types of capital proposals, each with different objectives and different criteria for approval. The categorization I find most useful is shown in Figure 9.4.

Profit orientated	Preservation
New products and processes	Replacement
Variety extension	Administration
Expansion	Welfare
Cost saving	
Rationalization	

Figure 9.4   Various types of capital proposals.

The Consequential Effects of Different Project Categories

Some of the questions that need to be postulated are the
following

1   What proportion of the capital budget is devoted to profit-
    orientated projects? Is this proportion changing?
2   What further investment opportunities will or could arise as
    a result of investing in this proposal?
3   What impact will this investment have on our resource plan-
    ning and cost structure in the longer term?

A moment's thought should enable the reader to recognize
that new products and processes may give rise to secondary expansion and variety extension projects. At the same time they
frequently generate a long-term demand for additional 'preserva-
tion' proposals.

In some instances supporting resources such as factory space
are already available and under-utilized, at least in the short
term. An apparently attractive proposal but heavily reliant upon
such free resources could damage profitability if a better use

emerged. On the other hand, should the resources be permanently free and fixed within the company, the project should be worth supporting.

Industries vary in their propensity to generate complete or partial capital-investment proposals. For instance, multi-product businesses generally change their product lines, and make piecemeal additions to their factory premises, more frequently than would a mining company, which tends to make large, and frequently separately financed, investments in a new site from which it extracts a limited number of products. Apart from major expansion, the infrastructure of a mine is largely set in the construction phase, and the costs are built into the initial project proposal.

GROUP FINANCIAL PLANNING

Table 9.3 amplifies the primary tasks of the group's financial management — finance procurement, source satisficing, dividend policy, tax planning, and cash and currency management. While these tasks are clearly the responsibility of the finance side, the corporate planner needs to understand the significance of each and how they mesh together.

Matching Investments and Sources of Finance

Downturns in business confidence regularly expose companies who have 'borrowed short and invested long'. For one reason or another investors who find that they can obtain a better return elsewhere attempt to withdraw their money, which is by now tied up in assets that cannot be liquidated rapidly, other than at a substantial discount. The company runs out of cash and has to be liquidated or taken over on unfavourable terms.

The Property Boom

During the period 1971−3 many British companies overinvested in the property boom, to their evident discomfiture in 1974. Lacking a buoyant market, which would have enabled them to liquidate their investments profitably, many speculative property companies found themselves trapped between high interest rates and frozen rental income. Having overborrowed during the growth

Table 9.3   Key tasks of financial management

Group Financial Tasks

1. Finance procurement.

   Obtaining the right quantity at the right time from the most appropriate source. Determining whether the finance be raised from shareholders or lenders; and, if the latter, the period of the loan.

2. Source satisficing.

   Maintaining the continued confidence of the company's financial backers. This necessitates that shareholder categorization be defined and that the separate interests and aspirations of shareholders and lenders be recognized, and in normal circumstances acted upon.

3. Dividend policy.

   Ideally a policy of gradual, progressive growth is sought. Firms are generally reluctant to raise dividends if they believe that they may later need to reduce them. Cyclical businesses are frequently an exception to this rule, in that sharp rises and falls in dividends are common.

4. Tax planning.

   Minimizing the tax burden on existing operations. Evaluating the interaction of tax legislation and investment policy, tax and dividend policy (the switch from income tax to corporation tax (1965), and from the classical to the imputation system of corporation tax (1973)) tax and liquidity — the introduction of Advanced Corporation Tax (1965) and changes in the timing of payment (1974).

5. Cash Management.

   Managing cash flows to ensure that the cash requirements of the operating divisions are kept to a necessary minimum. The short term investment of temporary cash surpluses, largely through the discount market.

6. Currency Management.

   Predicting whether sterling will rise or fall in value relative to the currencies of the countries with which one transacts business or in which one has investments.
       Matching investment needs and cash supply in different currencies. Arranging the purchase and transfer of currency at the optimum time.

phase, instead of limiting their investment or raising more equity finance from their shareholders, they paid the penalty when the market turned down. This had a domino effect on the secondary banks, many of which had overlent to these same clients.

The Cost of Borrowing

Unilever in 1948–9 raised large long-term loans at the then high rate of interest of $4\frac{1}{2}$–$4\frac{3}{4}$ per cent. It is believed that a substantial part of this was earmarked for groundnuts, but the groundnut scheme fell through and Unilever was left with substantial sums of cash raised at what later transpired to be a ridiculously low cost. While some would consider Unilever fortunate, the firm was clearly astute enough to recognize the trend of interest rates and to borrow rather than raise equity finance.

Risk and Return

It would be unwise for a company to invest substantially in highly speculative activities – with the attendant risks of a reduced dividend if things went wrong – if its shares were largely held by pension funds and life-assurance companies. Such is the reliance upon stable dividends of such funds and companies that they would be reluctant to continue holding these shares.

The Influence of Shareholders

The latent power of the institutional shareholders is well illustrated by the Rank-Watney case. The Rank Organisation, seeking to diversify, offended the large body of American institutional shareholders who viewed Rank as a cheap way into Xerox. The resultant fall in share prices substantially reduced the value of the bid.

Dividend Policy

A high retention/low dividend policy is appropriate to a cash-hungry business. As cash outlays normally precede cash inflows, rapid growth imposes a strain on cash resources. While the market, at least in normal times, is willing to accept these low dividends, it is critical of companies whose growth objectives are modest and who over-conserve their cash, much of which is often frittered away on prestige projects.

Taxation

All business transactions fit into one of several tax pockets, some of which are more onerous than others in respect of the amount of tax to be paid or the timing of the payment. On the one hand we have the tax inspector and on the other the tax-avoidance industry, both sides seeking to place transactions in the category that suits them best. Tax considerations are also particularly important to companies with large overseas interests who have to assess the prospects for the British economy against the tax penalties that arise if too high a proportion of earnings come from overseas.

THE INCREASING IMPORTANCE OF EXCHANGE RATES

Consequent upon the move to floating exchange rates, currency markets have become increasingly volatile. Such volatility places a premium upon adroit currency management in that large windfall profits or substantial losses are becoming increasingly common. All businesses operating in international markets have to take both a long- and short-term view of the relative strength of the various currencies in which they deal. Will a currency's exchange-rate trend continue for several months or will it be reversed in the next few days?

While the answer to the above question may not appear to be the direct concern of the corporate planner, the long-term financial strength or weakness of a country in which the company has invested, or is about to invest, is of considerable significance; as it would also be if the company had raised large long- or medium-term loans in that currency. It is frequently necessary to base some planning decisions upon a currency's short-term weakness and others upon its long-term strength — a psychologically difficult argument to formulate and to propound, for it is dependent upon the planner having the ability to specify the time span for which the decision will be effective, and to conduct his analysis through this period of time.

CORPORATE FINANCIAL OBJECTIVES

It is easy to fall into the trap of postulating objectives solely in
such growth terms as increased profits, return on investment or
earnings per share. Setting financial objectives is essentially a
balancing operation, covering a range of objectives and criteria
(Figure 9.5). This may be a good point to define financial
criteria.

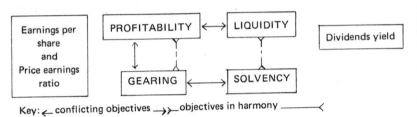

Figure 9.5   Setting financial objectives.

Profitability

The relation of profit to the resources used in generating it is
profitability. Normally measured by the ratio profit to capital
employed.

Liquidity

The ability of the business to meet its cash commitments shows
that it has sufficient liquidity. Current and quick-asset ratios
(current assets : current liabilities and cash and debtors : current
liabilities) in excess of 1·6—2·0 and 0·8—1·0 respectively suggest
a satisfactory liquidity ratio. Nevertheless it should be recognized that these ratios are at best arbitrary, and that the analysis
of the cash cycle is a much more powerful analytical tool.

The following questions need to be answered about liquidity.

Given that working capital is continuously being used and replaced, and that fixed capital investment predominantly consists
of a few, large cash outflows, is the business fixed- or working-
capital intensive?

How long a period elapses from the time that raw materials are
acquired, to the receipt of cash from our customers? To what
extent is this cycle financed by our creditors or by progress payments from our customers?

Table 9.4   Analysing the cash cycle

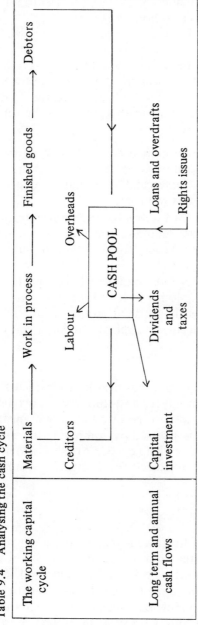

How predictable, seasonal and cyclical is the demand for our products? How much cash, or the potential to raise cash instantaneously, do we need to hold in reserve?

What rate of growth is projected, and how will inflation affect cash flow? In the vast majority of cases, particularly in the manufacturing sector, the cash-flow effects on growth and inflation are adverse in that investment, both fixed and working capital, precedes returns (I use the term cash-negative to describe this). Some notable exceptions to this rule are to be found outside the manufacturing sector:

1 *Insurance.* Premium income is received before claims are met. A healthy cash position ensues, unless the claims record is bad or inflation escalates beyond the expectations at the time premiums were set.
2 *Supermarkets.* Not noted for the promptness of their cash payments, yet selling for cash rather than on credit, supermarkets have frequently used their suppliers to finance their rapid growth.
3 *Financial institutions* (banks and discount houses, hire purchase, etc.). Money in its various forms is both the raw material and the finished product of the financial institutions, which form a sophisticated and complex sector.

Solvency

The potential ability of a business to discharge its financial obligations fully to employees and third parties (as distinct from shareholders) if it were to go into liquidation means that it is solvent. Solvency is assessed by comparing the total liabilities with the estimated realizable value of the assets in liquidation. Should the liabilities exceed the assets, the company is technically insolvent.

Gearing

The proportion of borrowed finance to the net worth (issued share capital, capital and revenue reserves) is known as the gearing or debt/equity ratio. Traditionally bank overdrafts, which are repayable on demand (at least in theory), are excluded from this measurement. But in an era in which businesses are frequently having to rely on short-term finance to meet their long-term investment needs, it is prudent to include overdrafts in the calculation of gearing ratios whenever they appear to be both permanent and significant.

Earnings per Share (e.p.s.)

A simple measurement is profit after tax less preference dividends, divided by the number of shares issued. The price/earnings ratio (P/E) is the share price divided by the earnings per share.

Both e.p.s. and P/E ratios are profitability measures in that no distinction is drawn between retained and distributed profits. This is in contrast to dividend yield, which is the dividend divided by the share price, and is a cash measure.

The matching of financial objectives

1 *Profitability-liquidity conflicts.* The conservation of cash automatically improves liquidity, but would the business do better by expanding more quickly? Conversely, a business that overtrades, investing too much, is likely to suffer severe liquidity problems.

2 *Liquidity-solvency harmonization.* A business suffering from an acute shortage of cash is likely to be forced into liquidation if its solvency is suspect.

3 *Gearing-solvency conflict.* As the business increases its gearing, so its total liabilities increase. In the event that the business invests in assets having a low realizable value, its solvency ratio declines.

4 *Gearing-profitability harmony and conflict.* The effect of gearing in increasing the return of shareholders' equity can be demonstrated by means of a simple illustration (Figure 9.6).

	Company A		Company B	
Shareholder finance	100		50	
Long term liabilities	–		50 (at 10%)	
Profit before tax and interest	20	5	20	5
Interest	–	–	5	5
Profit before tax	20	5	15	–
Pre-tax return on shareholder finance	20%	5%	30%	nil

Figure 9.6   The effect of gearing.

5   *Earnings per share, P/E ratios and dividend criteria.* The relative importance of earnings versus dividend criteria should initially be considered from the standpoint of the shareholder rather than the company. To which, earnings or dividends, does the shareholder attach the greater importance? Throughout the period 1955–73 earnings criteria were dominant.

Another dimension to this conflict is that of the competition between management and shareholders for retained profits on the one hand and for dividends on the other. Most managements are interested in growth, from which they attain self-fulfilment and opportunities for promotion, and this militates in favour of retentions rather than dividends, and in extreme cases can lead to unsound growth policies.

FINANCIAL STRUCTURE

It is readily apparent that the financial structure (the combination of profit, liquidity, solvency, gearing, earnings and dividend structures) of any business is in a continuous state of flux. Given a stable economic environment and modest rather than over-ambitious growth plans, financial structure, while altering gradually, could be considered to have a degree of permanence. This permanence provides a basis against which financial decisions can be taken and from which additional finance can normally be raised in large tranches, whether by a rights issue or the issue of a loan stock. Should a business seek to make a significant change in the style of its operations or to its rate of growth, it would need to reassess this financial structure.

Today inflation is insidiously altering the financial structure of many businesses by whittling away liquidity, causing a sharp cut back in business investment. Previously the twin fear of inflation and of a depression so reduced investor confidence that for a time it became impossible for business to raise significant amounts of long-term finance, and businesses were increasingly forced to meet their investment needs by borrowing short-term money, thereby exposing themselves to acute financial danger. Once this borrowing had peaked, a cut-back in investment was inevitable. It is predictable that, should a high rate of inflation continue, expansionary moves will soon run into renewed liquidity crises.

SETTING FINANCIAL OBJECTIVES FOR SUBSIDIARIES

Each subsidiary has a distinct financial structure of its own, though this is frequently masked by the method the parent company uses to finance it — predominantly parent-company loan finance, which may or may not be interest-free. Consequently solvency and gearing measurements applied to the balance sheet of a subsidiary are mostly meaningless, as are liquidity ratios — though not cash flow analyses — in that the parent company will largely denude the subsidiary of cash.

As a result it is inevitable that subsidiary-company managers concentrate their attention upon profitability (profit relative to capital employed), or upon profit volume. So great is the management-accounting emphasis upon turnover, profits and margins, that the control of capital employed is often left to the accountants rather than to general management. In both cases the balancing of financial objectives is left, *ipso facto,* to the parent company.

Allowing the subsidiary to concentrate entirely upon profitability, to the exclusion of all other financial considerations, has the merit of simplicity — but deceptively so. Firstly, it entails that all major financial decisions ought to be made, as distinct from sanctioned, by the parent; and this limits the effective degree of decentralization that can be attained. Alternatively, it calls for a remarkably efficient form of communication between the parent and its many subsidiaries. Secondly, it assumes that the subsidiary is unlikely to find its plans suddenly curtailed by a lack of cash, an assumption that is increasingly becoming untenable.

INVESTMENT STRATEGY

Previously we suggested that it was vital for the organization to ensure that its investment policy was coherent (Step 4, p. 138). What then governs the determination of investment strategy?

The Product Life-cycle

The five stages of the product life-cycle are development, growth, maturity, extension, and decline.

It is self-evident that a developing business will concentrate its

investment in new products and technologies, whereas a growth
business will be primarily busy with expansion projects and
variety extension. A mature business, without diversification
plans, is likely to increase its proportionate allocation of funds
to replacement, rationalization and cost-saving projects; lacking
market opportunities it tends to become increasingly efficient
and cost-conscious as it masters its technology and benefits from
economies of scale. Extension signifies a determination to pro-
long the product life cycle, frequently through process and
product improvements; and in other respects, the extension
phase resembles maturity. Disinvestment and closures feature
strongly in a decline.

Strategic Risks

It is necessary that a business should continually monitor the
risks inherent in its investment strategy (including the risks associated with its existing business). Occasionally large projects are
so risky that failure could cause the liquidation of the company,
or result in such depressing returns that a top management shake-
out will become inevitable. Thus for major projects it is just as
important to quantify the cost of failure as to quantify the benefits of success, to identify the circumstances that bring about
disaster, to outline a fail-safe strategy, to consider means of minimizing or sharing risks, and to define risk-return priorities.

The Availability of Finance

Rapid growth can rarely be undertaken without an infusion of
new cash. While the business may be highly profitable, or potentially so, increased investment in fixed assets and working
capital normally precedes the flow of cash from customers.

There are limits to the amount of cash which can prudently be
borrowed or raised from shareholders, so that the role of growth
is constrained by cash availability. In particular, this constraint
has particular relevance to companies in a development or growth
stage.

The corporate planner needs to ensure that the consequential
effects of an investment strategy upon cash flow are projected
ahead over a number of years. The unwary can easily fall into
the trap of securing sufficient finance for the medium term with-

out considering that the long-term investment strategy may call for the rapid expansion of several products in as many markets. This must eventually lead to a severe cash crisis or a pruning of investment plans, often at a critical stage of development.

Rampant inflation has a similar effect on cash flows as has rapid growth. More and more cash is required to refinance the existing level of working capital, so that growth plans have to be postponed or cancelled during an inflationary era.

The Business Cycle

As investment opportunities improve and as cash becomes readily available, businesses seek to expand. New fixed investment is authorized and stock levels rise to match increased sales. The demand for resources intensifies and prices rise. Cash becomes scarce and interest rates rise. Eventually customers lack the resources to buy and industry is unwilling to raise money at high interest rates, orders are cancelled, destocking begins and material prices fall. (In the past wage rates also tended to fall or to decelerate.) Expansion plans are cancelled wherever possible, though fixed investment often comes on stream after the downturn and firms are left with stock acquired at premium prices. British industry suffers badly in this respect; almost invariably it is among the last to expand and the last to deflate, in contrast to the German and Japanese economies.

In a cyclic economy each business needs to develop the ability to recognize whether or not a sales upturn is due to the attributes of its products or services, or to cyclic or seasonal factors (and vice versa in a downturn). Furthermore it needs to take into consideration the lead time that elapses before production facilities can be installed. Indeed, in the more capital-intensive industries this frequently means investing during the downturn, provided one is confident that markets will turn up rather than suffer the grip of a prolonged depression.

Rationing the Claims of Competing Subsidiaries

Normally the potential demand for investment funds exceeds the available supply of cash. Consequently some form of capital rationing is necessary. In many businesses the power, influence and track record of the larger successful subsidiaries ensure that they receive the lion's share of the cake. In other cases priority may be accorded to those projects which promise the highest returns.

Taken to extremes, both allocation systems are counterproductive. The larger successful subsidiaries are frequently well established, with less call for investment than their younger brothers, while stated project returns are absolutely dependent upon the assumption used in projecting revenues and costs. In order to ensure that bias in the preparation of plans or project submission is eliminated, many of the more successful companies appear to rely extensively on centrally organized multi-disciplinary project teams or senior planning executives to prepare or review plans and project submissions.

Risk Spreading or Specialization?

Much of the theory of risk spreading, and its attendant measurement techniques, is based upon the principle of portfolio management. As such it has limited relevance to business decisions. The City has access to 'a perfect market' in which shares can be disposed of quickly, and at a price close to the existing quote unless the divestment is large. Operating in such a market, it pays the investment manager to spread his risks. In contrast, most major business investment decisions need a lengthy and painful process of deliberation. Such investments, once they have gone sour, are not easily reversed, and generally lead to substantial losses. Consequently it normally pays businesses to specialize in those areas they know best, particularly during development and growth stages, when diversification can be likened to a dilution of energy. The case for diversification is enhanced once the company reaches a mature stage.

Asset-based Strategies

Manufacturing companies normally assess the value of capital investment by relating the derived profits to the sum invested — implicitly assuming that undistributed profits will add to the net asset value (assets less liabilities) of the business; the relative propensity of assets to increase or decline in value frequently being ignored (often through a lack of expertise).

In the financial sector it is common to assess the merit of

potential investment by reference to its appreciation potential rather than the running returns that are derived therefrom, though the perceived return does influence the value of the asset.

The manufacturing sector stands to benefit from the judicious but partial use of financial-sector criteria whenever it is considering investment in appreciating assets or assets with a volatile price structure. A financier invariably considers the intrinsic qualities of the assets to be acquired – not only appreciation qualities, but the flexibility of asset use, and its marketability should the asset no longer be required. These qualities are frequently disregarded, erroneously, by the analyst located in the industrial sector.

Balanced Investment Strategies

A moment's reflection indicates that a group consisting predominantly of rapid-growth businesses is likely to suffer severe cash shortages, except where it is exceptionally profitable or has a particularly favourable cash profile. A mix of developing, growth and mature businesses provides a better balance. Similarly, a situation in which there are few high risk-return investments but a predominance of safe good-return investments leads to a balanced situation. *Prima facie,* such a business could grow exponentially over an infinite period of time; untroubled by setbacks, it would amass wealth in perpetuity.

The preceding argument is of course fallacious. Once a business reaches a critical size, its actions increasingly impinge upon other organizations and interest groups. Nor can there be sufficient promising development opportunities for it to maintain the ratio of growth/mature sectors. Like it or not, all businesses must go ex-growth and moderate their ambitions.

THE COST OF CAPITAL

Underlying many of the preceding observations on growth, risk and specialization is the theory of the cost of capital. While loan finance bears an interest coupon, equity finance, whether through the issue of shares or profit retentions, bears no direct interest charge. Shareholder satisfaction is obtained from the receipt of dividends and the supposed growth in the value of shareholdings.

The theory of the cost of capital seeks to postulate the returns required by the shareholder, though it will be appreciated that such postulation is inevitably subjective. Two principal approaches to this subject have been used. The first, an externally based approach, uses the cost of capital to calculate a share-price objective, adjusted by dividend yields. The second, the internal approach, relies on setting return on investment objectives. These objectives take into consideration the proportionate relation of shareholder to borrowed finance. All costs of capital calculations are stated in real terms, being calculated after tax and an inflation uplift is added to the basic calculation. Let us take an example.

Say shareholder finance is 70 per cent and long-term borrowings are 30 per cent of total long-term finance. The borrowings carry a historic interest coupon of 10 per cent gross and 5 per cent net. Suppose an 8 per cent after-tax return and an inflation adjustment are postulated. Then, the return on investment required is calculated as follows:

$$(\cdot70 \times 8) + (\cdot3 \times 5) = 7\cdot1 \text{ per cent}$$

after tax, to which should be added an inflation factor.

Cost of capital models, particularly those externally based, are helpful in explaining the interest and dividend requirements of institutional investors. It will be realized that an increase in dividend-yield requirements will push share prices down, all other things being equal.

Obviously directors have to take shareholder needs into consideration when formulating policy. However, so volatile are share prices and shareholder expectations that share-price objectives appear to be of limited use as a basis for long-term corporate-policy formation.

As inflation escalates so, according to the cost of capital theory, the rate of return required on investment must increase. While businesses should seek to make high real returns, it should be recognized that there are only a limited number of investment opportunities capable of producing them; and, at the same time, there are a large number of potential investors. A business that blindly follows the cost of capital theory will almost certainly find itself raising its risk threshold, and its decisions becoming increasingly speculative.

10 Managing the Process of Corporate Development

Bernard Taylor

To produce sensible policies for the development of individual companies and whole industries we need to have an understanding of how businesses rise and fall. Is there a life-cycle, and a life-style for each stage in the cycle? Are there some times when formal planning is vital and others when it is destructive? Are there times in the history of a business when building a larger operating unit is the only way to survive and others when concentration into large units could destroy the very quality and service on which the business is based? Is there a time for employee participation and another time for charismatic leadership? Our instincts say there must be different strategies for different situations. In this chapter we summarize modern thinking and practice about corporate development, and seek to offer a basis for policy-making in the individual business and at national level.

THE CORPORATE LIFE-CYCLE

The Product Life-cycle

An idea fundamental to modern management thinking is that products and technologies are introduced, grow, reach a saturation level, and then fall out of favour or are replaced. A technology is said to have a 'switch-over point', when the new technology takes over. A product or brand may be taken off the market when it reaches a minimum level of distribution or when servicing becomes too expensive. (See Chapter 11, p. 180.)

Market Segments

Another basic concept is that markets are not homogeneous, but may be divided into segments according to the different requirements of various customers. In fact every customer's needs may be quite individual. More commonly markets may be divided according to customer usage and attitude, distribution channels, and geographical area; and, as different countries and regions vary in sophistication, products may become obsolete in one market and still sell in a less developed or less affluent area. Figure 10.1 shows the way black and white television sets have been introduced in different countries — a sequence of product life-cycles, or rather the same product life-cycle in different markets.

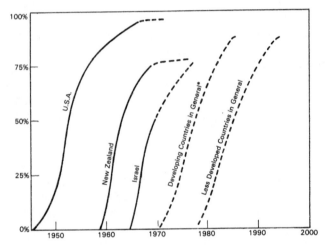

Figure 10.1   The product life-cycle in different markets: percentage of households with television sets.

Actual figures for the years 1946–70 (U.S.A., New Zealand, and Israel). Projections are estimated. Z. Z. Shipchandlar, *Diffusion Patterns of Consumer Durables in International Markets,* (University of Indiana, Fort Wayne). *Categories relate to average G.N.P. per capita (industrialized $3,700, developing countries $1,500, less developed countries $160).

Stages of Corporate Development

Harvard University's studies of the administration of large industrial enterprises in the U.S.A. and Western Europe suggest that companies also tend to pass through phases of development, as follows:

1   The owner-entrepreneur with a single product and an informal
    organization acts as the pioneer.
2   If the sales of his product grow, he eventually has to delegate
    control to department heads, and he usually divides his
    business by functions, e.g. engineering, production, sales
    and service.
3   Often the first product becomes obsolete and others are
    added; the company offers a series of related products and
    it is normal at this stage for the enterprise to adopt a divi-
    sional organization, with a number of quasi-autonomous
    businesses based on different products or product
    groups.
4   Later, businesses not connected with the original technologies
    or markets may be acquired; at this point it may seem more
    appropriate for the central management to work through
    an industrial holding company, regarding the businesses
    largely as investments.

Figure 10.2 shows one version of the theory of corporate
development by Malcolm Salter. Figure 10.3 illustrates the evolution of the organizational structure through different stages.
Figure 10.4 illustrates the progress of diversification and division
in large manufacturing companies in the U.K.

Phases of International Expansion

Parallel investigations by Harvard researchers have revealed a
similar pattern of progress in international expansion:

1   Initially the export business is a small proportion of the total,
    and is handled through an international department or
    division.
2   As the export business grows, a new organization is needed:
    if there is a simple product line and many markets, the
    tendency is to set up geographic divisions or national
    companies; but if there are a number of different products
    and the technology is complex, worldwide product divi-
    sions may seem to be more appropriate.
3   Further growth will probably result in a matrix or 'grid'
    organization, with product divisions, geographical units,
    and functional groups.

Figure 10.2   Stages of corporate development.

	Stage I	Stage II	Stage III	Stage IV
Structure of operating units	Single unit managed by a sole proprietor	Single unit managed by a team	Several regional units reporting to a corporate H.Q. each with structure I or II	Several semi-autonomous units reporting to corp. H.Q.: each with structure I, II or III
Product-market relationships	Small scale, single line of related products, 1 market 1 distribution channel	Large scale, single line of related products, 1 market 1 distribution channel	Each region produces same product line, single market, multiple channels	Each unit produces different product line for separate markets, multiple channels
Top management	One man operation, very little task differentiation	Responsible for single functions, e.g. production, sales, finance	Regional units performing several functions	Product divisions performing all major functions
Quantitative measures of performance	Very few, personalized, not based on formal criteria	Operating budgets for each function	Operating budget, return on sales, R.O.I.	Return on sales, return on investment

Adapted from Malcolm S. Salter 'Management Appraisal & Reward Systems', *Journal of Business Policy*, Vol. 1, No 4, 1971 page **44**.

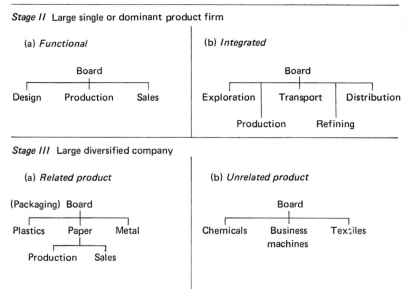

Stage I Small entrepreneur
Single product/Informal organization

Stage II Large single or dominant product firm

(a) *Functional*

(b) *Integrated*

Stage III Large diversified company

(a) *Related product*

(b) *Unrelated product*

See Derek F. Channon, *The Strategy & Structure of British Enterprise,* Macmillan, London, 1973 (Chapter 1).

Figure 10.3   Stages of corporate development.

Figure 10.5 illustrates the phases of growth which business goes through as it expands geographically.

DEVISING A CORPORATE STRATEGY

A central tenet of teaching and research in business policy over the past decade has been that, to avoid becoming victims of technological obsolescence and changing markets, companies should have, implicitly or explicitly, a corporate strategy. It has been defined by Igor Ansoff as 'the concept of the firm's business — which provides a unifying theme for all its activities', and

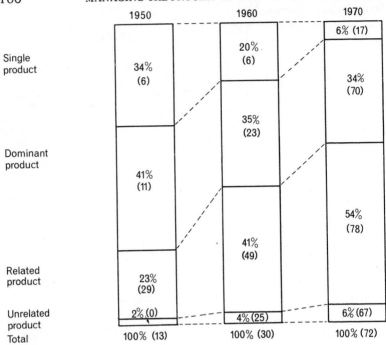

Adapted from a table in Derek F. Channon's, The Strategy & Structure of British Enterprise' Macmillan, 1973, (p. 67).

Figure 10.4   Diversification and multidivisional structures (U.K. Times 500)
Figures in brackets refer to percentage of multidivisional structures in each category.

its purpose is to provide a basis for strategies in the functional areas, to act as a guide for operational planning, and to guide the choice of products and markets and the types of businesses companies enter.

In attempting to put this idea into effect, senior managers and planners are invited to ask a number of fundamental questions as follows:

1   What are the objectives to be achieved and how should we define the scope of the business?
2   What limits are set on these objectives by our personal values and social responsibilities?
3   On which strengths can we build, and what are the weaknesses needing to be compensated for?

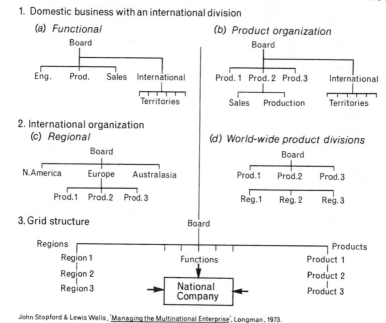

1. Domestic business with an international division

(a) *Functional*

(b) *Product organization*

2. International organization

(c) *Regional*

(d) *World-wide product divisions*

3. Grid structure

John Stopford & Lewis Wells, 'Managing the Multinational Enterprise', Longman, 1973.

Figure 10.5   Developing the international business organization.

4   What opportunities are to be taken advantage of and what threats should be avoided?
5   What are the main decisions to be taken and to what major courses of action must we commit ourselves?
6   What resources will be required and where will these resources come from?
7   What are the risks in this strategy and what contingency plans are required?

In practice, business strategies seem to evolve as the business develops. The original entrepreneur starts with a simple concept of the business, and then, as the business grows, he has to share it with others, and it becomes modified to suit changing conditions. What was once one man's inspiration becomes a set of flexible guidelines to be applied variously in different fields of operation. Then, all too often, the business outgrows its strategy, which is assiduously imposed as 'company policy' or 'the way we do things around here', until a market failure, competitive action or

Table 10.1   Essential elements of corporate planning

1. Specific objectives (company, division, function).
2. Environmental appraisal (economic, social/political, technological, competitive).
3. Company appraisal.
4. Assumptions and forecasts.
5. Alternative strategies.
6. Integrated plan.
7. Action programmes.
8. Budgets.
9. Review.

Government intervention cause a crisis. Then the ruling coalition is replaced and a new strategy has to be evolved.

In recent years, academics and consultants have tried hard to sell the idea that strategies should be written down and regularly reviewed. Table 10.1 lists the main elements in the corporate-planning process, and Table 10.2 indicates the kind of annual cycle companies frequently establish in an effort to engage top management, central staff specialists, and the general managers of product divisions and national subsidiaries in regular discussions about strategies and plans. Increasingly, the dialogue occurs in three stages, as follows:

1   A discussion about forecasts and broad-policy guidelines, and the assumptions on which the plan is to be based.

Table 10.2   The corporate planning cycle

I Divisional Strategy

Corporate and divisional executives discuss key strategy issues, tentative allocation of resources, and new corporate projects.

II Divisional Action Programmes

Divisional and departmental executives discuss alternative programmes, new divisional projects, and resources required.

III Divisional Budgets

Departmental staff and divisional staff develop detailed 5-year and annual budgets.

2   An examination of the key issues in the divisional develop-
    ment programme, including new facilities to be built, new
    marketing initiatives, new business ventures, acquisitions,
    divestments and closures.
3   A consideration of the operating plan and budget for the
    year ahead.

   The idea of having an explicit corporate strategy seems to be
widely accepted but not so generally implemented. In practice,
boards of directors find it difficult to agree on a broad strategy,
except in the most general terms. Chief executives often prefer
for political reasons not to discuss alternative strategies with
other executives, and they are even less forthcoming in the presence of Government officials and trade-union leaders. In addition, as numerous studies have revealed, senior managers rarely
stay still long enough to formulate a comprehensive strategy;
they are much more likely to take decisions in a piecemeal way
as important issues arise. This is not to say that they are necessarily unaware of the longer-term implications of the commitments
they are making. They may simply feel that formalizing the process of analysis and decision-making is likely to introduce a
spurious sense of science and rationality in what is a fundamentally intuitive process.

Strategies for Growth

A good deal of the early literature on corporate development
was concerned with helping companies that were threatened
with obsolescence to plan their way into new businesses. As the
Harvard research has shown, the 1960s were a time when large
numbers of companies recognized that they had no future in
their present businesses and began to expand into new products
and new markets — including overseas markets, and entirely new
businesses outside their usual areas of activity.
   Igor Ansoff's analysis of alternative directions for growth
served to emphasize the importance of expansion and diversification (see Figure 10.6). Figure 10.7 shows the gap-analysis
approach made popular by Stanford Research Institute. Management is invited to

1   Set an objective, e.g. in terms of return on investment, or
    cash flow

Product Mission	Present	New
Present	Market penetration	Product development
New	Market development	Diversification

H. Igor Ansoff, *Corporate Strategy,* McGraw Hill,
New York, 1965 (p. 109).

Figure 10.6   Directions for growth.

2   Forecast the 'momentum line' for the present business
3   Plan to 'fill the gap' with projects for the following:

(a) *Efficiency.* Raising the profitability in the present business
    up to the best in the industry through reducing costs,
    increasing prices, increasing market share, etc.
(b) *Expansion* through the introduction of new products, new
    applications of present products, and entry into new
    markets, including export markets
(c) *Diversification* through internal development, by buying
    up customers, suppliers, or competitors — or through
    acquiring companies in quite unrelated fields.

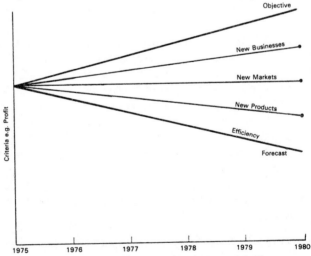

Figure 10.7   Directions for growth-Gap analysis.

Stanford Research Institute also proposed that the corporate plan should contain two types of strategic plans: product-line strategic plans for the present businesses, and corporate development plans designed to fill the planning gap with new projects, ideas for mergers and diversifications, etc.

In many companies, even in the affluent 1960s, the problem of growth was not so much a shortage of projects and ideas but lack of cash for investment. The planners and consultants at this point set about analysing the 'negative gap', i.e. the possible ways of increasing funds. This would start with a forecast of cash flow from the present business compared with the cash that might be required for new projects. One could then examine the possibility of reducing cash tied up in stocks and debtors, selling off certain assets, reducing dividends, obtaining loans, issuing more shares, etc.

The Experience Curve

In more recent years another American consultancy organization, the Boston Consulting Group, has emphasized the need for companies to 'invest in growth and cost reduction' in existing businesses that have a growth potential.

The argument is based on the assertion that, as industries grow, *experience* increases, companies are able to benefit from economies of scale through bulk purchasing, mass production/high volume distribution, mass marketing, etc., and so costs may be reduced by as much as 20–30 per cent every time the cumulative sales volume doubles. The downward-sloping experience curve thus indicates a decline in price per unit of output as volume and experience accumulate. This gives substantial competitive advantages to the market leader in an industry, and enables the dominant company to reduce its prices and at the same time make good profits.

Some major Japanese industries seem to have followed a strategy of 'market penetration'. They have obtained a commanding position in world markets for steel, ships, motor cars, motor cycles, radios, television, cameras, etc.

It is only fair to say that the experience curve is a subject of much controversy. Those who contest the theory argue as follows:

1   There is only limited evidence that expanding volume in an

industry or in an individual firm can produce these dramatic falls in total costs, and there are certainly areas where costs per unit of volume seem to rise because of large-scale working, especially in labour-intensive operations, where turnover, absenteeism, and industrial stoppages may all increase.

2   Where companies commit themselves to long runs and high volumes of standard products, as Henry Ford did with his Model T, the organization may lose its flexibility and the firm may become vulnerable to a competitor which, like General Motors in the 1920s, chooses to compete not on price but on product performance.

3   Even if the experience curve does apply, there is no guarantee that management will be able to reduce costs in line with the curve. We have numerous examples in Britain of companies that have grown in size but management has not been able to reap the profits from higher outputs.

4   The experience curve theory invites companies to commit more and more funds to a few large products in limited market areas. This concentration may increase the risk to the business in the case of a change in technology or market. The heavy commitment of the Japanese ship-builders to large oil tankers and their huge overcapacity after the energy crisis illustrates the danger of specialization.

5   The theory assumes a competitive market, whereas in many markets prices are controlled by monopolies, by price controls and by Government intervention.

These arguments do not of course invalidate the theory, which has many adherents, particularly in high-technology industries, but they do emphasize the need for care in applying the concept, e.g. in defining the product, the market segment, and the stage in the life-cycle, and in ensuring that management has the capacity to realize the potential cost savings, and at the same time maintain a high rate of product innovation.

The Business as a Portfolio of Investments

The companies that expanded and diversified in the 1960s and early 1970s are now trying to sort out the businesses created or acquired into some kind of sensible pattern. The usual approach is to create various nuclei in the form of groups or subsidiary companies, around which the various activities can be collected. The next stage is to group those operations that seem likely to benefit from economies of scale, and to decentralize those functions where transportation and distribution costs, or customer service, are important factors. Then an attempt has to be made to find a reasonable method for allocating resources, i.e. management effort, skilled personnel, and scarce materials, as well as capital for investment.

Priorities must be set and decisions must be made about acquisitions and mergers, the allocation of capital, the closure of unprofitable businesses, etc. A basis for this discussion can be found by viewing the whole enterprise from the centre as if it were a portfolio of shares, a number of investments in particular businesses.

Valuable insights can emerge from this kind of analysis. For example, it seems sensible to have a range of businesses at different stages of development, as follows:

1   There should be some new projects offering good profit opportunities with high risk, and hungry for cash.
2   To support these new businesses the company will need a number of solid well-established products in mature markets, which are making good profits, face little risk, and produce a good cash flow.
3   There should be products or subsidiaries that are fighting to hold a dominant position in growth markets, and will provide the sound basis for company growth in the future.
4   Finally, there will inevitably be other businesses that are due for 'retirement', because the total market has declined, the products have become uncompetitive, or the risks for some reason are unacceptable.

Another approach is to balance the portfolio of investments by type of industry. Management may be worried about the fact that their basic business is too cyclical, which could mean that earnings are variable and the share price is unstable. A number of companies finding that their business was too closely tied to the capital investment cycle, or to Government purchasing, have diversified into industries with a more stable pattern of demand or a different cycle of trade. Tube Investments have stabilized their pattern of earnings by expanding into consumer markets such as bicycles and cookers. Rockwell International have combined an aerospace business, which is a cyclical business heavily dependent on U.S. defence policy, with electronics, automobile components, printing and textile equipment and household appliances. Figure 10.8 shows how the demand cycles experienced by the different marketing groups have to a large degree cancelled each other out, with consequent improvement in stability for the whole enterprise.

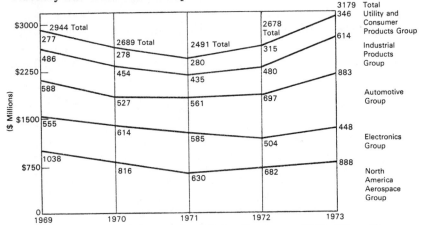

Figure 10.8   Rockwell International Sales, fiscal years 1969–73, ending September 30. Source: W. F. Rockwell, Jr., Management of a Multi-industry Business *Journal of General Management,* Spring 1975.

Geographical diversification is another way of achieving a spread of risk and opportunity. Here again the objective is not to be too dependent on one national or regional market, or on one type of market. The advantage of a geographical spread in producing a steady stream of earnings is evident with companies such as Metal Box. Profits from Britain are stable but unexciting, whereas overseas markets yield higher profits but are subject to higher risks from wars, expropriation, etc. U.A.C. International, which had a dominant position in West African trade, and Fiat, which has two-thirds of the Italian automobile market, are typical examples of companies that have seen a clear need to expand geographically to 'diversify their portfolio'.

For the purpose of analysis it is helpful to display the pattern of a company's business in diagrammatic form. Figure 10.9 is an example of a two-way matrix of products and national markets, as used by a firm based in Scandinavia.

The matrix provides a useful basis for discussion between central staff and divisional management. For example, the following questions might be put: 'Why is it that we can achieve a 50 per cent share of the market in Product C in Norway, when in Sweden our share is less than 1 per cent?' or 'We sell Product A

Market Product	Italy	France	Finland	Denmark	Sweden	Norway	West Germany	England	Holland	Rest of Europe	Other exports
A	0	0	0	0	1	1	1	1	1	0	0
B	1	0	0	2	3	1	3	1	0	0	0
C	0	0	0	0	0	4	1	0	0	0	0
D	1	3	0	1	4	1	0	0	0	0	0
E	0	0	1	3	3	1	1	1	0	1	0
F	1	0	0	3	4	1	0	0	0	0	0
G	0	0	3	4	0	0	1	1	1	1	0
H	0	0	1	3	0	1	1	1	1	0	1
I	0	0	0	3	0	3	3	0	0	0	0

Figures represent market shares e.g:
0 = up to 1%, 1=1−10%, 2=10−25%, 3=25−50%, 4≑50% or over.

E. Rhenman, 'Organisation Theory for Long Range Planning', Wiley, London. 1973, p.123.

Figure 10.9   A European company's territory − an analysis by products and markets.

to the textile industry in Germany. Why don't we sell it for the same applications in France?' These kinds of question are likely to lead to discussions about the allocation of resources by product and by region. In general one expects that there will be a correlation between the business potential and the resources provided. Sometimes, however, certain markets − overseas markets are an example − do not receive an appropriate level of support. Table 10.3, from a recent survey of British exporting practice, shows the extent to which some companies have neglected the growing sales potential of overseas markets.

Table 10.3   British salesmen in overseas markets: 1975*

Companies chosen at random

Company	No. of salesmen		Overseas sales	
	Home	Export	% of total sales	Value £m
Textiles	31	1	55	1·25
Light engineering	4	1	80	7·20
Electrical	70	1	60	3·00
Chemicals	10	6	58	6·00
Pharmac.	60	8	57	5·10
Earthenware	30	20	62	14·00
Publishing	14	3	60	6·60
Engineering tools	22	1	60	7·20
Light engineering	30	3	62	6·80
Electrical	27	1	70	57·40
				114·55

*Concentration on Key Markets
A Development Plan for exports, ITI Research, 1975 (p. 30).

MORE COMPLEX MODELS OF STRATEGY

The idea of the business as a portfolio of investments is a helpful
analogy to use in allocating resources, but, of course, businesses
do not consist merely of money that may be transferred at will
from one business to another. They comprise managers and
workers with very specific knowledge, skills and attitudes; and
investments in raw-material reserves, property and equipment
that are useful in certain businesses but not in others. They also
have long-standing commitments to suppliers, customers, local
communities and public bodies. Management is therefore searching for more comprehensive and realistic forms of analysis.

The Business Screen

Figure 10.10 shows one of a number of analyses used by General
Electric (U.S.A.) in deciding on the allocation of resources
between different businesses. Other elements discussed include
risk and sensitivity to changes in assumptions about the future
state of the environment. In this chart, however, attention centres

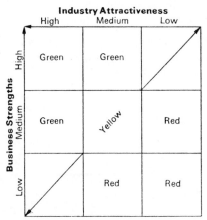

Figure 10.10 Portfolio management — General Electric's Business Screen.
Source: D. C. D. Rogers, *Essentials of Business Policy*, Harper & Row,
New York, 1975, p. 52.

on an attempt to evaluate and rank each business in relation to
both industry attractiveness and business strengths, in terms of
market size and growth, competition, profitability, and technical
and other factors. The matrix is used to enable divisional general
management to develop a dialogue first with the corporate-
planning group and then with top management about key
strategic decisions. The business plans are checked against the
priorities for the business as a whole, e.g. to develop worldwide
strength in certain specified 'businesses of the future'. The
businesses' plans are also considered against their previous track
record as shown in a quality of earnings matrix, which ranks the
estimates from hard to soft. In the business screen businesses
are divided broadly into three groups, businesses in the 'green'
category being given the highest priority for investment. These
include the following:

1 Businesses with high market shares or the possibility of
    achieving market dominance in growing industries
2 Businesses in areas the corporation regards as its present or
    future 'prime territory'
3 Ventures offering very high earnings or cash returns in the
    short term.

Businesses in the 'yellow' area are often stable or declining,
and the policy is to be very selective when making further investments in them. Businesses falling into the 'red' area are those
management is worried about, because of poor earnings, high

risks, vulnerability to competition, etc. The guideline for these activities is to reduce investments and possibly to sell off the assets or the whole business.

Profit Impact of Market Strategy

Another strategic approach, which came originally from General Electric, is known as PIMS — Profit Impact of Market Strategy — and is now marketed as a research programme by Harvard Business School and other management colleges around the world. The programme at present includes 300 pieces of data taken from 700 businesses in different industries (mainly in the U.S.A.) over a three- to five-year period. The intention of the programme is to find the answers to two basic questions:

1   What factors influence profitability, i.e. return on investment, in a business, and by how much?
2   How does the return on investment change in response to new policies and trends in the environment?

This study, like the experience-curve theory, indicates that there is a strong relation between a product's market share and its return on investment. The results of an investigation based on 600 U.S. businesses over the period 1970–2 showed that products with under 10 per cent market share averaged 9 per cent return on investment (pre-tax), whereas those with over 40 per cent market share produced a 30 per cent return on investment. Return on investment was seen to increase more or less in line with increasing market share.

Other factors having a critical effect on return on investment are the following:

1   *Market share compared with competition,* especially in the 'mature' phase of a business, and particularly with consumer durables and capital goods
2   *Product quality compared with competition* (a subjective judgement). High-quality products and services are the most profitable and usually achieve a dominant market position.
3   *'Investment intensity'*, i.e. a high ratio of investment to sales, tends to depress the return on investment; as investment intensity rises, profitability declines

4   *High marketing expenditures* seem to be harmful to profits when the product quality is low, and disastrous when combined with high levels of capital investment.

Cash-flow analyses confirm the need to balance the product portfolio, as the Boston Consulting Group suggests. Products with a high market share relative to competition produce large positive cash flows, and products in rapidly growing markets are big users of cash — particularly in capital-intensive businesses.

On reflection, the initial results from these computer analyses are not surprising, and up to now the results are based almost entirely on businesses in the U.S.A. An important benefit of the system, however, is that it encourages management to ask what are the critical factors affecting profitability in their different businesses — product quality, the level of capital investment, market share, the level of marketing expenditure, or some combination of these.

The Stakeholder Approach

Much of the writing on strategy during the 1960s by Igor Ansoff, Peter Drucker and Theodore Levitt, emphasized the need for a marketing orientation to correct the traditional focus on production and productivity, which largely ignored the changing needs of the customer. A viewpoint more typical of the 1970s is expressed in the stakeholder approach developed by Stanford Research Institute. The stakeholder theory suggests that a firm has obligations not only to shareholders and customers but to all the individuals and organizations with which it has transactions and relations, in fact to the following:

1   Suppliers of raw materials, components and services
2   Employees, leaders of trade unions and professional associations.
3   Private shareholders, institutional investors and banks
4   Private and industrial customers
5   Distributors, agents, wholesalers and retailers
6   Competitors and collaborators in the same industry, and officials of industrial and trade associations
7   Public servants in local and national government
8   Members of the communities in which the company's offices and factories are located.

This modern view, then, is that management cannot afford to focus its attention on satisfying the needs of the customers, or meeting the demands of the shareholders, while ignoring the claims of other powerful groups. In practice, it is usually necessary at any one time to give priority to the needs of one interest or another, depending on the problems of the business. There may be a shortage of raw materials, labour problems, or a need to raise capital. But a prudent management team is aware that all of the stakeholders have the power to damage or help the business. They are therefore continually monitoring and promoting these stakeholder relations — often using marketing research and other marketing techniques that were initially developed for use in selling products to market the company and its policies to employees, shareholders, local communities, suppliers and Governments.

In effect, management is recognizing that corporate strategy is concerned not simply with producing a return on the shareholders' capital and delivering satisfactory products to customers, but also achieving social acceptance in the community, ensuring a continuing and uninterrupted supply of key raw materials and components, influencing Government policies, and, of course, ensuring that the work force and the whole management team are motivated and committed to the company and its policies.

The stakeholder approach suggests that management should be searching for a set of policies for research, production, marketing, finance and personnel that are compatible with each other yet satisfy the minimum requirements of the stakeholder groups, giving priority to those interests which, for various reasons, seem to merit more attention than the rest. Some firms seem to manage this — Marks and Spencers and IBM, for example, appear to have evolved satisfactory relations with suppliers, customers, shareholders, employees and the community.

Another consequence implied by the stakeholder view of business, but by no means fully worked out, is the recognition that corporate strategy cannot be stated simply in terms of products and markets, as was widely believed in the 1960s. Now the key management decisions may be concerned with worker and trade-union participation, relations with Governments, securing supplies of key raw materials from Third World sources, and maintaining a positive cash flow in conditions of rapid inflation.

The arena for debate about corporate strategy, in the U.S.A.

at least, still centres on the development of products and the penetration of markets, but there is increasing recognition, particularly in Europe, that neither the supply of resources nor the reactions of society or of employees can be taken for granted. In consequence there is a growing interest in public affairs and 'societal strategy', in strategies for supply markets, strategies for participation, etc.

THE DEVELOPMENT OF MANAGEMENT SYSTEMS

An important trend in recent thinking about corporate strategy is the suggestion that businesses at different stages of development require different organizational structures, different management systems and different styles of leadership. The Harvard research into stages of corporate development mentioned earlier appears to have established that a company's organizational structure is related to the spread of the products it sells, and firms tend to move through the following stages:

1 Entrepreneurial/informal structure
2 Single or dominant product/functional structure
3 Related product/product division
4 Unrelated product/conglomerate structure.

Some of the Harvard researchers into the stages of corporate development theory also found indications that companies at a particular phase of development tended to have characteristic management systems, e.g. performance measurement and reward systems for management. In view of this work it has been suggested that the use of product divisions and profit centres in diversified companies in Britain has been far less effective than in the U.S.A. for the following reasons:

1 British management was reluctant to install the necessary systems of performance measurement, sanctions and rewards
2 It did not have at its disposal the large numbers of trained general managers required to manage such a decentralized system
3 It had less experience in using formalized planning systems, which are required to coordinate policy-making and resource-allocation in complex diversified businesses.

Category	Characteristics			
Managerial	Entrepreneur	Sophisticated Mkt. Mgr.	Critical Administrator	Opportunistic Milker
Planning Time Frame	Long Enough to Draw Tentative Life Cycle (10)	Long Range-Investment Payout (7)	Intermediate (3)	Short Range II
Structure	Free Form or Task Force	Semi-Permanent Task Force Product or Market Division	Business Division Plus Task Force for Renewal	Pared-Down Division
Compensation	High Variable/Low Fixed Fluctuating with Performance	Balanced Variable and Fixed Individual and Group Rewards	Low Variable-High Fixed Group Rewards	Fixed Only
Communication System	Informal/Tailor-Made	Formal/Tailor-Made	Formal/Uniform	Little or None Command System
Measuring and Reporting	Qualitative Marketing Unwritten	Qualitative and Quantitative, Early Warning System, All Functions	Quantitative Written Production Oriented	Numerical Written Balance Sheet Oriented
Corporate Department	Market Research New Product Development	Operations Research Organization Development	Value Analysis Data Processing Taxes and Insurance	Purchasing
Maturity Curve				
Industry/Market	High Growth/Low Shares	High Growth/High Shares	Low Growth/High Shares	Low Growth/Low Shares
Financial	Cash Hungry Low Reported Earnings Good P/E High Debt Level	Self-Financing Cash Hungry, Good to Low Reported Earnings High P/E. Low-Moderate Dept Level	Cash Rich High Earnings Fair P/E No Dept-High Debt Capacity	Fair Cash Low Earnings Low P/C Low Dept Capacity
Title	Embryonic	Growth	Mature	Aging

Figure 10.11 The strategy centres approach. Source: R. V. L. Wright, *Strategic Centers – a Contemporary Managing System,* Arthur D. Little, Cambridge, Mass., 1975, p. 9.

STRATEGY CENTRES

Figure 10.11 illustrates one of the most ambitious attempts to associate management systems with businesses at different phases of development. This type of analysis, known as the Strategy Centres approach, is being marketed by Arthur D. Little for use by diversified companies in developing management systems for their various subsidiaries or divisions. It makes the following suggestions:

1 For purposes of strategy and resource planning, diversified businesses should be divided into strategic business units (a term coined by General Electric), which are units of the company with their own missions, their own competitors, and capable of developing an independent long-term

strategy. These units usually differ from the existing divisions and profit centres.

2   Strategic planning should be concerned with the allocation of managerial as well as financial resources. This means, in effect, having a 'portfolio' of managers of different types to allocate to different types of business – entrepreneurs, sophisticated professional staff, careful administrators and experts in 'turnaround situations'.

3   The level of sophistication in the managerial system needs to be tailored to the stage of development in the business.

DEVELOPING THE COMPANY AS A TOTAL SYSTEM

Recent research in large diversified companies by Bower and others suggests that resource-allocation systems such as capital budgeting provide most inadequate controls for top management. By the time a project for a new product or a new facility reaches the main board of a company that is grouped into divisions that project has normally acquired so much commitment on the way up the organization that it is difficult for the board to consider other options.

For the most part, the top-management team has to rely on less direct methods of influencing thinking within the organization. These controls are likely to include the following:

1   *Periodic discussions about divisional strategy*, to ensure that alternative approaches are considered before they become frozen into specific development plans and projects

2   *The establishment of profit centres and strategy centres,* to ensure that managers are held responsible both for operational performance and for business development

3   *Changes in the whole management system:* better information on new technology, competition and market trends; improved measures of performance in terms of cash flow, profit contribution by products and by customer groups, and salaries and bonuses reflecting achievement as well as seniority; and the recruitment and promotion of managers with potential, and the early retirement of others who are no longer effective.

Staff Development

One of the main ways for top management in a large organization
to exercise influence is through getting other people to grow,
learn and develop. Operating managers are primarily concerned
with the day-to-day running of the business, and it is the senior-
management team that has the main responsibility for ensuring
the 'self-renewal' of the organization – in terms of management
development and succession, as well as through innovation in
products and services, in production processes, and in marketing
and distribution.

This entails recruiting and training individual managers, placing
them in appropriate positions and planning the succession for
key appointments. In effect the chief executive and the board are
in a position to manage a 'portfolio' of executives and relate their
various strengths to the needs of different parts of the business.
The stages of business development provide a useful guide to the
classification of managers, who may be variously suited to starting new ventures, developing systems in growing enterprises,
penetrating markets in mature businesses or stabilizing and exploiting declining markets.

Organizational Development

Of course, top management also has the chance of influencing
the business organization as a total system. In a large company
there are severe limits to what can be achieved by direct personal
leadership. The chief executive exercises his influence largely
through the impact he has, or does not have, on the ideas and
attitudes that become accepted and are approved within the
organization.

In a modern diversified company with different parts of the
organization at different phases of development – some highly
innovative, others very stable and set in their ways – it is natural
that there will be tensions. The top management of the company
has to reflect these different points of view, and the chief executive must try to resolve the conflicts, and produce a coherent
company philosophy and a set of business strategies that are
internally consistent.

If he and his team are successful, the original business idea and
the accompanying value system will evolve in line with the chang-

ing needs of the business and with trends in the external environment. In addition, innovation will be fostered at an appropriate level, but the company will not be overcommitted to new ventures. If the management is unsuccessful in marrying the different cultures and value systems, there will be a kind of organizational schizophrenia as incompatible strategies are put together. Different factions will develop, and management may spend too much time on lobbying and internal politics. In extreme cases the inconsistencies will be made explicit, through operational problems and as key executives leave.

The notion of strategic management coined by Igor Ansoff links strategic planning, staff development and organizational development, and serves to emphasize that these are the key elements through which the top management team can influence and control the modern corporation. Occasionally these functions can be put together in a coordinated programme that can be extremely effective in changing the culture of an organization, fostering innovation and building morale. More frequently the integration of these policies for corporate development has to take shape, if at all, on an informal basis, through collaboration between corporate staff groups, or through the efforts of an energetic chief executive.

11 Strategy and Planning for Technology

Brian C. Twiss

During recent years top management in an increasing number of companies has accepted the need for formal corporate strategic and long-range planning. This has, to a great extent, been forced upon it by the rapidly changing environment within which its businesses operate. A major agent for this change has been technology. We are living in the midst of a 'knowledge explosion' resulting from a substantial investment in research and development both by companies and by Governments. This is reflected in the proportion of the United Kingdom's G.N.P. devoted to research and development, which has risen from 0·25 per cent in 1938 to over 3 per cent today. Some companies in technologically advanced industries are investing 15 to 20 per cent of their turnover in research and development, but many people are now questioning whether we are getting good value for this investment, and the words 'management gap' are heard more frequently than 'technological gap', which was current four or five years ago.

If these criticisms are true, and there is good reason to believe that they are, one possible explanation is that a gap exists between corporate strategic thinking and what actually takes place within a company's R. and D. organization. How many companies have a formal R. and D. strategy formulated with the same systematic care as the corporate long-range plan? The answer seems to be very few, although in fairness this does not necessarily mean that, in the absence of an explicit research and development strategy, the corporate plan is not reflected implicitly in many R. and D. decisions. However, the danger exists that much of the corporate plan may be nullified by R. and D.

effort expended upon the development of new products that do not meet the best commercial interests of the business.

TECHNOLOGY AND BUSINESS

Scientific advances are increasingly threatening the technological base of whole industries, as well as individual companies. On the other hand, new opportunities for the profitable exploitation of technology are constantly presenting themselves. For some companies and industries the threat will be of such urgency that the choice will be between major diversification or disaster — and the actual outcome will depend very much on the ability to foresee the threat and to select sound diversifications. But it is perhaps appropriate to sound here a word of warning: innovation is not in itself the complete answer, for all too often indiscriminate innovation can prove unprofitable. Other companies may not be under immediate threat but their long-term growth will depend upon the development of new products.

Technology makes existing products obsolete. The increasing tempo with which new technology and completely new technologies are being created is continuously shortening product lives. Consequently companies are faced with the problems of planning for more frequent product changes. This problem is compounded by the need for longer production runs to recover the heavy development and facility costs associated with advanced technology. Furthermore, for many advanced products (e.g. aircraft, power stations) the lead time between the start of development and the first sales is growing longer.

We must not think, however, that technology affects only the science-based industries; it affects almost every company. Much of industry consists of companies that assemble (true to a large extent of both the motor and electronics industries) or transform (e.g. clothing) the products of other industries. These also must be attuned to changes in technology, often outside their own industry, which can affect them profoundly. If they do not do so, someone else will; very often, the 'someone else' will be from outside the industry. This 'innovation by invasion' is quite common, e.g. the chemical company that diversifies into the manufacture of plastic household goods because the established companies are slow in exploiting the new material; the company that starts life by making sheets from nylon and within ten years becomes the market leader in the bed-sheet industry.

Technological innovation is the process by which ideas for the application of technology are carried through to commercial exploitation. The company problem is to ensure that it has a creative organization to generate new ideas, that these ideas are screened to ensure that resources are applied to those most likely to succeed commercially, and that the development of new products based on these ideas is managed effectively. The ideas themselves may originate from within the company or from outside. The most likely internal sources are the R. and D. department through its awareness of changes in the technological environment, and in the marketing department because of its close contact with the needs of the customer. But no company can afford to rely entirely on its own resources, which, even for the largest firm, are slight compared with what is available throughout the world. The net must therefore be cast wide, and serious consideration given to licence arrangements, takeovers and mergers, as an integral part of a policy for product innovation.

The relevance of the marketing concept to this process of technological innovation is clear, since the aim of the latter must be the satisfaction of customer needs. But this aim is not easy to achieve in practice. Difference of outlook, and educational and professional backgrounds, often exacerbated by a company's organizational structure, can easily frustrate the permeation of a marketing approach through an R. and D. department.

RESEARCH AND DEVELOPMENT STRATEGY

The long-range company plan can be expected to specify profit-growth objectives for a number of years ahead. This relation of profit with time can be illustrated by a simple graph of the type shown in Figure 11.1. During this period many products will

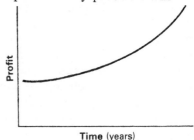

Figure 11.1   Corporate profit
growth projection.

make their individual contributions. Some of these will be in production at the beginning of the period and may be expected to make a continuing contribution only in the short term. These will be replaced by new products that were under development at the beginning of the period, and in turn will also be replaced eventually. The simple case for a one-product company is illustrated in Figure 11.2. It can be seen that as Product 1 reaches the end of its life-cycle, it is replaced by the new Product 2, which sustains the company target growth. In time this process repeats itself with the introduction of Product 3.

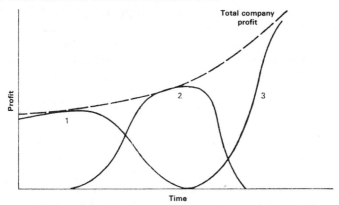

Figure 11.2   Profit contributions from successive products for a one product company.

For most companies, however, the situation will be far more complex, and it will be necessary to develop a portfolio of new products that together will make sufficient contributions to sustain the corporate profit-growth plan. Furthermore experience shows that only a small proportion (approximately 10 per cent) of those projects on which development work is initiated will reach the stage of commercial exploitation. If the resources devoted to research and development were unlimited, a creative organization should have no difficulty in building up a portfolio of projects of commercial potential ready to be drawn upon as required. In reality, however, the situation is usually far removed from this and, with R. and D. expenditures rising throughout industry, a means must be found whereby scarce resources can be allocated in such a way as to yield maximum benefit. The days when this expenditure could be regarded as an act of faith, in the hope that something would turn up, have gone forever.

There are many calls on the R. and D. budget. A brief examination of Figure 11.2 indicates some of the alternatives on which the resources available can be spent. In the short term it may be possible to increase the market share of Product 1 by enhancing its performance or reducing its cost; this might be achieved by detailed refinements utilizing the company's traditional technology or alternatively by applying new technology, process or materials. The product might, however, be reaching the end of its life-cycle in its present form, and the size of the total market might be expected to fall as the new Product 2 is introduced either by the company itself or its competitors. But Product 2 is likely to be expensive until it is in volume production, and because of the capital invested in Product 1, further development which would extend its useful life may have some great attractions. Mullard, for example, did not abandon the development of thermionic valves with the advent of the transistor, and was consequently able to gain a larger market share of the declining total valve market. It should be noted, however, that this was undertaken as a deliberate policy, and not at the price of neglect of the growing transistor market.

Whatever decisions have been made regarding the first product, its life cannot be protracted indefinitely, and resources will need to be devoted to developing a replacement. The timing of the commerical introduction of the new product may well be the critical factor to be considered, but the choice rests primarily on the decision whether to be first in the field or to follow. If first in the field, the chances of technical or commercial failure are greater, owing to the uncertainties attendant upon new products, but the rewards for success can be considerable. This can be illustrated by comparing the profit and sales volume life-cycles for a given product type (see Figure 11.3), from which it can be seen that, after an initial loss during the launching stage, profits rise ahead of the volume curve.

High profit margins for the new product reap handsome rewards for the innovative firms until they are eroded by competition. Looking further ahead as the uncertainties increase, a wider range of possibilities opens up. Here the pay-off from research and development is even more difficult to forecast, and we are in the area more of applied research and development. Decisions have to be taken whether to undertake sophisticated technological forecasting or to monitor the technological environment in

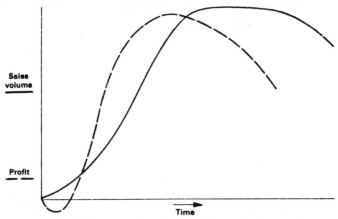

Figure 11.3   Product volume and profit life cycles.

the hope that changes that will have a major effect on the company's products are spotted in sufficient time for action to be taken. A technological forecast may reveal major threats to the technology base on which the industry is founded, or opportunities for future developments of the existing technology to satisfy entirely new consumer needs. In either case the forecast is of little more than academic interest unless it is used as a guideline for action in the near future; this may range from the initiation of a major research project, at one end of the scale, to the recruitment of research staff in a technology new to the company, at the other.

The alternatives even for a one-product company are thus seen to be many. For a multi-product company there will be a bewildering multiplicity of short-, medium- and long-term possibilities, covering a range of new or existing technologies. But such decisions on the allocation of resources must be made that the optimum balance between the conflicting demands is struck. The problem is illustrated diagrammatically in Figure 11.4. The box can be likened to a cash box representing the funds available in any year, and the smaller cubes the ways in which it can be allocated.

At this stage it is only possible to make a very general appraisal of the situation, but that can still be of value in ensuring that a systematic examination is made of the balance between new and existing products/new and existing technologies/short-, medium- and long-term possibilities. Much of the money available in any year will, however, be earmarked for projects in hand, and the proportion of the budget available for any redistribution of

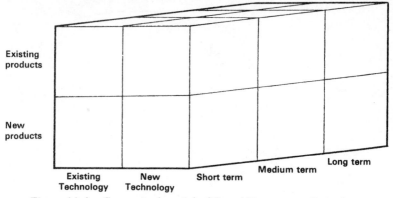

Existing
products

New
products

Existing   New   Short term   Medium term   Long term
Technology   Technology

Figure 11.4   Conceptual model of R and D resource allocations.

emphasis will be limited. Since in most cases the total size of the
R. and D. budget is unlikely to vary appreciably year to year,
change cannot be introduced abruptly without severely affecting
existing projects. This limited room for manoeuvre strengthens
the need to keep the allocation of resources under review on a
more general basis than just project headings. An example of a
not uncommon situation is to be found in companies with central
research laboratories concentrating on the longer-term projects
and divisional R. and D. departments deeply committed to immediate development work associated with problems arising from
the products the division is currently manufacturing. In this
situation inadequate resources may be devoted to new products
for the medium term. Since resources are limited, they must be
allocated in a way that makes sense for a particular company.
In other words, a series of decisions has to be made as to where
the spending should be concentrated in order to yield the maximum benefit over the long run, taking into account the total
company situation. This implies the development of an R. and
D. strategy analogous to and consistent with the company's
corporate strategy.

So far we have considered at the conceptual level ways in
which resources may be allocated to sustain a corporate profit-
growth pattern. Now it is necessary to examine a range of factors
and alternative strategies that could be pursued. A strategy
appropriate to a particular company can be formulated when
these considerations are related to its own capabilities.

CRITICAL FACTORS

The formulation of an R. and D. strategy demands a high degree

of management judgement. The strategy and the plans that will
be developed from it will not by themselves ensure a successful
outcome for what is essentially a creative activity. Whatever
formal systems are established, they must not ignore the importance that must be attached to the creation of a human environment in which original ideas can flourish. Nor is it possible to list
definitive methods for formulating the strategy itself. Nevertheless a careful consideration of the factors discussed below can
help in the selection of a strategy that will enable resources to
be utilized in the full knowledge that projects for new products
are initiated only after taking account of all relevant information.

Analysis of the Total Environment as It Affects the Company and Its Products

Market research and economic forecasting are well-established
techniques in most major companies. A study of advances in
technology has always been an important aspect of the work of
the R. and D. department, although the more formalized
techniques of technological forecasting are of more recent origin.
Analysis of social and political factors, and forecasting in these
areas have, however, often been rudimentary or neglected
entirely. There are indications that social factors, particularly
when reinforced with legislation, are likely to offer increasing
opportunities to companies that study them closely. The tobacco
and pharmaceutical industries are obvious examples where attention has already been focused on health standards. Other social
trends that may have extensive ramifications over a wide section
of industry include demand for safety, particularly in vehicles
and in the home; increasing human leisure; and the opposition
to all forms of pollution (atmospheric, river, etc.).

Technological Cost-benefit

As a general statement it is probably true to say that as the body
of knowledge in a particular technology increases, the incremental
benefit derived from further research in that field decreases. The
same expenditure devoted to a new branch of technology may
offer the prospects of far greater opportunities for new products
or product improvements. One of the major difficulties is that
the relevance of advances in a technology in which the company

has no experience may be missed. This can arise because the new technology or branch of science is not represented in the research department, and consequently there may be no one to recognize its significance. Furthermore a group of specialists in a particular field will always generate proposals for their continued employment on new projects even when the pay-off in commercial terms is of decreasing significance. It is not easy to avoid this technological obsolescence, particularly in smaller companies. But it does indicate the need for an awareness of what is happening in all branches of science, and a frequent review of the balance between specialisms represented in the R. and D. organization.

Offensive, Defensive, and Absorptive Strategies

We saw earlier that a company can aim either to be first in the field with a technological innovation (an offensive strategy) or to follow (a defensive strategy). The choice of strategy for a particular new product depends upon many factors, most of which are related to corporate strengths and weaknesses. To be first in the field, it is not sufficient to possess an original idea and a strong research team, if the financial and development resources are inadequate to carry the innovation through to a marketable product. There are many cases of companies that have found themselves in financial difficulties during this phase in the development of a product that subsequently proved a commercial success for a competitor. Marketing and production weaknesses may also prevent a company from exploiting a technical success through its inability to generate a consumer demand, or to meet demand through manufacturing inadequacies. In such cases a competitor that has adopted a defensive strategy but has reacted quickly with a slightly improved product, backed up with marketing and manufacturing expertise, will gain the commercial success for a product the first company has pioneered. An absorptive strategy is where the company opts out from the R. and D. work but will utilize the research done by others through licence arrangements, takeover, or mergers with the innovative company, or even by careful navigation round the patent laws. A criticism that is sometimes made of British industry is that the opportunities for fruitful licence agreements are not sufficiently recognized. Many companies will adopt a mix of all three strategies, but a choice must be made of where to place most emphasis, and this choice should follow a careful appraisal of all the company's strengths and weaknesses.

Appraisal of Competition

There is little merit in developing a product if a major competitor is developing a similar product at the same time, or if there are alternatives with similar potential. No two companies have identical technological strengths. If a company can spot an area where its major competitors are weak and it is strong, then these suggest themselves for a concentration of R. and D. effort. This requires as careful an appraisal of the main competitor's strengths and weaknesses as of one's own. It also suggests the need for legitimate technological intelligence, e.g. who are their personnel of high calibre, what companies have been taken over recently, who are they recruiting?

International Comparisons

Similar considerations to those above apply if significant overseas sales are planned. The international pacemaker in technology is the United States of America, but even that country, with its immense research and development expenditure, is not equally strong in all fields. United States technology is distorted by the pattern of defence expenditure, and gaps exist for non-American companies to exploit. The uneven distribution of technological expertise has recently been recognized by several international companies that have decentralized their research activities to several countries in order to utilize particular national strengths.

O.E.C.D. research reports indicate that long-term success in international trade can only be achieved by companies adopting an offensive strategy.

Risk versus Pay-off

Although cost/benefit analysis is an essential part of any project-selection procedure, we need to examine the relation between risk and benefit in a rather different light when trying to establish a strategy for research and development. In general the more innovative projects are likely to present the highest opportunities

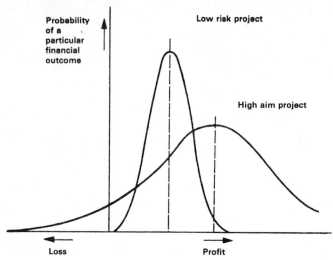

Figure 11.5   Profit probability distributions for low and high risk projects.

for profit, but they also contain the greater risk; the less risky projects, on the other hand, have a higher likelihood of profitability but a lower gross figure. Figure 11.5 illustrates this point.

In many cases such as this, conventional risk analysis will suggest that for a particular choice between two projects the more risky should be chosen because of its greater expected benefit. However, the company's financial position may dictate that it could not entertain the possibility of loss. Whereas a large company undertaking numerous research projects will be prepared to accept high risk because it believes that the contribution from those that succeed will more than outweigh the losses from failures, a smaller company with fewer projects may prefer to opt for more certain though less spectacular profitability. These considerations should be reflected in the R. and D. strategy, since the degree of acceptable risk is likely to influence the allocation of resources between new or existing technologies and between new or existing products.

COMPANY STRENGTHS AND WEAKNESSES

Examination of possible strategies will not lead us to an optimum choice unless we relate the alternatives to the company situation generally. This point, although it has already been mentioned several times when considering individual aspects of R. and D. strategy, cannot be overstressed. Before a decision is taken, a careful and realistic appraisal needs to be made of the strengths and weaknesses throughout the company. It is in this respect that perhaps the largest number of companies make serious errors, for the possession of a creative idea for a new product to meet an established market need can be a fatal trap for a company not possessing all the resources necessary to carry it through to successful commercial exploitation. Strengths should be exploited and weaknesses must be taken into account, although one would hope that their inevitability and immutability would not be accepted. It is only when the company's capabilities have been related to possible strategies that an R. and D. strategy can be formulated for allocating resources to specific areas.

Analysis of the factors to be taken into account when evaluating the company's strength in marketing, finance, and production will not be considered here. However, the R. and D. department will have its own strengths and weaknesses, and these must also be taken into account, since the identification of a technological opportunity does not necessarily imply that there is the capability within the company for its successful realization. Some of the most important factors to be considered are the following:

1 The existing resources within the department both in terms of its numerical strength and the capability of its personnel
2 The technologies in which it has expertise.
3 Evaluation of past performance in the development of entirely new products
4 The extent to which it is accustomed to working at the frontiers of knowledge
5 The mix of research and development
6 The product life-cycles and the gestation periods of new products that have been developed in the past
7 The organizational relation between the R. and D. department and the rest of the company, particularly marketing.

The last two factors perhaps require some amplification. In general the relation between marketing and research and development is much closer where product life-cycles and gestation periods are short. This is not surprising, since in these circumstances new products development must be geared closely to a rapidly changing market. The reverse is usually true where new product development and product lives are long; here one expects to find a more strictly formalized organization that slowly reacts

to market changes. It is thus unlikely that a company in the latter
category could exploit successfully a short-term new product
opportunity, however promising it may appear.

SELECTION OF PROJECTS

The formulation of a strategy for research and development
merely provides a framework within which individual project
proposals can be evaluated. The solution must be carried out in
the light once again of the total company situation, taking into
account short-term factors that may not be appropriate when
considering a strategy for the long term. Most companies carry
out some form of cost/benefit analysis in which the research
and development, capital equipment, and marketing investments
are compared with an expected benefit that takes into account
the probabilities of both technical and commercial success. This
form of evaluation procedure suffers from the shortcoming that
it tends to consider the project in isolation from other projects
and the current situation elsewhere in the company. The factors
that should be taken into account will vary from company to
company, but the list in Table 11.1 covers many of the points
most companies will need to consider.

Table 11.1   Criteria commonly used in selecting research and
development projects

A. **Corporate Objectives and Strategy**

    1. Is it compatible with the company's current strategy and long
range plan?
    2. Is its potential such that a change in the current strategy is
warranted?
    3. Is it consistent with the company 'image'?

B. **Research and Development**

    1. Is it consistent with the company's research and development
strategy?
    2. Is its potential such that a change in the research and development
strategy is warranted?
    3. Probability of technical success.
    4. The patent position.

5. Development time and cost — unique estimates can be misleading and the probabilities of various outcomes should be assessed.
6. Availability of research and development skills and efforts.
7. Effect upon other projects.
8. Possible future developments of the product and future applications for any new technology generated.

C. Marketing

1. Total size of the market.
2. Estimated market share.
3. 1 and 2 indicate the likely volume of the sales for the company. Considerations need to be given to the question whether there are advantages in having several major new products rather than a larger number of smaller projects. The latter will absorb more scarce management effort but will minimize the effects of a failure.
4. Estimated product life.
5. Probability of commercial success.
6. Time scale and relationship to current plans.
7. Effect upon current products.
8. Pricing and customer acceptance.
9. Competition.
10. Compatibility with existing distribution channels.

D. Finance

1. Capital investment required.
2. Revenue expense during the development phase.
3. Availability of finance for 1 and 2.
4. Effect upon other projects requiring finance.
5. Potential annual cash flow.
6. Profit margins.
7. Time to break even and maximum negative cash flow.
8. Does it meet the company's investment criteria?

E. Production

1. New processes involved.
2. Requirements for additional facilities.
3. Availability of raw material.
4. Manufacturing safety.
5. Availability of manufacturing personnel — numbers and skills.
6. Value added in production.

Most of the considerations shown in Table 11.1 are obvious when listed, and are widely used, although surprisingly few companies take more than a few of them into account. Many of them cannot be evaluated accurately when a project is first selected. Nevertheless it is vital that they be considered carefully at the outset; otherwise a situation will arise in which major decisions affecting future production and marketing policy are made in isolation.

THE DECISION-MAKING PROCESS

Much of what has been written above is obvious; much of it rests upon the work of others too numerous to acknowledge in detail. But perhaps where most companies fail is in putting the parts together to form a coherent strategy for research and development linked to their corporate strategies, and to which individual

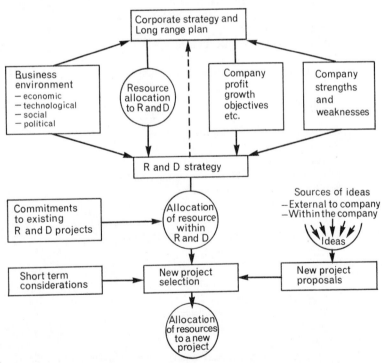

Figure 11.6   The decision-making process for research and development.

project selection can be related. If we are to gain greater benefit from expenditure on technology, there must be fewer failures, not so much in the quality of the technological effort but in the way it is harnessed to fulfilling business objectives. In the writer's view this will only be achieved when all the relevant factors are taken into account through a systematic approach (see Figure 11.6).

12 Strategy and Planning for Production

Brian C. Twiss

THE NEED FOR A PRODUCTION STRATEGY

The survival of the organization as an independent unit is generally accepted as a primary objective for most businesses. By this criterion a high proportion of top management must be judged to have failed. In the United Kingdom, for example, it has been estimated that in the ten years from 1960 to 1970 40 per cent of companies with assets of over £65 million and 65 per cent of companies with assets of less than £1 million ceased to exist as independent businesses. While the reasons for failure are often complex, two major causes associated with technology are frequently found — obsolescence of the product line and excessive production costs. In many cases this results from a reluctance to innovate technologically by developing new and improved products or to reduce manufacturing costs through process innovations. This aspect of technological strategy is discussed in the previous chapter. Failure to innovate, however, is by no means the only cause of poor performance.

Low profitability due to excessive production costs is still prevalent among companies, even when they have invested heavily in new technology. It is the purpose of this chapter to discuss why this is so. It will be suggested that a major cause is the absence or inadequacy of long-range anticipatory strategic thinking in relation to the production function in business. 'Production strategy' or 'manufacturing strategy' are phrases with an unfamiliar ring, but a strategic approach can and must be applied to the production function, which is the major cost centre for most manufacturing businesses.

The usual response to high production costs is an attempt to economize at the operational level. The whole range of modern management techniques may be applied. Although these will undoubtedly effect some improvement, the basic causes of the problem are frequently more deep-seated, resulting from decisions made years earlier. By the time the underlying problem is diagnosed it may be impossible to rectify without a major upheaval, leading to factory closures and redundancies sometimes, and a belated decision to invest in a crash programme for extending the production facilities at others. We may conclude that the fault lies in an over-concentration on the minutiae of production efficiency — work study, inventory control, scheduling, etc. — rather than on the 'big' decisions, and a preoccupation with the many urgent day-to-day problems at the expense of planning for the future. While these are managerial shortcomings, not unknown in other functions of business, they tend to be more marked in the production area, owing to the complexity and immediacy of many short-term operational problems and the background and attitudes of many of the senior production managers.

There is a marked difference between industries in their attitudes to long-range production planning. In the chemical and process industries, for example, the production plants are often large and capital-intensive. Investment usually means a new plant rather than extension or modification of the existing factory. Thus investment decisions are rare, but when they arise, they are large and follow detailed analysis. When, as all too frequently occurs, these investments result in excess manufacturing capacity, the fault can be attributed to shortcomings in the planning process, owing to incorrect forecasting or poor timing of the investment decision, rather than to the absence of planning.

But in many other industries, notably engineering, the production capacity grows 'like Topsy'. One only has to look at the factories with their mixture of architectural styles, building extensions and temporary structures, to appreciate that new investment over the years was a piecemeal short-term response to immediate difficulties. What is perhaps more serious is that the equipment installed within these buildings has been bought in the same way. Rarely has anyone reviewed the complete production system and modernized it as a whole. New machines may have been acquired but the system is virtually unchanged. It is comparable with attempting to modernize a Model T Ford by fitting it with radial ply tyres, independent suspension and a new carburettor.

Thus we see that the majority of manufacturing companies operate at anything near their optimum efficiency for only short periods. For the rest of the time they experience one or more of the following situations — idle equipment, excessive inventories, overtime or short-time working, the use of unsuitable equipment and so on. All these result in high production costs and reduced profit. They are caused by past failure to forecast and plan for the competitive and business conditions now facing the company. A strategic approach is clearly essential. Furthermore, since so many of the investment decisions in production are largely irreversible, because they represent buildings and equipment often peculiar to one production process, it is essential that the time horizon for planning should extend at least to the limits of the expected useful life of these investments.

THE SCOPE OF THE PROBLEM

A production strategy is primarily concerned with guiding investment decisions. Today's investment decisions provide the framework within which future operational decisions must be taken. A view must be taken of the future environment for production. Alternative solutions must be postulated and these related to the general corporate strategy and the competence of the manufacturing organization. Thus the elements in the formulation of the production strategy are, as one would expect, the same as those found in other areas of strategic thought — forecasting, capability analysis and objectives based upon the furtherance of the corporate strategy.

Since the purpose of a strategy is to guide decision-making, it is useful to examine briefly some of the major areas where such guidance is needed. These are the following:

1   To what extent should the company channel its resources into production rather than elsewhere in the business?
2   What productive capacity is required to meet the corporate and production objectives?
3   When should new capacity be brought into production?
4   Where should the production plant be located?
5   What manufacturing technologies should be used?

Corporate Investment in Production

Why manufacture? This question is seldom asked. Most companies were founded at a time when there was a seller's market, and their growth was based upon the ability to produce efficiently. The founding entrepreneur was frequently an engineer. Thus over the years production facilities will have been given priority for new investment. This attitude persists and may not even be questioned, although nowadays, and increasingly in the future, business success is as much dependent upon the ability to devise new products and market them effectively as upon the skills needed to make them.

The only justification for any investment in production should be the belief that the same money cannot be deployed more profitably elsewhere in the business. It might even be argued that more stringent criteria ought to be applied in the case of an investment in production facilities, since the decision once taken is difficult to reverse because of the physical and specialized nature of the assets bought. Nevertheless their relative permanence often leads to their continued existence being regarded as a 'given' when formulating a strategy for the future. This assumption is wrong. If the funds released by the sale of an uneconomic production facility can be put to more profitable long-term use elsewhere, perhaps in new product development or additional marketing effort, then this should be done, provided, of course, that alternative satisfactory arrangements can be made for sub-contract production.

Although the circumstances for moving out of production completely or initiating manufacture for the first time are rare, there is usually a great deal of choice in the extent of commitment to production, i.e. of vertical integration. Figure 12.1 illustrates the wide range of options. At one end of the spectrum all the items used in production including standard parts, small special components and major components can be manufactured and complete assembly undertaken. At the other extreme the finished article can be bought and the company's nameplate attached. For the purpose of illustration Figure 12.1 also shows the typical situation arising in several industries. The nature of the manufacturing operation dictates to a certain extent the area where the optimum is likely. But even so, there is often a considerable range of variation. Why, for example, should the degree

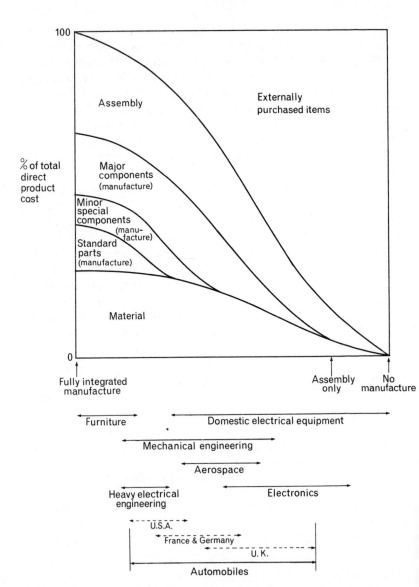

Figure 12.1   Involvement in production — a strategic choice.

of integration in the motor industry vary so widely between countries? The reasons, which are largely historical, may no longer relate to present-day economic realities.

Change, however, can only be introduced slowly. It must result from a conscious decision that a change of emphasis is necessary to meet future conditions in the industry. That decision can only be effective when it follows a long-range forecast of the industrial environment incorporated in an explicit strategy.

A trend towards a more flexible attitude is already apparent. As an example, one can note the domestic-appliance manufacturing company which is prepared to supplement its local production of some items in its product line with others bought from a subcontractor abroad and sold under its own brand name.

Production Capacity

Having decided in principle the extent of commitment to production, the firm must consider the size of the plant. Long-term forecasts of product line and demand give an indication of what capacity might be needed for several years ahead. Upon this trend must be superimposed cyclical variations, which tend to be much greater in amplitude for industrial than consumer products. Should capacity be installed in order to meet the maximum expected demand at all times? The answer may be in the affirmative if there is confidence that excess capacity can be utilized by expanding exports, should the national economic cycle not coincide with the world cycle, or by accumulating stocks if the duration of the surplus capacity is expected to be limited. On the other hand, it may be possible to supplement a plant of smaller capacity by imports or increased sub-contracting in periods of high demand. Lengthened delivery times or even the loss of some sales might sometimes be an acceptable alternative.

Forecasting is liable to substantial errors. In recent years the chemical industry has suffered seriously from excess capacity in major large investments, owing to overoptimistic forecasts of the market growth rate. Consequently future plants are likely to be smaller, for, however attractive economies of scale may appear on paper, the under-utilization of capital-intensive equipment can have a disastrous effect upon the profits earned.

Thus in deciding upon the size of manufacturing capacity it can be seen that, although forecasts are essential, due attention must be paid to the risks resulting from forecasting errors. The total profits derived over a period of time are more important than the theoretical profitability of a plant operating at optimum efficiency. Furthermore long-term contingency plans are necessary to cope with either under- or over-capacity demand, for it is usually too late to react when the emergency arises.

The Timing of Investment

Capital-investment decisions reflect the level of business confidence. Historically this has coincided with the peak of an economic cycle (Figure 12.2), but because of the time needed to implement the decision, the industry may well be entering the next recession before the new capacity becomes available. Thus we have the all too common phenomenon of a new factory operating at well below its planned rate for a year or two after completion. Psychologically it seems inevitable that new investment must remain linked to management's confidence in the future. But decision-making is likely to be much more accurately timed if this confidence springs from a clearly enunciated strategy based upon forecasts of the future rather than from the temporary euphoria caused by rising market demand.

Another problem of timing occurs in many industries where capacity increments must be large in order to gain economies of scale. In the chemical and process industries, where this has been true for many years, severe problems have been experienced when several large manufacturers have responded at the same period of the economic cycle. This is now extending to other industries, such as engineering, where it is necessary to replace rather than extend complete plants if the maximum benefits are to be gained from advances in production engineering. Although some reaction has been noted against the very large new investments, it seems likely that the general trend towards larger investments will continue. Timing becomes correspondingly more important. It becomes increasingly essential to pay considerable attention not only to what major competitors are doing now, but also to forecast what they are likely to do in the future. This can lead to a choice of (1) attempting to get one's own new plant on stream before the competitor, perhaps using a less advanced technology; (2) accepting the risk of overcapacity in the industry and striving to gain a larger market share; or (3) continuing to

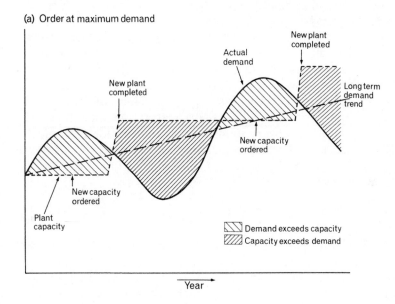

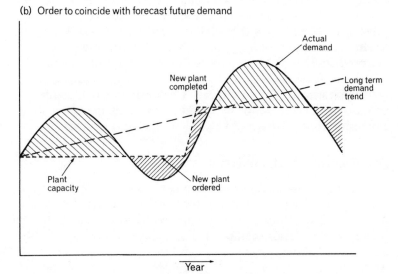

Figure 12.2   New plant ordering patterns.

use older plant at full capacity, recognizing that this will lead to temporarily uncompetitive unit costs, and introducing a new plant with improved technology at a later date.

Cost escalations, commissioning delays and teething troubles seem to be the rule rather than the exception with new plant. A major cause is that too little time is allowed for adequate planning. The decision is delayed, but once taken the new capacity is required as soon afterwards as possible. Many of these problems can be overcome by intelligent anticipatory planning, forward ordering of long-delivery items and the preparation of contingency plans; for the cost of planning, representing the efforts of a limited number of people, is a small proportion of the cost of physical assets.

Plant Location

Since most investments necessitate an expansion of current production, the natural tendency is to extend existing facilities in the same location. But the reasons for the original siting of the factory — local raw materials, availability of skilled labour or financial incentives — may no longer be valid. Many of the environmental trends discussed in the next section could have a substantial effect upon the relative economics of plant in different areas. It is necessary, therefore, to identify clearly those factors critical to the location decision and examine them in relation to forecasted trends over the working life of the proposed investment. Only then can it be decided whether the operational advantages of expansion on an existing site justify expansion there rather than elsewhere, perhaps overseas.

Manufacturing Technologies

Technological advances have often made a new plant obsolete before it was ready to start production. Sometimes the product itself has become out of date owing to an innovation. Often the process technologies themselves have changed. An outstanding example is Pilkington's development of the float glass process, which, within a few years, revolutionized flat glass production worldwide. Other manufacturers, notably St. Gobain, either unaware of the new process or misjudging its potential, continued to invest in new plant already technically obsolete. In another example a major computer manufacturer had to cancel plans for a new factory, planning permission for which had been obtained with difficulty from a German city authority, because advances in micro-circuitry made it no longer necessary.

This is where technological forecasting can be of great assistance in deciding what new technologies may have a significant impact on the industry in the next ten to fifteen years. Emerging technologies must be identified and forecasts made of the probable time-scales both of feasibility and subsequent rate of diffusion. But technological capability must be related to a variety of economic, social and political factors that have a bearing on the decision process. For example, recent evidence suggests that the adoption of numerically controlled machine tools is determined more by a growing shortage of skilled labour than by the theoretical economies that under-utilization has often shown to be illusory.

THE CHANGING ENVIRONMENT OF PRODUCTION

Few of the environmental trends influencing corporate planning will not have some effect upon the production strategy. We will now consider some of the most important of these and discuss briefly the effect they may have upon the production strategy.

The Labour Force

Manufacturers in Europe can expect to experience increasing difficulty in obtaining the quantity, quality and cooperation of their workers. The total work force is static and the proportion of the G.N.P. devoted to services is increasing, thereby reducing the availability of labour for manufacturing.

A significant development is the increasing unwillingness to accept the dehumanizing activities inseparable from mass-production processes. The difficulty experienced in the Lordstown plant in the U.S.A. is but an extreme case of what many companies are now facing. We read daily of the need for job enrichment and of the pioneering experiments at SAAB and Volvo; but examination of the whole range of industrial jobs suggests that the retention of current mass-production methods is normally essential if unacceptable economic penalties are to be avoided. Inevitably it appears that the developed nations will experience rising labour costs, both direct and indirect in terms of longer holidays, shorter working week and higher fringe payments; a shortage of skilled labour; and increasing industrial strife from well-paid workers demanding greater job satisfaction. It is interesting to note that Europe is in an unfavourable position compared with the U.S.A., where the working labour force will continue to grow and where labour costs are falling by international comparison because of successive dollar devaluations.

Few labour-intensive industries can now compete with products from low-cost areas of the world. In the years ahead we may well see the same thing happening to our mass-production industries. This trend has already started with Rollei manufacturing cameras in Singapore and European motor manufacturers establishing plants in Brazil, Turkey and Spain. Swiss pharmaceutical companies no longer regard Switzerland as their manufacturing base, new investment being spread to other centres and the homeland taking on the role of the centre for technological innovation. The message seems clear. No longer can it be assumed that the historical location will provide a profitable base for future production. Furthermore, because of labour unrest, multiple international sourcing for supplies will increase. The growth of international trade unionism will also have to be watched closely.

Technological advance has led to the gradual replacement of man by machine. The influences already discussed are likely to lead to an acceleration of this trend. These, combined with Government regulations for redundancy payments and the trend towards restrictions on the company's freedom to discharge employees, are tending to make labour a fixed rather than a variable cost. Thus one can infer that long-term manpower planning will become increasingly necessary. Moreover the nature of many jobs is changing, so that the worker is becoming less of an active operator and more of a machine-watcher. This calls for profound organizational changes in the production unit and the placing of a greater emphasis on individual worker morale.[1]

Measures of the extent to which the machine/man substitution process has occurred are provided by figures of capital employed per employee, potential output per employee and value added per employee. Target figures for these measures should consequently form part of any production strategy.

Government Intervention

Government intervention in industry is growing worldwide, and is unlikely to diminish. Nowadays, with countries' membership of larger units such as the E.E.C., businesses must be constantly aware of the future pattern of regulations, which might affect their operations both nationally and internationally. Regional policies, environmental control, labour regulations, etc., will all have an impact upon a production unit. For example, a factory at one site may in the future face much more stringent control of atmospheric pollution than one at an alternative site, whereas under current legislation there may be little to choose between the two.

Demands for an increased proportion of locally made parts (e.g. motor cars in Australia) can affect the content of export sales and consequently the requirements for manufacturing capacity both at home and overseas. These changes also must be anticipated.

Market Factors

Product lives are shortening, not only for consumer goods but also for many industrial products. This is a result not only of the pace of technological change but also of the buyer's market, whereby competition is increasingly bringing about a rapid rate of product obsolescence. But much of the improvement in production efficiency is gained at the expense of flexibility. Machines and processes are becoming more specialized. Consequently the useful life of production equipment is also shortening and reduced payback periods must be used in new investment appraisal. A strategic question to answer is 'Should new investment be channelled towards (1) flexible general-purpose machinery, which is usually more expensive and often less efficient, or (2) towards short-life inflexible special-purpose equipment?' The trend of economic analysis would appear to indicate (2), yet frequently one finds specifications for specialist machinery that would operate satisfactorily for decades whereas economically its life is limited.

Greater product variety is also being demanded. Fortunately recent developments in production technology and organization are enabling this need to be met without insuperable economic penalties, e.g. modular production, group technology, production scheduling, and real-time machine-loading by computer and numerically controlled machine tools. The adoption of these techniques will grow, stimulated not so much by their technical merits but because they are needed to meet the changing requirements of the market, changes that are likely to be much less predictable than they have been in the past.

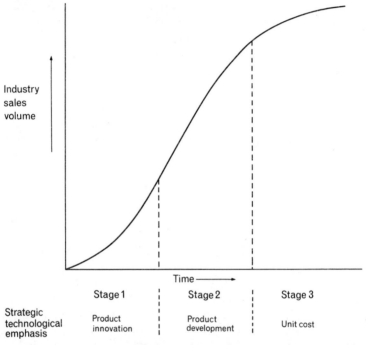

Figure 12.3   Strategic emphasis on production efficiency as an industry matures.

Industry Maturity

Most industries go through a life-cycle comparable to a product life-cycle (Figure 12.3). At each stage the corporate strategic emphasis is different, starting with product innovation based upon technological innovation and ending with a situation where it is virtually impossible to differentiate between products (e.g. detergents, motor fuel). The need for production efficiency and consequently the need for investment in production grows accordingly, for in maturity, products and their selling price cease to be variables and profit is earned by reducing unit cost. In any consideration of production strategy it is essential therefore to understand what stage of maturity the industry is reaching and adjust the level and type of investment in production accordingly.

Technological Progress

Most of the technological trends of significance have already been referred to. Their impact will, however, vary considerably from one industry to another. Summarizing, the main factors are as follows:

1 The growth of systems geared to the production of a particular product, e.g. an automobile-engine factory, which must be replaced as a total system when the product changes
2 The increasing use of specialized equipment, often semi- or fully automated and demanding fewer and less skilled operators
3 Decreasing flexibility with special-purpose machinery, but the promise of some greater flexibility of operation and scheduling in batch production resulting from computer control
4 A reducing economic operating life of equipment owing to technological advances.

There is one factor calling for particular attention, and that is the effect of technological progress in the product on the total value added in production. Some products are becoming more complex, e.g. aircraft and road vehicles, so that the total manufacturing effort and investment required for one unit of output is increasing. But the reverse is also true. In the electronic industry dramatic reductions in the value added per unit of output are noted, and are reflected in the selling price of electronic desk calculators and transistor radios. In these cases manufacturing investment may even fall in spite of considerable increases in production volume.

CAPABILITY ANALYSIS

The process of strategy formulation must be iterative, but it is not critical where the process starts, i.e. with objectives, identifi-

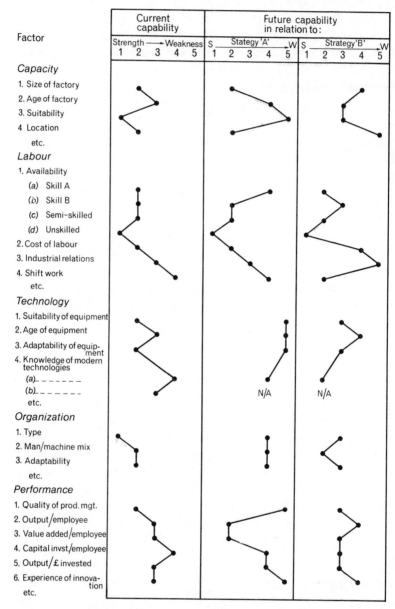

Figure 12.4   Capability analysis — use of profile chart.

cation of threats and opportunities or the analysis of the organization's strengths or weaknesses. There is a case, however, for
carrying out the *environmental analysis* before the *capability
analysis,* for what is important is not the company's present
abilities but its productive competence in relation to the future
in either meeting the threats or exploiting the opportunities
revealed by the forecasts.

One of the most difficult facts to appreciate is that in times of
change attributes that have formerly been assets may in the future
prove to be liabilities. One can consider, for example, a company
that is the sole industrial employer in a community. Over the
years the life of the community has been centred upon the
company – an enviable asset. But this interdependence becomes
a constraint when other considerations point to a need to cut
back the work force. Thus an asset becomes a liability. To take
another case, modern specialized plant for making product X gives
Company A lower unit-manufacturing costs than its main competitor, Company B. However, Company B has more flexible
general-purpose machinery, which can be quickly modified to
manufacture a new product Y. Thus Company A's competitive
advantage today may turn into an expensive burden tomorrow.

Assessing one's own capability objectively is not easy, but an
attempt to do so as dispassionately as possible must be made. In
doing this, a systematic approach can be of invaluable assistance.
One way in which this can be done – a profile chart – is illustrated in Figure 12.4. Firstly, all those factors, past, present and
future, relevant to an evaluation of the company's production
capability are listed. The items will, of course, differ between industries and from one company to another. The company's
present capability in relation to each of these factors is then
evaluated. For most of them the assessment must of necessity be
subjective, but for others it will be possible to derive quantitative
guidelines from industry data, e.g. output per employee, capital
investment per employee.

It is next necessary to look at the future. Profiles can then be
constructed in a similar fashion for alternative production strategies suggested by the environmental analysis. This is a process of
evaluating *current capabilities* against forecasted *future needs.* It
must be emphasized, however, that this is not a technique for
selecting the optimum strategy; that must remain a matter for
managerial judgement. But it can perform the following tasks:

1   Indicate those areas where a proposed strategic change is likely to have the greatest impact, thereby directing managerial attention in the right directions
2   Give an indication of the order of magnitude of changes required by alternative strategies
3   Ensure that all relevant factors are considered systematically.

A large discrepancy between present capability and the requirements of a particular strategy should not necessarily be interpreted as ruling it out. But it does suggest that managerial and financial priority may need to be channelled into the production function. Moreover, since the probability of failure to achieve the objectives fully is likely to be higher in this case, the potential rewards should be correspondingly attractive for what is in essence a high risk/high pay-off strategy.

CONCLUSION

This chapter has not focused on the methodology of production strategy formulation, for it differs little from what is needed in defining a corporate strategy. The elements are the same — objective setting, environmental analysis, capability analysis, alternative strategy generation, selection of the optimum strategy and the setting of key policies (Figure 12.5). The problem of implementation is also similar. It does, however, suffer from additional difficulties stemming from the traditional isolation of senior production executives from strategic thought and a long-term perspective. This may be why so many companies fail seriously in their critical production decisions, namely those that concern the size, timing, location and type of investment in production capacity.

Strategy is concerned with change. Discussion of a few of the environmental trends indicates that the pace of change is accelerating. Hence the increasing need for a clear strategy.

The importance of attempting to forecast these trends has been stressed. However, experience of forecasting indicates that as the pace of change quickens, so does it become more difficult to predict. Thus a word of warning must be sounded. Forecasts do not resolve uncertainty. They can be misleading if a 'mock'

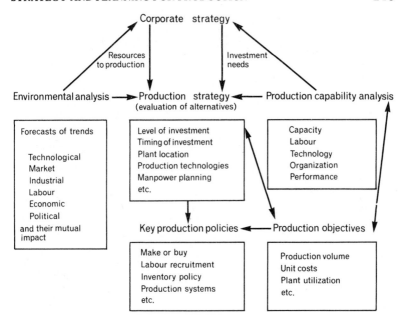

Figure 12.5   Information flows in production strategy formulation.

certainty is substituted for a genuine uncertainty. This faces the decision-maker with the following choices:

1   To direct his efforts towards areas where little change is anticipated – usually a low pay-off solution
2   To base his decisions upon a belief that the forecasts provide a sound basis for a changed strategy – the most rewarding choice if the forecasts prove correct
3   To adopt a flexible approach whereby resources can be adjusted without too much dislocation in the light of future events or later forecasts – a lower risk strategy but one that will almost always mean additional expenditure.

The choice lies with top management, with the advice of senior production management. It will depend upon their judgement and attitude to risk and uncertainty. But it must be a conscious decision taken within a framework of strategic analysis of the place the production function is destined to play as a contributor to corporate profit.

REFERENCE

1 For a detailed discussion of this trend see Weinshall, T.
   and Twiss, B. *Organisational Problems in European Manufacture* (Longmans, 1973), ch. 5.

13 Key Issues in Industrial Relations

Kevin Hawkins

Is it necessary for companies to have a strategy for employee relations? For many years the conventional wisdom in British industry was that every manager worthy of the name should be able to handle men. Dealing with employees was something a manager did as a matter of course — almost instinctively. What need was there for a strategy or for specialist advice in this field? For many years neither governments nor the trade unions themselves appeared unduly worried by the traditional managerial approach to industrial relations.

Over the past decade, however, many things have happened to challenge these complacent assumptions. First, the growing weakness of the British economy has compelled successive Governments to intervene in collective bargaining between employers and trade unions. The Government now takes an active interest in the behaviour of wage costs, the level of direct conflict, the efficiency with which manpower is used, and indeed in the whole spectrum of labour relations at work-place level. What managements do is subject to an increasing degree of regulation by the state. Second, the growth of collective bargaining at factory level has put pressure on managements from another direction. Traditional managerial prerogatives — to hire and fire, to determine how much work shall be done and at what speed, to fix the rate of payment for a given job — have been eroded by the changing expectations of work groups and their representatives. Many employers have found that their power to make decisions on matters affecting the work force is increasingly subject to bargaining and agreement. Consequently more and more issues of substance at shop and factory level are being determined by negotiation between managers and shop stewards. Where managers refuse to negotiate, the result may well be direct action by the work force.

Pressure from the Government is therefore combining with pressure from the work force to place severe limitations on management's freedom of action. In these circumstances it behoves managers to give careful thought to *what* they are trying to achieve in industrial relations and *how* they are going to achieve it. In short, company managements should have a *policy* for employee relations. Such a policy must seek to anticipate events — otherwise management will be forced back into a 'fire-fighting' role and will merely react to problems as they occur. The shape and content of an industrial-relations policy is obviously a matter for the management concerned. Objectives, strategies and procedures will vary from one industry to another and from one company to another. It is possible, however, to indicate a number of key policy issues that all thinking managers should now be actively considering.

THE REFORM OF WAGE-PAYMENT SYSTEMS

More strikes arise from disputes about wage claims and wage structures than from all other matters of substance put together. One very obvious reason for the importance of wages is, of course, the tendency for a greater proportion of the weekly wage packet to be provided through bargaining at company level. As the Donovan Commission pointed out some time ago, industry-wide bargaining has been declining in importance since the 1940s. With the exception of the nationalized industries, it is a safe assumption that this decline will continue. The corresponding growth of wage and salary bargaining at the work place has prompted Governments and the public agencies, such as the National Board for Prices and Incomes (1965—71), to take an active interest in the character and effectiveness of company payment systems. The character of these systems can often reflect managerial attitudes towards the improvement of efficiency and the reduction of unit labour costs. Cost inflation at the work place also has obvious implications for a national incomes policy. Indeed, many observers would endorse Clegg's view that 'one of the greatest obstacles to a reasonable and fair system of pay in the country as a whole is the absurdity and injustice of many of our plant and company pay structures.'[1]

It has often been argued that the widespread use of payment by results systems, especially in the manufacturing sector, has in the past been responsible for much of the inflationary disorder characteristic of work-place bargaining. First, it is generally believed that P.B.R. contributes to wage drift by pushing earnings far above basic rates and by disturbing wage differentials within the enterprise in a way that leads to pressures for further wage increases. Second, it is said that P.B.R. gives rise to anomalies in earnings between different jobs and skills, in many cases leading to competitive bargaining between groups of workers. Third, it has been discovered that with the passage of time the effect of P.B.R. on output and productivity declines, but the ability of workers and groups to make the system produce higher earnings does not. One could therefore say that P.B.R. is in practice incompatible with any attempt to contain cost inflation at plant level in so far as it cannot ensure that pay increases do not exceed the growth of productivity. One could also criticize it on the grounds that it rests on an outdated and extremely dubious view of human motivation. People do not come to work *only* for money, and a payment system based on the assumption that monetary incentives are the only ones that matter is therefore bound to cause problems in the long run.

If, therefore, the case against payment by results is so clear cut, why, one may ask, are some 8 or 9 million workers still employed in establishments where some form of incentive system is in use? One reason may well be, quite simply, that it meets the needs of many managers and workers. Most researchers have confirmed that an incentive scheme can, at least in the short run, raise output quite significantly, especially in situations of low performance. Many managers still think that, although the cruder versions of 'economic man' are no longer appropriate, it is still necessary to establish a direct connection between effort and reward. As the N.B.P.I. observed: 'A number of firms regard themselves as committed to whatever payment system they operate and much less impetus for change seems to come from management than might be expected from the experience we have reported . . . Conventional P.B.R. systems seem to induce strong resistance to change on management's part perhaps because it fears that the effort will decline if the customary incentives are tampered with.'[2] By the same token many workers see payment by results as the best way of retaining some personal control over the speed at which they work and the amount of work they do. Indeed, it is perhaps significant that in recent years there has been a pronounced decline in the hostility towards payment by results that was once so marked in official trade-union circles. There seems, in fact, to have been more pressure against payment by results from *outside* industry than from either managements or trade unions.

Another reason for the continued use of incentive schemes at work-place level may also be the apparent lack of a persuasive alternative. Certain technological circumstances favour incentive schemes, most notably where there is a good deal of repetitive assembly work. If management's overriding objective is to secure higher output, even if this entails higher labour costs, then they are unlikely to be impressed by the non-incentive payment systems available.[3] These may be grouped under the collective title of 'measured day work'. In essence, measured day work requires the employee to maintain an agreed level of performance in return for a specified wage. Herein lies the main difference between measured day work and conventional payment by results, under which there is in effect a sliding scale of effort bargains. Measured day work, as the name implies, normally entails the use of techniques such as job evaluation and work study. As such, it represents the principle of rational assessment in the performance of work tasks and holds out the prospect of a simplified non-competitive wage structure. It has therefore been strongly endorsed by many would-be reformers of collective bargaining. It has also been seen as a positive aid to an incomes policy.

Certainly there is much to be said for measured day work. It gives management more control over the movement of earnings and therefore over labour costs, it reinforces the need for better supervision, and it greatly reduces the opportunities for haggling and conflict on the shop floor. Yet its very advantages may in practice be a major source of contention, for there is evidence to suggest that some shop stewards and work groups view measured day work with intense suspicion. They see it as an attempt by management to restore unilateral control over the effort bargain and thereby deprive them of the bargaining power that payment by results has given them. The evidence from the motor-car industry concerning the effects of measured day work on the climate of shop-floor relations is certainly ambiguous. At British Leyland's Cowley plant, for example, where measured day work was introduced early in 1971, the number of small-scale local stoppages has been greatly reduced. It has been reported, however, that the stewards are now concerned to re-establish the bargaining power which P.B.R. gave them. The implication is that measured day work may in certain circumstances pose a threat to the status and authority of the shop steward. It can reasonably be argued, therefore, that the Leyland stewards will, in common with their counterparts at Ford (a company that has always used measured day work), mount a close watch on management and will strongly resist any further attempts to erode their authority.[4]

Admittedly the Leyland stewards have one important advantage over the stewards at Ford's. As part of the price for introducing measured day work, the company agreed (in the so-called 'mutuality clauses') to negotiate all changes in manning standards and work loads with union representatives. But despite all the publicity the 'mutuality' principle received at the time, it appears to have had little real effect on the climate of labour relations in British Leyland, although, of course, one cannot say that the climate would not have been worse without it. Perhaps the real lesson is that at a time when more workers are looking for opportunities to participate in an ever-widening circle of managerial decisions, it is inadvisable to look at measured day work simply as a means of restoring management *control* over a vital issue of substance at the work place. Changing a payment system cannot in practice be divorced from the framework of power relations in the work place, a particular feature of which at the moment is, of course, the rising demand for participation. This point will be discussed below.

The same argument applies to job evaluation, itself frequently associated with the introduction of measured day work, for the successful implementation of both job evaluation and measured day work presupposes the existence of a consensus within the organization on the social and economic value of all the jobs concerned. Such a consensus must exist not merely between management on the one hand and the work force on the other, but also between different *work groups* within the firm. In order to achieve this depth of agreement management will presumably have to broaden the scope of joint regulation to cover most other issues of substance in the work place. Yet it is deceptively easy to invest too much confidence in the capacity of managements to abolish conflict there through 'objective' techniques such as job evaluation. Over the past few years several managements have made the same optimistic assumptions about job evaluation as their predecessors did about F. W. Taylor's theory of scientific management. In the words of one recent study, 'there is a tendency for management to promote, and even to believe, the idea that in job evaluation it has an authoritative independent tool for determining job grades and differentials, legitimised by science; and that anyone who questions the form and findings of a job evaluation system is either a fool or a knave'.[5]

One cannot deny that the more sophisticated forms of job evaluation offer a reasonably precise method of analysing and describing the content of a job and the level of ability required to achieve a given level of performance. But the formal analysis, with its precise, quantitative benchmarks, must sooner or later be given practical meaning in the form of a new wage structure. This means that weightings must be attached to the objective hierarchy of jobs produced by the initial analysis. At this point, however, two other values intrude upon the scene. The first of these is the *market* value of the work group whose jobs are under consideration. True, some authorities seek to exclude or at least greatly dilute the laws of the market from the process of job evaluation. Daniel, for example, has argued that 'it is not generally held to be fair that someone should command high earnings simply because his services are in short supply and regardless of the level of skill or responsibility he exercises'.[6] But while market value in its *pure* form is rarely used, the example of the dispute between the Government and the National Union of Mineworkers in the winter of 1973—4 suggests that labour shortages can play a strategic role in a wage claim if the group concerned occupies a sufficiently important position in the economy.

This leads us to the second of these values, which is, of course, the value to society as a whole of a given job or group of related jobs. The social value of a job is, however, extremely difficult to define in terms that would permit a specific price to be placed upon it. It can be argued that every job has a social value of some kind — otherwise it would not exist. General agreements may conceivably be forthcoming on which jobs occupy the two extremes of the hierarchy — those of greatest and those of least social value. But one can foresee that immense difficulties will arise if an attempt is made to induce the numerous groups in between to accept estimates of their social value that appear to allot them a relatively subordinate and perhaps fixed position in the wage and salary hierarchy. Such an attempt can be successful only if all groups are agreed on the same ideas of fairness; but this in itself is a relative concept, and one man's fairness is another man's injustice. While it is conceivable that some form of general agreement on a fair structure of wage relativities might emerge at the work place through the normal processes of bargaining and compromise, it is extremely difficult to be sanguine about the prospects for extending the consensus between different work places in the same industry, let alone between different industries. It is certainly true that the idea of a national system of job evaluation has been attracting more attention in recent years. But in so far as such a system presupposes the development of a national consensus on the social and economic value of all jobs — a consensus that will presumably emerge through the general application of objective scientific analysis — its realization in the foreseeable future appears highly unlikely.

The Achilles heel of all systems of job evaluation is the strong *de facto* relation between fairness and bargaining power. An assumption implicit in job evaluation is that all the groups to whom it applies will accept its verdict as rational, equitable and impartial. The fact that the results of job evaluation are frequently rejected by groups who consider themselves unfairly placed in the new objective hierarchy is sometimes overlooked by its more uncritical advocates. Some would argue that objections from the work force can be overcome if only management sets out to bring all groups into the evaluation process from the very beginning. That, it is argued, will bring total commitment. Some managements, however, have actually sought to achieve this level of participation and have found their overtures rejected. The attitude of many shop stewards towards managerial initiatives on job evaluation may be summarized in a sentence: 'You go and do your evaluation and then we'll negotiate about it.' In short, it is rather naïve to assume that any system of job evaluation can be insulated from the pressures of conventional collective bargaining.[7] If job evaluation throws out too radical a challenge to the *status quo* within a company or an industry, then it stands little chance of being accepted by the majority of the work force.

THE PROBLEM OF WAGE RELATIVITIES

Much of the advice that has been gratuitously offered to managers on the subject of the reform of their internal payment systems seems to imply that a company or establishment can somehow insulate itself from inflationary pressures that may emanate from outside. In reality, however, the success of most managers in restraining the growth of labour costs in their own plants depends to a great extent on the level of wage inflation in other comparable firms in the same region, industry or locality. Wage *relativities* are becoming more and more significant in the inflationary process. Groups are competing with other groups for large relative shares of the available wealth. Competition in turn thrives on comparison. In Britain the habit of comparing one's own income with someone else's has become deeply ingrained over the past few years.

As Robinson has pointed out, 'People demand wage increases because other people have received wage increases. Justice is based on relativity and comparison in the area of wages and so individuals, groups and trade unionists are constantly looking at others to help determine whether their own pay is fair'.[8] The habit of comparison seems to be spreading. Hilde Behrend's research into popular attitudes towards incomes policy and inflation suggests that we are all becoming more interested in the size of the pay increases obtained by others. She argues that 'ideas about what represents fair pay increases are based on generalised pay increase images which are acquired through experience or through contact with pay increase information'.[9] This general learning process has obviously been very much accelerated by the growing preoccupation of the press, radio and television with wage claims, wage settlements and strikes. It has also been encouraged, paradoxically, by the reform of work-place payment systems. Under piecework, earnings levels tend to vary not only from group to group but also within a single group. This variability makes comparison difficult. Measured day work systems, by contrast, tend to produce a clear set of wage reference points. Many groups have in recent years found it much easier to compare their earnings with those of other groups precisely because their respective pay structures have been 'rationalised'. Under measured day work and similar systems the establishment of a series of clear wage reference points facilitates the dissemination of information on relative pay. As Brown and Sisson have observed, 'The more information workers have about other workers' pay (and, in some instances, the more information they have about other workers' jobs), the more likely they are to adopt fresh comparative reference groups'.[10] As information flows in from more sources, so the orbits of comparison are being steadily widened.

The relevance of comparability as a principle in wage bargaining has also been strongly emphasized by the experience of two major strikes in the coalmining industry. The miners' argument in the 1972 dispute was that their earnings had fallen way behind those of other comparable groups for reasons peculiar to the mining industry itself, namely rationalization and the abolition of piecework. In 1973—4 they made use of external events, arguing that the radical change in the price of alternative forms of energy made coal a cheap but vital indigenous source of fuel. If the country wanted more coal, it would have to pay its miners more money. In both cases the miners argued that their relative earnings position was grossly out of line with the economic importance of their job.

Their overwhelming success in both disputes has raised some important questions about the existing structure of relative wages, which have clear implications for the future of incomes policy. Hitherto it has been difficult to dispute the general validity of Hyman's statement that 'The application of pay comparisons in industrial relations is typically unambitious and powerfully shaped by custom: major inequalities which form an established part of the incomes hierarchy are rarely a focus of contention'.[11] It seems likely, however, that over the next few years the orbits of comparison will be gradually extended. The flow of information on relative pay will not only increase but work groups will also tend to adopt a more opportunistic attitude towards it. They will increasingly use whatever reference points are most likely to help them win a particular claim. Opportunism, however, may also encourage groups to question traditional relativities if these conflict with their bargaining objectives.

One of the most time-honoured assumptions built into the existing structure of relative incomes is that white-collar work is intrinsically more valuable than manual employment. Historically it may well be true that this assumption has derived its strength from the broad ideological associations between white-

collar workers and top management. In Hyman's words, 'They
enjoy the advantages of a partial and contingent parallel in work
task and qualifications — as well as in some cases a place, however modest, in the same hierarchy of control — with those in
elite and dominant occupational roles'.[12] For some years now,
however, the relative position of many white-collar workers in
the incomes hierarchy has been subject to a gradual erosion. Loss
of pre-eminence in terms of income has frequently gone hand in
hand with a corresponding diminution in power and status in
the work place. The response of many white-collar groups has
been to seek protection through trade unionism. The extent to
which the growth of white-collar unionism explicitly challenges
the old ideological association between white-collar workers
and top management may, of course, be debated. What *is* beyond
doubt is that many manual unions are extremely hostile to the
implied objectives of white-collar unionism, for if it is successful,
it must inevitably result in a *widening* of income differentials
between manual and white-collar groups, in defiance of the slow
but unmistakable trend towards a more compressed structure of
relativities.[13] Moreover the strength and militancy of white-
collar unions in both the public and private sectors have sharply
increased over the past few years; and in view of the long-run
tendency of white-collar employment to absorb an increasing
share of total employment, many would argue that the future is
on their side.

It is equally clear, however, that the most powerful manual
groups have no intention of sitting back and permitting white-
collar unions to make the running. Over the past few years some
manual groups have discovered that they have more power to
improve their own relative position through collective action
than they had once assumed. Consciousness of power has been
accompanied by a growing willingness to use it. Their determination has, of course, been greatly strengthened by the misdirected
efforts of successive Governments to restrain wages, but we shall
all have to live with the disruptive consequences of past incomes
policies for many years to come. In the summer of 1974, for
example, the Scottish section of the N.U.M. made it clear that in
their view the miners should be striving to effect a radical change
in the structure of relative incomes: 'We miners refuse to accept
the values which place the lowest rewards on the dirtiest and
most dangerous jobs and the highest rewards on the lightest,

most comfortable, least dangerous work. In other words, we no longer accept the income differentials which place white collar work higher up the scale than manual work.'[14] The existing structure of wage relativities and differentials will probably become increasingly unstable as a result of the continued growth of competitive and coercive behaviour.

It follows from this analysis that senior managers at plant and company level will find it increasingly difficult to preserve whatever order they have achieved in their internal wage and salary structures. It may even be that the conventional wisdom regarding the need for 'rational' systems of payment (i.e. measured day work) should be reconsidered. The retention of an incentive scheme of some kind in plant payment systems may well provide managements with a valuable element of flexibility when they are faced with adverse comparisons in wage negotiations.

PARTICIPATION

In recent years managements have found their authority to make decisions unilaterally on matters of substance at the work place challenged. There is now a growing demand by employees for participation in the making of decisions that affect their working lives. This demand assumes many forms and varies greatly in intensity from one work place to another. Nevertheless employee participation seems likely to become more and more central to industrial relations over the next few years. Governments will undoubtedly enact legislation that in some way furthers the cause of participation. Even the most sceptical manager, therefore, must begin to think about the fundamental issues participation will raise.

What is the *purpose* of greater participation by employees in managerial decision-making? Clearly, one of the most significant features of industrial relations in all West European countries over the past few decades has been the spread of 'low-trust' attitudes in the work place. It has been argued that the extreme division of labour and the organization of work on increasingly bureaucratic lines has deprived all but the most favoured groups of employees of much of the discretion and autonomy in their jobs they once enjoyed.[15] The diminishing discretionary content of many jobs (manual and white-collar alike) has resulted in widespread alienation and a lack of trust between employers and employees. Strikes, absenteeism, restrictive practices and labour turnover are all to some extent symptomatic of this fundamental alienation. In so far as participation implies that employees are able to exercise more discretion in their daily work it is increasingly seen as an effective strategy against alienation. Managements see participation as a means of encouraging the moral commitment of the work force to the enterprise. Moral commitment should in turn facilitate the implementation of change within the enterprise. Change cannot be imposed upon employees regardless of their interests. In the current climate of opinion managers must manage by agreement. This does not necessarily weaken managerial authority. On the contrary, the moral commitment of employees to the success of the enterprise is a vital asset to managements, not a liability.

There are, however, several different forms of participation, the choice between them being determined largely by the level of decision-making desired. Collective bargaining is, of course, the traditional British form of participation. Until recently the consensus of opinion on both sides of industry was that once collective bargaining had been formalized and extended at the work place, it would continue to meet the future needs of employers and trade unions very well. Its main weakness, however, is that it is concerned primarily with *collective* relations in industry and may neglect the interests of the individual worker. Certainly the relation of the employee to his job is rarely covered in a collective agreement. Collective bargaining in practice usually means that certain limits are imposed on managerial authority. It establishes a code of rights that protects workers against the power of management. Yet many of these rights are defensive, even negative in character. Within the broad framework of these limitations, management is free to act. Indeed, the generally informal character of collective bargaining at the work place means that in practice the effectiveness of these checks on managerial authority depends in the last resort on the sanctions the work force can bring to bear. The steady growth of unofficial and unconstitutional strikes over the past decade suggests that work groups are resorting more and more to direct action in pursuit of what they consider to be their legitimate interests. In this sense it could be said that collective bargaining is failing to promote an adequate degree of orderly joint decision-making.

One symptom of the growing disenchantment with collective

bargaining in trade-union circles is the sudden upsurge of interest at the T.U.C. in worker representation on boards of directors. Some European countries have already made provision for the election and/or appointment of worker directors. West Germany has had nearly twenty-five years' experience with one form of worker representation. It would appear, therefore, that sooner or later Britain will move in the same direction as her fellow members of the E.E.C. in respect of worker directors.

There are several points in favour of worker representation at board level. It is said that worker directorships will bring the following advantages:

1   Encourage the development of employer-employee coopera-
     tion and harmony
2   Improve the quality of decision-making at board level;
     workers' interests will be safeguarded in all board decisions
     and the decisions themselves will be more effective because
     they have the support of the work force
3   Encourage the work force to identify themselves with the
     company and its policies.

It must be recognized, however, that there are also a number of arguments against worker directors. Trade-union critics, for example, have expressed the following opinions:

1   As long as industry is privately owned, workers can never hope
     to achieve as much effective power through representation
     on the board as they have done through collective organiza-
     tion. The idea of worker directors ignores the fundamental
     division of interests between employers and employees. In
     practice, therefore, the worker directors would find them-
     selves increasingly at variance with the aspirations of the
     work force.
2   Worker directors would create a channel of communication
     and representation separate from (and probably in conflict
     with) the established machinery of collective bargaining.
     In organized firms a system of worker directors might
     weaken the loyalty of the work force to their trade unions.
     In unorganized establishments worker directors might be
     used as a covert method of keeping collective bargaining
     at bay.

Managerial critics have also added the point that, in firms

where trade unions are well-established, worker directors would inevitably come under strong pressure from the union organization to represent *trade-union* interests in the boardroom. This would in effect turn board meetings into bargaining sessions, and decision-making would become much more prolonged and difficult. In these circumstances it would be impossible to stimulate the kind of joint problem-solving approach to key policy decisions which, from a managerial viewpoint, is the *raison d'être* of worker representation in the boardroom. This indeed is what has tended to happen under West Germany's system of 'co-determination'.

Although originally designed as a method of electing *worker* directors, co-determination has become increasingly dominated by *trade-union* representatives. Where collective organization is present, collective bargaining inevitably follows. It is naïve, therefore, to suppose that one can somehow introduce a system of genuine joint decision-making without simultaneously conceding the right of employees' representatives to *bargain* with management. Since this usually implies the use of collective sanctions, it would be foolish to assume that a system of worker directors could in any sense displace traditional collective bargaining.

There are, in fact, several key questions that must be answered before the concept of worker representation on company boards is given practical effect:

1   What is the role of worker directors to be in relation to decision-making? Are they on the board merely to be consulted, or are they there as equals with senior management? If their role is merely consultative, how can they retain any credibility with the work force? If, however, their role includes bargaining, how are their functions to be reconciled with those of the established representatives of trade unions?

2   To whom are the worker directors primarily accountable? Should they be responsible to the company (as represented by the 'managerial' directors) or should they be responsible to the work force? If the work force is organized, should the directors' responsibility be to the trade union? If more than one union is represented in the company, will every union (regardless of size) be entitled to board representation? Will the worker directors be elected by ballot on the

shop floor, elected by a show of hands at union branch
meetings, or appointed directly by the trade unions
concerned?

3   What should be the constituency of a worker director? Should
    each main interest group on the shop floor (e.g. skilled men,
    semi-skilled men, labourers) be entitled to representation?
    What of the white-collar staff and middle management? If
    board representation is to be confined to trade-union
    members, how will the interest of non-union middle to
    senior executives be safeguarded?

It is to be hoped, therefore, that managers who anticipate a
system of worker representation at board level in their own
companies will consider these problems carefully.

THE WORK SITUATION

The difficulties and uncertainties associated with the concept of
worker representation on boards of directors have led some observers to argue that a much more promising field for management
initiative lies in the work situation itself. The assumption is that
most employees are more interested in participating in decisions
that directly affect the jobs they do and the environment in
which they work than with worker directorships. Many managers
and industrial consultants are therefore turning their attention
to job enrichment, job enlargement and indeed any method of
giving employees more freedom to decide *what kind* of work
they want to do, *how much* they want to do and *how long* they
should take to do it.

   A manager should ask himself what factors influence the behaviour of his employees in the work situation. Orthodox
opinion holds that workers as a whole want jobs that are satisfying and rewarding not merely in financial terms but in relation
to their psychological needs as individuals. The work of Maslow,
McGregor and Herzberg points to the importance of non-
monetary factors in the process of human motivation. Most
people, it is said, want jobs (1) which are intrinsically challenging
and tax their physical and/or mental capacities, (2) attract recognition for good performance, and (3) offer good prospects for
personal advancement as well as economic security. Beneath this
theory lies the assumption that the bureaucratic, authoritarian

and compartmentalized nature of modern industrial organizations effectively precludes the optimum use of human resources. It has often been argued that if people are treated as morons, they will respond with moronic behaviour. It follows from this argument that if only managements were capable of appreciating the real needs of their workers, efficiency, output and morale would all rise and strikes, absenteeism and labour turnover would fall.

However, with the passage of time and the accumulation of empirical evidence, some of the more optimistic assumptions about worker motivation of the kind indicated above are now being questioned. The findings of Goldthorpe and his colleagues in a survey of workers' attitudes in several manufacturing plants in the Luton area are very significant in this respect.[16] They suggest that some workers are quite capable of reconciling themselves even to the most extreme division of labour, i.e. the assembly line. Goldthorpe found that those who worked on the assembly line did so primarily because of the high wages on offer. The workers in his survey had deliberately foregone the chance of more interesting work and had accepted the discipline and boredom of the assembly line because of the high level of financial compensation. Having done this, they seemed quite satisfied with the jobs they had and showed relatively little hostility to their employers. They regarded their work and their work place in essentially *instrumental* terms — as a means to an end. They were prepared, in short, to put up with the assembly line for the money.

Goldthorpe's research at Luton casts doubts, therefore, on the importance of technology as an influence on workers' attitudes. Indeed he also suggested that all factors intrinsic to the work place were less important than workers' experience *outside* it. Such an interpretation appears to leave little scope for action by managements to encourage a higher level of moral commitment in the work situation on the part of their employees.

Not surprisingly, Goldthorpe's thesis has been the subject of severe criticism. W. Daniel, for example, has argued that Goldthorpe and his colleagues asked themselves an over-simple question, namely, 'What does the worker really want?' They should instead have recognized that the same group of workers could attach different priorities to different things in different circumstances. Daniel argued that a sharp distinction could be drawn between the 'negotiating' aspect of work, i.e. pay and job security, where workers could be said to be *extrinsically* oriented, and the 'work' aspect, i.e. job content and social relations in the work place, where workers were *intrinsically* oriented.[17] An additional qualification has been introduced by Wedderburn and Crompton, whose research in various industries in the North East has re-emphasized the importance of technology.[18] They found significant differences in attitudes between skilled men on the one hand and semi-skilled men on the other. The latter, engaged on continuous-flow production, 'had no expectation that their work *should* be interesting', and if it turned out to be interesting, this was merely 'an agreeable extra'. The craftsmen, on the other hand, 'took it for granted that their work *should* be interesting, and continually criticized their work as not enabling them to exercise their workmanship and initiative'.[19] The craftsmen regarded themselves as extremely important in the production process, and when management failed to recognize their status, the consequence was militant behaviour. In short, the policy and practices of management were also a significant influence on employee attitudes.

A sensible industrial-relations strategy must, therefore, start from the proposition that it is foolish to make broad generalizations about employee motivation. To say that management can do nothing to change workers' attitudes is as misguided as to assert that 'participation' will re-create the fundamental harmony in employer-employee relations that some managers believe to be a feasible objective. Clearly workers bring certain attitudes with them to the work place, but it has yet to be shown conclusively that these attitudes are totally immune to factors intrinsic to the work situation itself. Employees respond to the conditions in which they work. Technology is obviously a major constraint, but it is not necessarily a static unchangeable one. In certain circumstances managements can modify the impact of technology and thereby affect the experience of workers in the work situation. Workers' attitudes are susceptible to managerial strategies in all employment matters. It would be wise, however, to bear in mind Daniel's distinction between the negotiating and the work aspects of employment. Management may succeed in giving both work groups and individual employees a greater interest in their work by means of techniques such as job enrichment, but when collective issues such as pay and security are at stake, managements will usually find themselves bargaining

with trade-union representatives in the traditional manner.[20]
Many managers dislike having to bargain and are therefore less
effective negotiators than those who sit on the other side of the
table. Effective bargaining, however, is an integral part of any
industrial-relations strategy and must be recognized as such.

Before closing this section on the work situation, it would be
useful to note that security of employment is likely to become
more important as a bargaining issue over the next few years. It
is now generally recognized that the very high level of employment customary in the British economy between 1950 and 1967
will not return. The manifest speed of technological innovation,
combined with the accelerating pace of structural change in the
economy, will undoubtedly have a major impact on industrial
relations. It has long been recognized that some industries are
overmanned. There is an equally urgent shortage of various kinds
of skilled labour in a number of strategic industries. Left to themselves these underlying forces in the economy will undoubtedly
produce a high and rising level of unemployment over the next
decade. It seems certain, however, that Governments will devise
various institutional mechanisms through which the problems
of retraining and redeployment can be dealt with. The Manpower
Services Commission represents the first real attempt by the
state to improve the working of the labour market in the
interests of high efficiency and greater security of employment.
The inference is that over the next few years the concept of
employment security will be redefined. Traditionally it has
meant the right of a worker to retain the job he is doing and has
always done. In future it will mean the right of a worker to expect
another job, for which he may well have to be trained, when his
old job disappears. Many continental countries, notably West
Germany, Sweden and France, have already adopted this flexible
view of employment security. Before the end of the present decade Britain will almost certainly follow their example.

What does this mean for industrial-relations policy at company
level? First and foremost it means that many senior managers
will have to pay more attention to manpower planning than they
have done to date. Any organization wishing to develop a corporate plan must recognize that a manpower plan is an integral
part of it. Once the main objectives of the company have been
decided, the implications of these objectives for the future manpower requirements of the organization must be carefully

analysed. The corporate planner will at the very least need to pose a number of key questions, for example the following:

1 What kind of skills will be needed if the corporate plan is to succeed?
2 In what quantity will they be needed?
3 How far can the organization provide these skills for itself through internal training and retraining programmes?
4 How effective is the organization in using its current manpower resources?
5 What are the implications of the corporate plan for all matters connected with employment at work-place level, especially the wage and salary structure and the level of manning?
6 What are the main areas of difficulty likely to be encountered in changing the current pattern of employment and mix of skills in order to meet the objectives of the corporate plan?
7 Are the employment aspects of the plan likely to be acceptable to the trade unions and their members?
8 To what extent, if at all, is the plan negotiable with the trade unions?

It is easily seen, therefore, that the development of an effective plan for manpower and employment implies the development of a comprehensive industrial-relations policy.

CONCLUSIONS

In the course of this chapter, an attempt has been made to sketch out those problem areas which, in the present writer's view, are likely to loom largest on management's agenda for employee relations in the near future. Wages, participation and security of employment will all demand more and more managerial attention. It is essential, therefore, that managements should think through the implications of these problems for their own companies and develop strategies to deal with them. The first step managements must take is to ask themselves two simple but fundamental questions:

1 What are our objectives in industrial relations?
2 How shall we go about achieving them?

In the present writer's experience, the simple process of asking and answering these two questions can itself be an illuminating, if not traumatic, experience for some managers, for when top management embarks on the task of developing an industrial-relations policy for their company, they are in effect undertaking a critical reappraisal of their traditional attitudes towards managing all the people in their organization. This in itself can be quite a rigorous intellectual exercise, from which many tangible benefits can be derived.

Unfortunately, self-appraisal and, by implication, self-criticism are rarely found in senior managerial circles. There is still a tendency in British industry to regard employee relations either as a specialist function for middle management or as merely part and parcel of the line manager's job. The authors of a recent survey of industrial-relations policies formed the distinct impression that in many companies 'industrial relations did not receive the attention they need along with commercial and operational matters'.[21] The general neglect of the personnel function may have been understandable when the pressure for change from both the Government and the trade-union movement was weak. Those days, however, are gone. Managements are now facing problems whose complexity is such that they can rarely, if ever, be dealt with effectively by a series of *ad hoc* fire-fighting decisions. The new situation calls for a new response.

REFERENCES

1 Clegg, Hugh. *How to Run an Incomes Policy* (London: Heinemann, 1971), p. 72.
2 N.B.P.I. Report no. 65. *Payment by Results Systems,* Cmnd 3627 (H.M.S.O., 1968), p. 34.
3 Ibid. pp. 36–42. The evidence relating to the impact of measured day work systems on output is ambiguous. In some firms the replacement of an incentive system by measured day work has resulted in a significant improvement in productivity. Elsewhere, however, the reverse has happened. Output has fallen below its former level and has taken a long time to recover. In many cases it is clear that the abandonment of P.B.R. entails both costs and benefits. In some of the more strike-prone plants of the British Leyland group, for example, the level of performance appears to have declined after the abolition of P.B.R. but the number of stoppages has also fallen. It may, however, be unwise to assume that the atti-

tudes engendered by P.B.R. will disappear with the arrival of measured day work. In practice it would seem that group consciousness and sectional loyalties outlive the payment system that encouraged them in the first place.

4 Taylor, Robert. 'The Cowley Way of Work', *New Society*, 2 May 1974.

5 Daniel, W. W. and McIntosh, Neil. *The Right to Manage?* (P.E.P./Macdonald, 1972), p. 173.

6 *Reshaping Britain*, P.E.P. Broadsheet no. 548 (P.E.P, December 1974), p. 40.

7 By common consent this is the most critical weakness in Elliott Jaques's 'time span of discretion' theory. See Lupton, Tom (ed.). *Payment Systems* (Penguin, 1972), pp. 306–37 and 347–65; see also Daniel and McIntosh, op.cit., pp. 176–7.

8 Robinson, Derek. 'Differentials and Incomes Policy', *Industrial Relations Journal,* Spring 1973, vol. 4, no. 1.

9 Behrend, Hilde. 'The Impact of Inflation on Pay Increase Expectations and Ideas of Fair Pay', *Industrial Relations Journal,* Spring 1974.

10 Brown, William and Sisson, Keith. 'The Use of Comparisons in Workplace Wage Determination', *British Journal of Industrial Relations,* March 1975, vol. XIII, no. 1.

11 Hyman, Richard. 'Inequality, Ideology and Industrial Relations', *British Journal of Industrial Relations,* July 1974.

12 Ibid.

13 It has been estimated that in only four years of the decade 1960–70 did the average annual increase in real weekly earnings enjoyed by white-collar workers either equal or exceed that of manual workers. In two years, by contrast, manual workers raised their real weekly earnings by more than 2·5 per cent relative to those of white-collar groups. See Bain, G. S. and Price, R. 'Union Growth and Employment Trends in the United Kingdom', *British Journal of Industrial Relations,* November 1972. A survey of executive salaries by A.I.C. in 1971 concluded that on average manager's pay had only just kept pace with the cost of living during the explosion of 1969–71. The higher-paid manual groups, on the other hand, had moved ahead. Consequently, by 1971, some managers enjoyed only the same level of money earnings as craftsmen in the motor industry (about

£2,000 a year). The authors of the A.I.C. survey concluded that Britain was heading for a flatter system of wages and salaries 'based on a more egalitarian philosophy'.

14 *The Times,* 27 June 1974.

15 Fox, Alan. *Beyond Contract: Work, Power and Trust Relations* (London: Faber, 1974).

16 Goldthorpe, J. H., Lockwood, David *et al. The Affluent Worker: Industrial Attitudes and Behaviour* (Cambridge University Press, 1968). See also the authors' *The Affluent Worker in the Class Structure* (Cambridge University Press, 1969).

17 Daniel, W. W. 'What Interests a Worker?', *New Society,* 23 March 1972. See also Daniel, W. W. and McIntosh, Neil *The Right to Manage?* (P.E.P./Macdonald, 1972).

18 Wedderburn, Dorothy and Crompton, Rosemary. *Workers' Attitudes and Technology* (Cambridge University Press, 1972).

19 Wedderburn, Dorothy. 'What determines shopfloor behaviour?' *New Society,* 20 July 1972.

20 See Cotgrove, Stephen *et al. The Nylon Spinners* (London: Allen & Unwin, 1971).

21 C.I.R. Report no. 34. *The Role of Management in Industrial Relations* (H.M.S.O., 1973), p. 5, para. 19.

14 Strategic Planning for Resources

Bernard Taylor

Whatever view one takes of the long-term future — the Club of Rome prediction[1] that the world will run out of raw materials and productive resources in the foreseeable future; or the forecasts of optimists like Dr Wilfred Beckerman[2] that supplies and production facilities will eventually increase to make up the emerging gap between supply and demand as new reserves are located, new technologies developed, and reserves that were once not economic become economic to exploit because of increased prices — the prospect for the next five to ten years is one of continued difficulty in supply markets. In any case there is normally a lead time of at least five to ten years in developing alternative technologies, new mining and production facilities. The producing nations are beginning to realize the prudence of conserving their limited reserves of oil and other minerals, and oil-producing countries have demonstrated the power of the producer cartel to restrict production and force up prices.

PURCHASING MYOPIA

This suggests that businessmen should now be planning more carefully for resources. In commodity markets generally prices remained surprisingly low up to the 1973 boom, registering an annual increase of only 1·8 per cent between January 1954 and September 1971. Some prices fell from the 1973 record levels, but a return to the very low prices of previous recessions seems unlikely. We seem to be witnessing a shift away from buyers' markets towards producers' markets. This compares with the swing from sellers' markets to buyers' markets that occurred in consumer-goods industries in the 1960s. In response to this change in demand markets, business produced the marketing concept, marketing departments, and such marketing techniques as marketing research and product planning. The challenge of more difficult supply markets would seem to demand a similar adjustment from business. This would in essence do for buying what marketing has done for selling – it has given business a new philosophy, a different view of strategy and a research and planning capability to cope with the threat.

Considering the importance of purchasing decisions, the significance of resources in business strategy has received little attention in management literature, and corporate planning for procurement is remarkably under-developed.[3] In manufacturing industry the cost of bought-in materials and services commonly accounts for over 50 per cent of the sales turnover. As these firms normally make a profit on turnover of 2–5 per cent, the potential impact on profits is obvious, particularly in these days when Government regulations frequently prevent manufacturers from passing on to their customers the increased costs of raw materials and components. Some idea of the size of the purchasing bill can be gathered from individual companies: for example, ITT Europe makes annual purchases worth 2 billion dollars, roughly equivalent to half the sales turnover, and Vauxhall Motors (U.K.) has a purchasing budget of over £150 million on a sales turnover of £250 millions.

Purchasing Strategy?

Figures of this size suggest the need for a large and sophisticated purchasing activity, but there is clear evidence from recent research studies than even in large multi-national companies purchasing tends to be regarded as a function allied to production and responding to the needs of marketing.[4] It is rare to find companies that have an explicit purchasing strategy or a long-range plan for purchasing, although it is fairly common now for companies to have long-term strategies and plans for marketing, or finance. Igor Ansoff, in his classic book, *Corporate Strategy*, was simply reflecting current thinking and practice when he classified purchasing decisions as 'Administrative'.

Management theorists have tended to define business strategy in terms of products and markets. Up to this point the assumption has been that physical, financial and human resources – raw materials, skilled labour, working capital, and equipment – could all be assembled once the entrepreneur had spotted a market opportunity or discovered a technological break-through. It would then be an administrative task to design an organization structure, select and train the key staff, and breathe life into the original business idea.

Some writers have already expressed reservations about early evangelistic statements of the marketing concept. After all, in most strategic situations it is not so much a case of identifying a market opportunity but rather of matching the resources which exist, or can be readily acquired, to the business opportunities that can be discovered and exploited. The energy industries – oil, coal, gas, electricity and nuclear power – face a situation where the market is secure and a major factor determining the size, the rate of growth and the profitability of the businesses concerned is the supply of resources and the efficiency with which they can be developed.

The critical importance of supplies is evident from an examination of nationalized industries and public utilities. For example, the managements of nationalized industries such as the N.C.B., the C.E.G.B. and the British Steel Corporation are obliged by Acts of Parliament to operate their industries 'in the public interest', and this clearly means maintaining production and supplies at a level sufficient to meet national requirements. The Water Boards are in a similar position. They are expected to make arrangements for the supply of water to industrial and domestic consumers at a reasonable cost and with minimum disturbance to the physical and social environment.

In private industry, too, security of supplies is often critical, as may be readily appreciated from the number of companies that have integrated backwards to ensure control of their supplies – Bowater with forests in North America, Tate & Lyle with sugar in the West Indies, Brooke Bond with tea plantations in India and Ceylon, and, of course, oil companies with capital invested in the North Sea and Alaska, as well as in the Middle East. In extractive industries, particularly, exploration and development of reserves is essential to survival because the enterprise is continually using up its basic resource.

There are no doubt many businessmen who will claim that the purpose of their enterprise is to make a profit for the shareholder, to meet a social need, to satisfy a customer, or to provide security and good working conditions for their employees. In these days of shortages one would hope that an increasing number of top managers would also see that, to survive, the firm must also have as one of its objectives 'to ensure the continuous availability of essential supplies and capital equipment in the required quantities and qualities, at the right place, in the right locations and at the right time'. To many managers this notion of a supplier-orientated as opposed to a marketing- or shareholder-orientated philosophy will be novel and strange. However, in one particular industry — retailing — this approach has a long and venerable tradition. Indeed the success of such companies as Marks & Spencers and Sears Roebuck is based very largely on their ability to find and cultivate suppliers who can produce superior quality merchandise in large volume at an economic price, and deliver it on time at the locations where it is required. On the other hand, the failures of the British automobile companies can be blamed partly on their inability to build and maintain a network of component suppliers with a similar standard of performance.

The Conservation Argument

The current concern about the environment, agitation about pollution, and protests against the consuming society, provide other cogent reasons for the management in private and public enterprises to reassess their organization's use of energy and material resources. Air and water pollution is waste, litter is waste, planned obsolescence is waste, and waste in a world with limited resources is anti-social.

There is, for example, natural outrage among motorists and motoring organizations about the short life of some motor cars. It is widely believed that manufacturers have been cutting production costs, thus lowering body resistance to rust. For instance, in 1971 the Automobile Association Committee on Corrosion and Protection reported that the life of car bodies could be extended by a period of two to three years merely by the avoidance of moisture traps in design, and by improved instruction manuals for motorists.

In the U.S.A. particularly an increasing number of firms are taking an interest in recycling. Reynolds Metals, for example, has recently sponsored a project to build houses out of recycled materials. The aluminium-makers have good reasons to be interested in recycling. There have been public protests against the waste of resources on beverage cans, which are used once and then discarded. It goes a long way to answer the protest if the initial investment is recovered again and again through recycling. It takes the energy equivalent of 6 lb of coal to make a 1 lb of new aluminium, but only a fraction of this amount of energy to melt down aluminium scrap.

What Business or What Resources?

In the 1960s, with abundant resources and strong competition for consumer and industrial markets, it seemed natural to start the strategy discussion with the questions 'What business are we in and what business should we be in?' Now, when more and more industries are coming up against resource constraints, it may be more appropriate to begin by locating the financial, physical, and human resources required.

The dialogue between the British Government and the nationalized industries illustrates the point. In most cases the marketing problems of the industries are trivial, for by statute they are virtual monopolies. In addition the potential for expansion through product development, or by acquisition and merger, is strictly limited, because they are not allowed to diversify outside their original technologies. In a very real sense they are in the 'steel business' or the 'coal business', and any attempt to redefine their fields or activity as 'materials' or 'energy' is likely to be strongly resisted by the Government and other interested parties.

The discussions over the long-term plans for steel and energy have naturally focused on problems connected with supplies, as follows:

1   Steel plants, oil refineries and power stations are being sited near ports, because supplies must be imported, and within convenient range of suitable coalfields, because of the dependence upon coking coal or steam coal.
2   Uppermost in the discussions has been the quantity of mineral reserves available locally, the rates at which they might be developed, and the likely cost of exploitation.
3   Linked with this is a discussion about the problem of maintaining a sizeable labour force to keep the mines and the

steel plants working in a society where it is increasingly
difficult to find men willing to do hard manual labour
under dirty and often hazardous conditions.

4   Finally, there is the key question of how far new technologies
of mining, energy conversion, and steel production might
boost the productivity of men and equipment and reduce
the proportion of fuel and ore that is wasted.

In all these discussions on future strategies for nationalized
industries it seems clear that the question 'What business are we
in?' has hardly been mentioned, and that the question 'What
resources have we got and how can we best use them?' is central.
Top management is concerned less with a product-market strategy
than with the development of a resource strategy. How then does
a firm set about developing and implementing a strategy for
resources?

RESOURCE MANAGEMENT

If we are right in assuming that supplies of energy and certain
key raw materials may continue to be in short supply or even
rationed over the next five to ten years, then we should be searching for new approaches, new forms of organization, and new
systems and procedures that will give due priority to the need
to maintain supplies and conserve resources, nationally and at
the level of the enterprise.

A New Concept

We now need a total systems concept for materials to provide the
global view for supply markets that marketing provides for
demand markets. The words buying and purchasing tend to imply
simply a concern with the supplier relationship. Materials management tends to concentrate on the movement of materials into
and through a production unit, and physical distribution management deals with the movement of goods from the plant to the
consumer.

Resource management should be concerned with the management of physical resources from their origin through the various
stages of production and distribution, to final consumption, recycling or re-use. This concept has the advantage that it focuses

attention on the need to conserve resources by reducing waste at all stages, as follows:

1 At the first stage – in the extraction industries, and in fishing and agriculture
2 At the second stage – in refining metals, burning fuels, and processing food and raw materials
3 At the third stage – when energy and goods are distributed and consumed
4 And at the fourth stage – when the consumed products re-appear as refuse or sewage to be recycled or re-used.

The essential idea underpinning the concept of 'resource management' is that matter cannot be destroyed. It can only be transformed.

Resource management is a concept that can be applied to corporate and to national strategy. There are signs that, at a national level in Britain, steps are being taken to evaluate the resource costs of different processes. For example, a Government research group is preparing 'energy budgets' to find the industrial processes, technologies and consumer products that waste the most energy. Similar approaches are being applied to water, steel, and other vital resources. No doubt this kind of resource costing will eventually eliminate some of the nonsenses of the consumer society, whereby a product's packaging frequently costs more than the product itself, and motor cars and other expensive machines are made obsolete through minor changes in design. If the pressure on resources continues, then no doubt businessmen too will feel that they ought to improve their control over the use of energy and resources. And at company level it may be necessary to produce resource budgets in order to manage the use of energy, water, and other essential raw materials more carefully.

The Resource Management Audit

A common point of departure in corporate planning is the analysis of the present situation of the enterprise and its future prospects, by means of the following:

1 A corporate appraisal, which assesses the organization's strengths and weaknesses in terms of its various capacities

and capabilities — finance, research and development,
production, marketing, and personnel

2   An environmental appraisal, which assesses the trends, and
the threats and opportunities, which are apparent in the
economic, socio-political, technological and competitive
environment.

It goes without saying that the latter appraisal should include
an analysis of the firm's position with regard to essential supplies
and key suppliers.

In addition, in times of shortages and increasing prices for fuel
and raw materials, senior management should also be monitoring
the rates at which essential materials are being used. This kind of
audit is likely to become important for social as well as economic
reasons as Western governments attempt to hold down import
costs and the public becomes increasingly concerned about pollution and waste.

Figure 14.1 illustrates the form the audit might take. This
would mean an assessment of the level of waste and pollution at
each step in the process, from the initial acquisition or extraction, via production and distribution, through to final consump-
tions. This suggests, too, that the management is likely to be held
responsible by society for the waste and pollution that is associated with its product, in consumption as well as in production.

The Resources Gap

One method of opening up the discussion of a resource strategy
is to ask 'What is the resources gap and how do we close it?' The
resources gap or the energy gap defines the supply problem in
quantitative terms. It means estimating what amounts of key
items will be required during the planning period, e.g. three to
five years, and then comparing this remit with the quantities
likely to be available, assuming that current supply arrangements
remain unaltered. This assumes that the company already has a
forward plan from which requirements can be estimated, and that
the purchasing and supply staff have the capacity to carry out
marketing research, to forecast trends, and to produce product
plans for supply markets. Figure 14.2 shows how the resources
or materials gap is defined. It may be visualized in money or in
units.

Stage / Impact	Acquisition of Raw Materials	Production Process	Marketing and Logistics	Product in use	Product Residue
Legal					
Technological					
Economic					
Ecological					
Social					
Political					

Source: Colin Hutchinson, Conservation Society (U.K.).

Figure 14.1   Scheme for a Resource Management Audit.

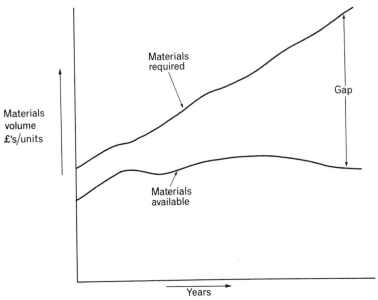

Figure 14.2   Defining the materials gap.

The following five methods, illustrate ways of dealing with the resources gap.

1   *The zero-growth alternative.* Having calculated the gap, the next step is to examine ways in which it might be closed (see Figure 14.3). One way, of course, is to revise the corporate financial and marketing objectives and to accept a slower rate of growth in profits and in sales turnover — this will bring down the 'materials required' line. It is still usual to accept a growth target as mandatory. With increasing pressure for conservation, however, a growing number of businessmen may question the growth philosophy and opt for zero growth with improved quality of life.

   Assuming that management still regard the corporate plan as realistic, then there are four other routes to explore (see Figure 14.4).

2   *Increased efficiency.* The present scarcities of energy, food and raw materials are a recent phenomenon, and it seems likely that considerable savings could be made in resource

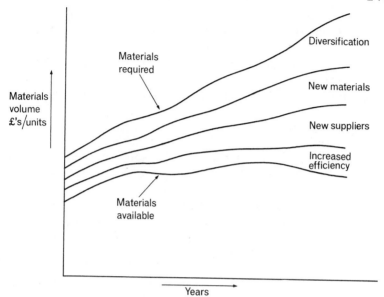

Figure 14.3   Closing the materials gap.
Compare H. I. Ansoff's analysis of product-market strategy in *Corporate Strategy*, McGraw-Hill, 1965.

Suppliers \ Technology	Existing	New
Existing	Improve present technology/ Develop present suppliers	Develop substitute materials/ less wasteful technology
New	Develop new suppliers/ Explore new geographical sources	Diversify into new technology requiring new suppliers and new materials or no materials

Compare the analysis of product-market strategies in H. I. Ansoff, *Corporate Strategy*, McGraw Hill, 1965.

Figure 14.4   Analysis of alternative supply strategies.

costs now that there is a strong incentive for management
to look for savings. An example from the water-supply
industry illustrates the kinds of economies that can be
achieved through changes in technology. Because there is
a shortage of water locally, British Steel at Scunthorpe
have recirculated water extensively so that they can make
1 ton of steel with 5 tons of water as opposed to the
normal 200 tons.

Similar economies may be made by the use of value
analysis in design, by waste reduction campaigns in factories, by rationalization in physical distribution, and by
the use of less expensive packaging. No doubt in the next
few years materials ratios and resource budgets will be
more commonly used as indicators of efficiency, and
managers will be set targets, in terms of resource costs as
well as accounting costs.

Supplier development is another way of increasing
productivity. Marks & Spencers, Fords, and other pioneers
in the field of procurement have already developed sophisticated systems for selecting, managing, evaluating and
controlling their major suppliers. When a new automobile
design is developed, component suppliers are selected by
a comprehensive profile, sometimes referred to as a 'pattern
of procurement', and once the contract is accepted, the
manufacturer works closely with his supplier, often providing expensive tools and helping with plant layout, production scheduling and the establishment of cost reduction
and productivity programmes. Marks & Spencers are
particularly well-known for their ability to identify growers
and manufacturers who have the potential to develop and
then providing the guaranteed contracts and the management expertise necessary to maintain the volume and
quality standards they require.

3   *New materials.* A second possibility is to look for alternative
materials or sources of energy. If oil is scarce, or too dear,
it may be possible to use coal or hydro-electric power. It
may even be possible to use the sun, the wind, the tides,
or even rubbish, as motive power. The United States and
German governments have already established huge research
budgets to investigate the possibility of developing alternatives to oil.

STRATEGIC PLANNING FOR RESOURCES

In materials, too, it is frequently possible to find substitutes — synthetic fibres instead of wool and cotton; plastics for rubber, glass, metal, and paper; saccharin for sugar; and even soya bean for meat in hamburgers. Less dramatic but more common perhaps is the use of one material in place of another very similar one from a different origin, e.g. palm oil instead of coconut oil, beet sugar instead of cane sugar.

In the search for new materials the initiative may come from suppliers offering substitutes, or from a product-development team that is exploring new formulations and new materials for components. In the case of Chrysler in Detroit, for example, a product-development material control unit in the purchasing department helps in the buying of prototype materials for special engineering programmes. It can start its investigations ten years before the production starts.

4   *New suppliers.* Another means of expanding supplies is to find new sources. The extractive industries are continually exploring for new reserves to keep their businesses alive. Manufacturers and retailers have a similar task of finding and cultivating new suppliers. New suppliers do not appear by chance. To do a proper job requires a staff of buyers with a clear remit to search for new suppliers. In the larger organizations the field force often requires the support of market analysts and market-development specialists.

5   *Diversification and acquisition.* Where there is likely to be a chronic shortage of supplies, and especially where a large proportion of the market is made up of captive suppliers tied to competitive organizations, there is a tendency for other firms to integrate backwards, by buying a minority or controlling interest in one of the suppliers that is still independent.

The situation in the chemical industry is a case in point. Today chemical companies such as ICI, Bayer, and B.A.S.F. have found it necessary to link up with oil companies to guarantee their supplies of feedstocks for petrochemicals. Other examples abound — newsprint manufacturers owning forests, soap companies with interests in groundnut plantations, and food manufacturers with their own can-making plants.

Another possibility is forward integration — into recycling. The Chloride Group has moved into the collection and smelting of lead from old batteries; and Thomasson & Drijver of the Netherlands, a metal-box company, have helped to set up a de-tinning factory to salvage the tin from household refuse.

A Practical Case

A case history described recently by David Hussey, Corporate Planner of Otis Elevators,[5] illustrates the wide-ranging strategic analysis that may be required to solve a supply problem. Figure 14.5 shows the kind of prospect many companies faced in 1973. After five years of relative stability the prices of three key raw materials were expected to rise steeply at rates of between 40 per cent and 100 per cent per year. The result would be a 'gap' between the materials called for in the corporate plan and the materials that could be bought with the funds budgeted. This prediction led to a consideration of the following alternative strategies:

1 An emphasis on research and development to find substitute raw materials, or new processes of manufacture that would give greater economy in the use of suspect materials.
2 A decision to invest in available new technology, which would also have this effect; to try for cost savings that might not have given a reasonable return at pre-point A; and to look for raw materials at prices that would satisfy all financial criteria at the higher future prices.
3 A reassessment of marketing prospects for products that were to be subject to massive price escalations, possibly resulting in withdrawal of the product, a change of advertising concept, or a reduction in promotional expenditure.
4 The postponement of plans to expand the factory producing articles likely to be under severe cost pressure.
5 An examination of alternative production sources, perhaps rationalizing a number of plants in different countries in order to produce economies of scale to offset the cost increase.
6 A move to protect profits by diversifying away from the products where pressure was foreseen.
7 A change in purchasing commitments or sources of supply.

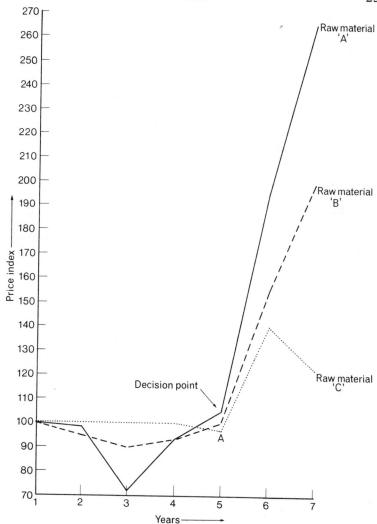

Figure 14.5   Price indices for three major raw materials.
(Source: David Hussey.)

New Multi-national Structures

So far we have been looking at the shortage of resources largely in a national context. Increasingly, however, companies and governments are being forced by events to view the world as a global system and to search for a multi-national solution to their problems.

One interesting trend is the tendency for large companies to transplant parts of their operations overseas — not simply sales branches but production plants and purchasing offices. In recent years Japanese and West German firms have been particularly active in making direct investments abroad. The motivation behind this investment varies, but in the case of Japan, with its lack of natural resources, a considerable incentive must be to obtain access to *raw materials*. In fact investment in mining alone accounted for around 40 per cent of Japanese direct foreign investment up to the end of 1970.

Another interesting development has been the tendency for Western companies to locate parts of their production operations and to make substantial purchases of *semi-manufactured goods* in developing countries with low labour costs (see Chapter 16, p. 275). Plessey, Olivetti, and Volkswagen all have substantial production units in developing countries, and the trend is likely to accelerate as national governments in the Middle East and Africa particularly insist on having their raw materials refined and processed locally. Further impetus is being added by the tendency of Western governments to outlaw certain dirty processes like the smelting of lead and zinc. There is also an increasing problem in finding workers to do heavy or dirty jobs. How long will it be before it becomes impossible to recruit coalminers in the West? In the long term it seems likely that, despite the political problems, the dangers of nationalization and revolution, western industry will come increasingly to rely upon the emerging countries for raw materials and for semi-manufactured goods.

Over the next decade governments and major companies in industrialized countries will be trying to determine what kinds of arrangements are most likely to work. In place of the traditional, vertically integrated Western company we are likely to see a variety of joint ventures, based on a partnership between Western Governments and industry on the one hand and Third World Governments on the other.

Planning for Flexibility

One factor that stands out in any examination of the supply environment today is a paradox. Modern technology relies on large-scale specialized plant and equipment. It is therefore very vulnerable to interruptions in supply. On the other hand, supply markets are increasingly subject to dramatic shifts caused by industrial unrest, fluctuations in exchange rates and shortages and high prices in international commodity markets.

Ever since World War II the drive in business has been towards bigger machines, bigger production units, and bigger companies. The tendency has also been to cut costs by selecting the supplier with the most competitive prices, by reducing stock levels to a minimum and working to integrate in-coming supplies into the mass-production process with split-second timing.

Now management is realizing that in an unpredictable environment it does not pay to operate on fine margins. There is talk of secondary suppliers, contingency plans, buffer stocks and stand-by generators.

In corporate planning for procurement the moral is to plane for greater risk and uncertainty by building extra flexibility into the system, as follows:

1   On a total company basis it argues for *diversifying* into many different though possibly related product areas, so that a shortage of one type of raw material or component will not put the company out of business. The oil companies seem to be seeing the argument, if rather late in the day, by investing in nuclear power and coal.

2   It suggests also that it is *unwise to rely unduly on one supplier.* As Lockheed found with Rolls-Royce, the whole business may be put in jeopardy by the collapse of this one firm.

3   It may also be *short-sighted to drive too hard a bargain.* As British consumers of glass bottles, newsprint and iron castings have found, it does not pay to put your suppliers out of business. It is more prudent to maintain a number of suppliers in business so as to have security of supply in the future.

4   It also pays in international commodity markets to have a number of *suppliers in different parts of the world.* In the recent crisis Occidental Oil, with supplies only in Libya, was far more vulnerable than B.P., which had a variety of sources in different parts of the world.

5   In uncertain times it often pays to *carry substantial stocks,*

which can be used in times of shortage. This lesson has
been learnt by the C.E.G.B., which, since the 1972 miners'
strike, has built up substantial stocks of coal.

6   Another moral is the need to have a *good information system*,
so as to anticipate movements in the major supply markets.
The impact of the present energy crisis has been softened
because the computerized information systems of the major
oil companies have enabled them to make the best use of
the oil available.

7   In addition the oil companies have had *contingency plans*
ready — as they had previously for the closure of the Suez
Canal.

8   The oil companies have tried to spread their risks by entering
into *joint ventures,* e.g. Conoco with the National Coal
Board in the North Sea.

9   They have also sought to reduce the risk by calling for
Government support, and a number of Western governments are reported to be negotiating in support of oil
companies based in the U.S.A. and Europe.

10 Of couse, flexibility costs money — money invested in stocks,
in stand-by generators, and in secondary suppliers. In due
course this means that management must look for *higher
prices and higher profits* to cover the increased risks in the
business. If these higher prices and higher profits are not
forthcoming, a prudent management should try to get out
of the business, or at least *reduce new investments* in the
area.

Marketing in Reverse

In a crisis there is a tendency for an organization to develop new
capabilities to meet the threat or opportunity that appears. At a
national level in industrialized countries the energy crisis has produced ministers of energy, huge budgets for research and capital
investment, and national campaigns aimed at reducing the consumption of fuel. In private and public enterprises, where key
fuels and raw materials are in short supply for a considerable
time, it seems reasonable to suppose that the following will
happen:

1   *Top management* will take charge of, or oversee, corporate
planning for resources.

2   *A senior member of staff,* probably a member of the board, will be appointed to maintain and conserve the supply of key resources.

3   *Specialist product planners* will be appointed to develop market research, market forecasts and forward planning for supply markets.

4   *Task forces and project groups* will be formed to carry out special programmes to develop substitute materials, to achieve improved utilization of fuel and materials and to investigate methods of reclaiming and recycling.

5   *Operating systems and procedures* will be evolved to emphasize the need for working more closely with suppliers, operating energy and resource 'budgets', and redesigning products and processes to eliminate waste.

At this point in time the functions which might be included under the heading Resource Management are spread throughout the firm. There have been various attempts to integrate a number of related functions under one department, e.g. physical distribution management, materials management, and logistics management. For example, the management of materials in, through and out of the firm has been integrated by means of a total cost approach at two aerospace companies, Boeing and Lockheed.[6]

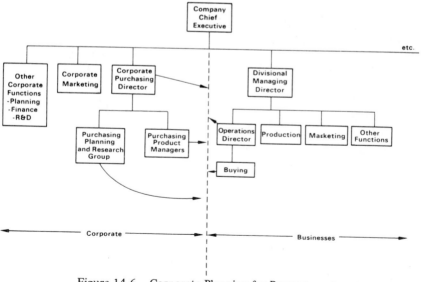

Figure 14.6   Corporate Planning for Procurement.

However, this is a very novel approach. Most companies are a
long way from this kind of integrated system. What seems more
likely is that the purchasing department will develop planning
teams, like the brand managers of the marketing department,
who will have the job of coordinating their work with other
product specialists in R. and D. and in marketing, and will provide data on supply markets for the company's long-range planning exercise. In addition, at an operating level, purchasing and
supply management will be co-opted to teams working on programmes of cost reduction, product and package development,
and the search for alternative or substitute materials.

Figure 14.6 shows how one company, Ciba-Geigy (U.K.) has
integrated purchasing into the long-term planning operation
through the use of Purchasing Product Managers and a Purchasing
Planning and Research Group.[7]

REFERENCES

1 Meadows, D. H. *et al. The Limits to Growth* (Universe Books,
   New York, and Earth Island, London, 1972).
2 In, for example, 'Economic Growth and Resources', from
   Farmer, D. H. and Taylor, B. (eds). *Corporate Planning and
   Procurement* (Heinemann, 1975).
3 See Farmer, D. H. 'The Impact of Supply Markets on Corporate
   Planning', *Long Range Planning,* March 1972.
4 Farmer, D. H. 'Purchasing Myopia in Multi-national Companies', *Journal of General Management,* Winter 1974.
5 Hussey, D. E. 'Corporate Strategy and Raw Materials', *The
   Director,* February 1974.
6 Davies, G. M. 'Purchasing's Role in a Logistics System',
   Journal of Purchasing (U.S.A.), May 1973.
7 Davies, Owen, 'The Marketing Approach to Purchasing', *Long
   Range Planning,* June 1974.

15 Planning for Growth by Acquisition

Adrian Buckley

INTRODUCTION

Growth by acquisition has been one of the major forces of corporate expansion in the last decade. In the U.K. this growth
formula was evidenced at the start of the decade by the emergence of the industrial holding companies, of which Thomas
Tilling has been the most consistently successful. Enhancement
of near-horizon earnings through diverse acquisitive growth was
the central philosophy of the conglomerates that became fashion-
able in the late 1960s. In either case the financial rationale of
improving short-term earnings per share through the issue of
equity quoted on a high price-earnings multiple — often totally
unjustified by reference to underlying fundamental earnings
prospects and sometimes engineered by stock-market manipula-
tions — and utilizing maximum gearing capacity seemed to
operate, at least for a while, to the acquiring company's
advantage.

But the industrial holding companies and the conglomerates
that have been more than flashes in the pan are the ones that
have achieved real economic and business gains in the longer
term, rather than transient earnings per share increments through
financing while failing to improve on the performance of the
companies that had been bought. Operators in the latter category
were able, even though unsuccessful in improving the underlying
results of companies acquired, to boost earnings per share through
acquisition. However, as their base expanded, they clearly needed
larger and larger acquisitions to achieve this. Furthermore, if they
did not get to grips with the businesses that they had bought —

which was often the case — a dip in performance inevitably followed. Plastering over poor results by changed accounting bases of income determination could, for a while, maintain apparent momentum — and this tactic was certainly resorted to. However, the realization that past earnings increments were precautious, that business improvements had not always been achieved and that ever greater takeovers were needed to keep up the trend, led to declining share prices. And where the results of businesses acquired went into reverse (and the previously ideal gearing began to appear too high), this downward share price spiral was compounded.

Successful acquisition policy, whether for a conglomerate or not, means improving the underlying results and cash flow of business acquired. And this must be achieved in accordance with a company's financial objectives and targets.

THE TREND OF ACQUISITION IN THE U.K.

The aggregate trend of acquisitions activity tends to follow the level of the stock market. Figure 15.1 summarizes published statistics over recent years and this relation is clearly discernible.

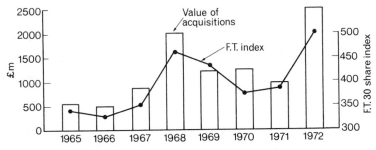

Figure 15.1   The acquisition and stock market trend.

The trend of takeovers in this country is also characterized by a tendency for acquisitions now to be larger, on average, than they were, say, ten years ago. According to Government figures on takeovers in Britain, the average purchase consideration in 1954 was £380,000; in 1960 the comparable figure was £460,000; in 1972 the average was £1,820,000. This trend has alarmed many economic commentators, pointing, as it does, to an increasing concentration in British manufacturing industry. In

1950 the 100 largest U.K. manufacturing companies' output accounted for 20 per cent of manufacturing output. By 1960 this figure had advanced to 30 per cent, but by 1970 it was over 52 per cent. Extrapolation of the trend in Figure 15.2, which

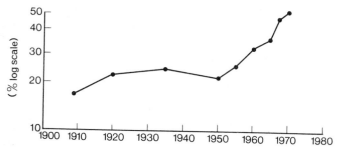

Figure 15.2   Share of 100 largest companies in manufacturing output in U.K. to 1970.

summarizes these figures, indicates that the figure may be as high as 67 per cent by 1980 and over 90 per cent by the end of the century.

In an environment of increasing international competitiveness this trend can be defended as inevitable if British business is to become a more significant influence on the world scene. However, the danger to the public interest from greater concentration must also be considered. This is now one of the most cogent reasons for the tougher government line on the policing of acquisitions. Another reason is the evidence that acquisitions and their subsequent integration, both in this country and in the U.S.A., have had a disturbing lack of real success.

SUCCESS AND FAILURE IN ACQUISITIONS

John Kitching's work on takeovers in both the U.S.A.[1] and in Europe[2] and Gerald Newbould's study[3] of acquisitions in the U.K. in 1967–8 are damning evidence of the achievement of companies on the acquisition trail. These studies also suggest that the quality of evaluation, in economic, business, financial and marketing terms, leaves a lot to be desired. Kitching's studies suggest that between 25 and 30 per cent of acquisitions are unqualified failures – which must hurt in financial terms. Indeed, using the statistics in Kitching's European takeovers study, the average consideration paid was $9 million per acquisition; the total number of acquisitions in Europe in 1972 was 4,350; with an outright failure rate of 26 per cent the failure cost is over $10 thousand million — or half the gross national product of Holland, or Spain, or Sweden.

If there are so many failures and they are, in aggregate, so costly, why do companies opt for growth by takeover? Presumably all acquisitions, except those motivated by defensive reasons, are intended to lead to enhanced performance. Some of the most frequently claimed motivations for mergers and acquisitions are quoted in Table 15.1.

Table 15.1   Some financial/economic reasons for acquisitions

---

To increase earnings per share — whether in the long-term or short-term — or profit performance.

Tax reasons, e.g. Trafalgar House bid for Cunard.

To increase market share and/or eliminate competition.

Diversification, e.g. British—American Tobacco's entry into toiletries.

Quickest and most economic way of entry into an industry, e.g. Grand Metropolitan Hotels' bid for Trumans.

Company bid for may be cheap if at low in the cycle, e.g. Thomas Tilling's bid for Pilkington Tile.

Economies of scale.

To improve efficiency or utilization of assets.

To increase purchasing leverage.

To utilize excess capacities.

To complete product lines.

Defensive.

However, several studies of the way organizations actually function conclude that company managers sometimes tend to pursue personal objectives, and this fact is also discernible in acquisition policy. Thus the desire for greater company size, because size brings a wider horizon to managerial opportunities and greater certainty of continued employment, to say nothing of enhanced remuneration, is also an apparent acquisition motivator.

Whatever the reasons for takeovers — and the evidence seems to indicate that of the reasons listed in Table 15.1 market dominance and defensive reasons appear to be the most frequent goals — it must be relevant to ask 'How can the pitfalls be

avoided?', for all of the indications are that hidden traps are
strewn along the path towards takeover success.

Certainly empirical evidence[2] shows why enhancement of
market share is the most frequently quoted acquisition objective,
for where market share purchased is high, so are the chances of
acquisition success. Conversely it seems that buying low market
share is less likely to result in success. Table 15.2 shows Kitching's
findings on this point. Of course, market share need not be
measured nationally — if the market is regionally segmented,
then measurement by reference to local market share is more
meaningful. Although purchasing a company with a low market

Table 15.2   Acquisition success and failure with respect to market share
and relative size of company acquired

	Acquisition considered:		
	Successful %	Not worth doing %	Failure %
Where market share was:			
Less than 1 per cent	43	22	35
1–5 per cent	42	23	35
5–10 per cent	58	24	18
10–25 per cent	61	20	19
25–50 per cent	70	12	18
50 per cent plus	73	24	3
Where company takeover's sales as per cent of parent were:			
Less than 1 per cent	49	20	31
1–5 per cent	54	17	29
5–10 per cent	59	25	16
10–25 per cent	59	31	10
25–50 per cent	80	10	10
50 per cent plus	73	14	13

share appears from Table 15.2 to be a higher risk policy, it must
be remembered that in the case of many acquisitions of this type
the acquirer already holds a large share of the market. 'Fill-in'
acquisitions of this type were described as successful in about
three-quarters of such cases by respondents in the Kitching
survey.

Table 15.2 shows that the incidence of acquisition success
seems to grow as relatively larger companies are acquired. Despite

this, however, acquisitions of very small companies tend to be more frequent. The incidence of cases where the turnover of the company acquired is below 1 per cent of the parent's turnover accounts for 47 per cent of acquisitions; cases where turnover is between 1 and 5 per cent of the parent's turnover account for 26 per cent of all acquisitions; instances of turnover between 5 and 10 per cent of the parent's turnover account for 9 per cent of takeovers.

Certain other connections can be discerned from an examination of the same evidence. The fact that diversification is a high-risk policy is brought out in Kitching's study. The incidence of success was highest for horizontal types of acquisition, i.e. where a company buys another in the same business and with similar customer types, with whom it directly competes.

Vertical acquisitions are next in the acquisition success table: i.e. those of businesses which supply goods or services to the acquiring company or to which goods and services are supplied by the acquiring company. Conglomerate acquisitions were considered the least successful formula.

The low-risk acquisition profile appears to be the relatively large horizontal or vertical type where the company purchased has high market share.

ACQUISITION PLANNING

Any company embarking upon a strategy of expansion through an acquisition policy should constantly review potential takeover candidates against a series of criteria that sum up its requirements from any new acquisitions. These criteria must be consistent with the company's long-term objectives. The formal procedure recommended for this purpose is set out in Figure 15.3.

Making the corporate objectives and the corporate plan the first step of the firm's acquisition strategy ensures that resources are not dissipated on an acquisition when they might more profitably be used to expand existing business activities.

An in-depth study of a company's own capabilities is an integral aspect of corporate planning. When used as a guide in selecting merger candidates, the chances of a successful acquisition programme are considerably improved.

The corporate plan will generally have focused upon the firm's strengths and weaknesses. It is in the area of the firm's

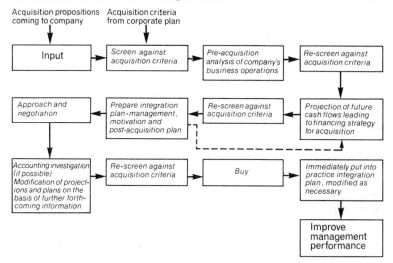

Figure 15.3   Framework for acquisition policy.

strengths that the greatest probability of successful acquisition lies. Once these strengths and the tactics that have so far under-pinned success have been identified, the key question is — can the existing formula for success be exploited in the case of the company acquired? One example of how failure to locate the key criterion underlying a business's achievements can lead to subsequent failure in a takeover is instanced by Mace and Montgomery:[4]

> A basic resin company . . . bought a plastic boat manufacturer because this seemed to present a controlled market for a portion of the resin it produced. It soon found that the boat business was considerably different from the manufacture and sale of basic chemicals. After a short but unpleasant experience manufacturing and trying to market what was essentially a consumer's item, the management concluded that its experience and abilities lay essentially in industrial rather than consumer-type products.

That companies skilled in the art of the takeover formulate and rigorously apply a set of acquisition criteria consistent with the company's general strategy and growth objectives is well-known and certainly substantiated by empirical evidence. Too frequently, however, the merger objective is corporate aggrandise-ment — what is sometimes referred to as the 'tallest chimney

syndrome'. While the desire to own more shops than one's competitors may mean enhanced profit potential because of market
dominance, this sort of acquisition policy should not be pursued
without reference to appropriate screening criteria.

PRE-ACQUISITION ANALYSIS

The acquiring company, in conjunction with its merchant bank,
will usually have studied the trend of financial indicators – for
example, total profits, profit margins, capital employed, or
profile of past cash absorption and generation, ratios of debtors
and creditors to sales, stocks to sales, net asset values, property
revaluations, surplus cash and other assets, capital commitments,
details of gearing together with debenture trust deed stipulations,
earnings per share trends, share price performance, shareholding
spread, including directors' holdings, and any other indicators,
available from the Chairman's Statement in the Annual Report
and Accounts, as to future plans, loss-making activities, reorgani-
zations, etc. – in coming to a realistic price bid.

Equally important from the standpoint of managing the
company following acquisition is the product/market analysis.
This type of analysis is aimed at focusing upon the business factors
necessary for success in each of the operations carried on by the
takeover candidate.

Most companies are engaged in a variety of businesses. Either
they have a diversified product line, or sell to a wide range of
customer groups, or use distinct distribution channels. Consequently it is important to analyse the company by looking at the
various separate 'businesses' that make up the whole.

The product/market analysis ought therefore to highlight the
following for each separate business:

1   The main determinants of market demand for each
      business's product(s)
2   The chief competitors, their market shares, and trends of
      performance over time
3   Any recent moves or innovations by competitors that might
      be likely to affect future demand for the takeover candi-
      date's products
4   Whether demand is cyclical

5   How the industry (in which the business operates) has
     performed relative to the economy
6   How the business has performed against the industry
7   The tactics necessary for competitive success, e.g. price
     competition, heavy advertising, product innovation, etc.
8   The rate of additional commitment of resources to the
     business
9   Price trends over time and future projections (here ex-
     perience curve analysis is valuable)
10 Whether effective barriers to entry exist, e.g. patent pro-
     tection, massive capital or advertising expenditure, etc.

Any other relevant areas in assessing market demand for the
takeover candidate's range of products should be examined. This
phase of the analysis should locate for each 'business' the key
variables that underpin profitability. In most businesses a small
number of factors exert a relatively large influence on profits; it
is essential to identify these if they are to be controlled after the
merger or takeover.

Equally important in the pre-acquisition appraisal are in-depth
studies of the production function, management and organizational requirements, and property uses and valuations.

The pre-acquisition analysis is facilitated where the takeover
candidate allows access (however limited) to factories, accounts
and the management team. Indeed, where the initial acquisition
approach has come from the takeover candidate, or where the
takeover is in the form of an agreed bid, full access should be
insisted upon. Not to allow such access in these circumstances
can only be taken as a sign of 'something to hide'.

Equally, in the case of a contested bid, the same procedure
should be followed — even if 'through a glass darkly'. Indeed,
some experts believe that no acquisition can possibly be justified
without a complete pre-acquisition appraisal.

At this stage the question should be asked — to what extent
are the results achieved by the takeover candidate a function of
the entrepreneurial abilities of one or two of the proprietors or
directors? Frequently these entrepreneurial situations depend
on specialist skills in the areas of salesmanship and innovation.
It is important to recognize where profit stems from this source,
because continued profit performance depends on the continued
motivation of the entrepreneur(s). The company making the

acquisition ought, in these circumstances, to make the purchase consideration contingent upon achievement of specified profit levels over a period of time. The long-term objective following acquisition of an entrepreneurial business should be to change the operation into a more routine profit-formula type of situation. If this is successful, it acts as an insurance against the entrepreneur losing his flair, or leaving the company.

In assessing potential economies of scale, or ways of releasing synergy, research indicates significant difference between theory and practice. It is generally considered that production is the most likely way of achieving gains from synergy, through longer manufacturing runs, increased raw materials purchasing leverage, the justification of more efficient plant and machinery and the opportunity to rationalize manufacturing facilities. The second most profitable area is often reckoned to be research and development, through the elimination of duplicated effort. Similarly, there is potential for more efficient marketing effort where product line, distribution channels and sales forces can be combined. Organizational gains are ranked fourth; these include economies of scale that eliminate duplicated functions, or improve management motivation, etc. Finally, financial economies of scale, where new money is raised on uncharged assets, or where asset backing for borrowing is increased, are generally ranked below other functional pay-offs.

However, in practice — and this is relevant in projecting and planning for results following mergers — these theoretical rankings are reversed. Synergy is most easily released in financial areas. Next comes the marketing function. Production and research and development gains, usually thought to be the most easily won sources of synergy, in practice turn out to be the hardest to release.

For the acquisition-minded company, these findings suggest that there should be a certain amount of scepticism about manufacturing and technological economies of scale. Such potential gains come as a reward for management effort: synergy is not inherent in a situation — it is the prize, not the entitlement.

The above procedure should culminate in five broad categories of financial projection incremental upon the acquisition, namely:

1   An estimate of likely future net of tax incremental cash
      flows (mainly profits plus depreciation net of reinvestment)

available, assuming that the acquired company is operated
in the manner most profitable to the purchasing
company
2 A valuation of all surplus assets, that is, assets not required in
running the main business activities of the takeover target
company
3 A valuation, on a break-up basis, of the acquisition candidate's
operating assets — showing how this valuation is made in
respect of individual divisions or businesses
4 An estimate of the necessary timing of the replacement and
cost thereof in respect of all non-surplus assets
5 The timing and amount of any loan redemptions, which will
not be made good from the proceeds of a replacement issue
of debt.

Most companies are not one-product companies and in compiling
the above estimates (particularly 1 above) it is desirable, if possible, to make separate projections for each business activity and
subsequently aggregate them to complete the picture of the takeover candidate.

The assumption in making the above projections is that 'the
acquired company will be operated in the manner most profitable to the purchasing company'.

In the estimation of future cash flows under 1 above the
analysis should be concerned with the *incremental* flows. This
necessarily includes the higher profit that may be earned in the
area of the acquiring company's existing operations as a result
of economies arising from the acquisition. It also includes allow-
ance for losses that would occur in the absence of the takeover.
For example, if company A does not buy out company B, allowing company C to merge with B, then A's profit would fall. In
these circumstances company A should calculate incremental
cash flows on the basis of (cash flows with the acquisition of B)
less (cash flows accruing to A on the basis of B merging with C).
Where this method of estimation is used, the merger of B and C
must be a realistic possibility. If it is not, the figures are merely
being biased.

Assuming that the acquired firm will continue to be operated
into the foreseeable future, and that surplus assets are realized,
it is possible by taking 1, 2, 4 and 5 together to determine the
cash flows resulting from the acquisition. Using the discounted

cash flow technique, the next step is to calculate the present value of the target company.

The acquired company may have only a limited economic life. Given the above estimates, comparison of the present value of items 1 and 5 with the present value of item 4 indicates whether this is so. Clearly if the present value of the costs of replacement exceeds that of net income, the business can only be viewed as being of limited economic usefulness. This does not mean to say that it is not worth buying but it should be seen as an investment with a limited life. In this case, however, the present value of the target company should be calculated by aggregating the discounted estimates of 1 — taken over the economic life of the business — 2 and 5.

The takeover target, either in total or in respect of individual divisions, should be viewed as one without an economic life if the break-up value (or the amount for which it can be sold off) — 3 above — exceeds the net present value of future cash flows. Again this is not to say that it is not worth buying.

Clearly difficulties exist in estimating future cash flows, especially when there are hostilities surrounding the acquisition and access to information is not available. Even in the cases of agreed bids where access to the target company's books, management, production and marketing facilities is given, a pragmatic view should be adopted. For example, where a loss-making division is due, according to the vendor, to move into profit, business logic ought to underlie the forecast. In any case, having seen the vendor's future projections, his management and other capabilities, the purchaser is best advised to base calculations on his own estimates of likely future out-turns — rather than the vendor's.

An alternative method of appraisal, which is basically a variation on the above, is to begin from the likely acquisition price and from this determine the sort of growth, given the relevant discount rate in estimated future cash flows, necessary to justify such a purchase price. Of course, growth cannot continue at a super-normal rate for ever and when this approach to valuation is used, the sound policy is to project future flows at the rate necessary to justify the acquisition (which is usually a fairly high rate and is to be determined by trial and error) for a relatively short period, say three or four years, and then to assume growth thereafter at a normal rate — perhaps the estimated growth in the industry in three or four years' time, or the growth in the economy. Or after the high growth period a terminal value may be put on the business on the basis of an estimated normal-growth price earnings ratio.[5]

It is also essential to consider the means of financing a take-over, how easily funds or paper can be raised to pay for it and the effect after allowing for the appropriate method of financing adopted — on the acquirer's reported accounts, balance sheet, debenture trust deed constraints and key financial ratios (such as debt to net tangible assets, debt to net worth, interest cover, current assets to current liabilities, etc.) for as long a period into the future as is possible. Such an analysis must take into account the effect of organic expansion plans upon financial ratios in the future; hence this procedure ought also to be done in the light of projections in the company's forward plan.

OUTLINE INTEGRATION PLAN

Assuming that the potential takeover satisfies the company's ac-quisition criteria — see Figure 15.3 — the next logical step is an outline integration plan. This should first specify what is hoped to be gained from the acquisition. For example, whether the gains lie in:

1 Increasing market share
2 Eliminating competition
3 Safeguarding a source of supply
4 Safeguarding the market of existing or future products
5 Buying technology
6 Buying as a defensive strategy to stop competitors increasing their strength
7 Buying into a different market as a specific policy of diversification.

The integration plan should detail how these gains are to be achieved. Here, positive results can best be won from a policy of active integration by management committed to the merger. Nothing fails like the merger of two equal partners, especially where the intention is that the business should continue to trade as if no merger had taken place.

As a general rule, the time to make change is immediately following the acquisition. There is general agreement among merger specialists that the longer the problem of change is put off, the harder it becomes.

The integration plan should specify the executive from the parent company who is to be assigned, immediately after acquisition, to the new subsidiary. The plan should also specify probable changes lower down the potential subsidiary company's executive structure: for example, who from the parent company (or from the subsidiary) is to fill vacant or new positions together with their duties and terms of reference. The plan should also make explicit probable lines of command and reporting relations and procedures in the subsidiary, and it should focus upon the management information and reporting system required immediately following takeover.

Where the potential for profitable rationalization exists, the plan should set out the grounds for this belief and how and when it is to be realized.

The ultimate release of the profit potential in a merger situation must depend on the existence of adequate management talent and its motivation. Before the acquisition is completed, it is imperative to introduce the personnel who are to be delegated from the parent company to the new acquisition to the problems of the merger, and to try to get a feel of their opinions and anxieties about managing the new company in the group. By doing this, it is possible to assess how these key managers will react in the new situation, and help to allay their qualms.

THE INTEGRATION PLAN

Before action is taken to reorganize the acquired company, it is essential to check the pre-acquisition appraisal from the inside. This should be the first task after gaining control. This will act as a check on the earlier analysis of management capabilities, business performance and profit potential. And it will lead to a reformulation − if necessary − of the outline integration plan. Also at this stage − if not done before − a property valuer should be assigned to report on the values and potential of all properties owned or occupied by the new subsidiary.

This part of the analysis should confirm short-term rationalization gains that would accrue by realizing surplus assets, cutting out loss-making activities, transferring work from one factory to another, consolidating head-office staffs, centralizing duplicated functions and services, etc.

The integration plan is the logical development of the outline plan prepared in the pre-acquisition stage. It should begin by re-stating the objectives of the acquisition, and it should show how these objectives are to be realized. It will highlight management reorganization plans, the past and likely future performance of all the 'businesses' comprising the new subsidiary company, rationalization plans, and the future corporate strategy recom-mended for the acquired company. This last aspect will take full cognisance of other group companies' future plans and will specify the detailed mechanism, including timing of integration and rationalization — for example, such aspects as the phasing out of the new subsidiary's existing product range and the launch of a joint range of products.

Thus, the post-acquisition appraisal will act as a check on key features in the pre-acquisition estimates, and will also specify future strategy for the business and for the absorption and moti-vation of management personnel.

CONCLUDING NOTE

Agreed bids are cheaper than contested ones — whether such contest comes from a third party or from the directors. It is therefore more than helpful to have the directors of a company bid for, recommending that bid. Some effective takeover per-suaders appear in Table 15.3.

Studying and making sure that the stance on an acquisition is in line with explicit Monopolies and Mergers Commission guidelines[6] is essential. The rules defining market shares, which

Table 15.3   Some effective takeover persuaders

Use our financial resources to fund your growth opportunities.
Use our distribution network for access to new markets for your products.
Use our product-line strength to get you into new customer groups.
Use our R & D (or other central facilities) to assist your expansion.
Guarantees of continuity of employment for directors and employees.
Inducements aimed at directors' personal objectives (e.g. golden hand-shakes, opportunities for greater power in a bigger organizational framework, etc.).

---

are guides for monopoly reference, now go down to 25 per cent of a market and include local monopolies. But explicit guidelines are by no means the only apparent criteria for reference, for a degree of political discretion seems to have entered into this question − perhaps motivated by the sort of trends outlined in Figure 15.2 and the growth of aggressive conglomerate acquisitions. Thus, reference to the social and political environment to ensure that a potential acquisition, and its inevitable media publicity, does not encourage hostility from a statutory body, or from some other influential section of the business community, is equally essential.

All the foregoing analysis clearly takes time; and time is usually at a premium in takeover situations. This is all the more reason why companies should do their homework early. Short cuts are often necessary expedients but they can be taken more easily when a rigorous approach has been pursued. It is far better to have the surprises out of the way before, rather than after, the acquisition.

Finally, and most importantly, there is the question of people. The main difference between the acquisition as a capital budgeting decision and the organic investment project is that in the latter case the managers are well-known, whereas with an acquisition the acquirer often has to deal with a new group of managers of unknown quality, operating in a changed environment. In this new environment their motivation and their attitudes may alter. Often men who have been their own bosses and have built up their own business find life in a large organization uncongenial. As a result they may no longer be motivated by profit. The question of the congruence of corporate culture, a subject for wholly qualitative judgement, must therefore receive attention. This applies wherever an acquisition is made.

REFERENCES

1 Kitching, John. 'Why do Mergers Miscarry?', *Harvard Business Review,* November−December 1967.
2 Kitching, John. Winning and Losing with European Acquisitions'. *Harvard Business Review,* Mar.−Apr. 1974; Kitching, John, 'Acquisitions in Europe'. *Business International* 1973.
3 Newbould, G. D. *Management and Merger Activity.* Guthstead. 1970.

4 Mace, Myles L. and Montgomery, George C, Jnr., *Management Problems of Corporate Acquisitions.* Division of Research, Harvard Business School 1962.
5 Franks, J. R., Miles, R. and Bagwell, J. A Review of Acquisition Valuation Models. *Journal of Business Finance and Accounting,* Vol. 1, Spring 1974.
6 See, for example, *Mergers: A Guide to Board of Trade Practice,* HMSO, 1969, and the *Fair Trading Legislation* of 1973.

16 International Expansion Strategy

James C. Leontiades

The emergence of a greatly expanded European Economic Community, reduced tariffs towards the developing non-industrial
nations, and improved transportation technology are only some
of the recent innovations causing decision-makers in multi-
national corporations to review their procedures for locating
optimal investment sites abroad. Even those firms that have
already implemented the latest in capital budgeting, linear programming and mathematical modelling techniques are encount-
ering difficulty adjusting their procedures to the new business
situation. In fact it is the more sophisticated techniques, with
their greater reliance on highly structured inputs, which most
urgently call for reappraisal. Such models are only useful as long
as their underlying assumptions are valid. The initial assumptions
they make about the real world are crucial to their effectiveness.
It is just these, however, which are now changing and throwing
doubt on current practice.

Consider the typical situation of Company X, which is
attracted by the growing European market and has decided to
study the feasibility of a new plant designed to service this
growing potential. The company proceeds to gather information
on the nature and distribution of the potential market, European
wages and productivity, European site costs, building costs, local
regulations, investment incentives and Government attitudes and
restrictions. These, together with facts that may be peculiar to
Company X's circumstances, will then be weighted and analysed
to determine the feasibility of alternative European plant sites.
This procedure, which worked well enough in the past, could
prove dangerously misleading today. A number of companies are

discovering that the best place for their 'European plants' may be in Asia, Africa or Latin America. The tacit link between the target market and the new plant built to service that market has been broken. New plants are going up in diverse corners of the developing world, aimed at the European market but making full use of the lower wages available elsewhere.

Satellite or runaway plants, as they have been called, are often associated with U.S. companies fleeing U.S. wage rates to produce abroad for the U.S. market. Yet, as a practical matter, planning for plant locations in the new E.E.C. will have to take into account this new competitive threat. An impressive list of leading European companies are already showing the way, including the following:

1   Germany's Rolleiwerke camera company has set up three subsidiaries in Singapore to export its products on a world-wide basis. Volkswagen's Mexican plants produce parts that are exported to Europe as well as the U.S. Besides Rolleiwerke, Grundig, Bayer, Hoechst and Siemens have also joined the move to Singapore.
2   Britain's Plessey Instruments has set up plants in Malta, Portugal, Barbados and Singapore, to produce a wide variety of products for Northern as well as Southern European markets.
3   Olivetti supplies its worldwide needs for desk calculators from Latin America.
4   Renault, Mercedes-Benz and Fiat are starting operations in Eastern Europe that are scheduled to produce components for Western European markets.
5   Philips, the Dutch firm, is setting up a major industrial base in the Far East to supply European and other markets.

This trend poses problems for corporate planners in multi-national corporations. As the wage gap between the industrial countries and the developing countries that are potential sites for such plants continues to grow, so will the need to take into consideration, more explicitly than heretofore, the feasibility of plant locations completely dissociated from the markets they service. This will necessitate the study of such 'hard-to-predict' variables as future wage rates, union activity, local incentives, development of free-trade zones and other incentives, transportation costs and future tariff movements.

WHICH COMMON MARKET?

Despite the growing importance of satellite plants, most companies building new plants for the European Common Market will continue to locate them within the enlarged community's tariff barriers. But what are these? Before even beginning to calculate the trade-off between plants located in one E.E.C. country or another, companies must first determine the outlines of the new tariff structure defining the Common Market. This will not be as simple as it might seem. The community long ago outgrew the six country members that signed the Rome treaty. It is not a matter of six or even nine countries which must be considered, but the large group of countries that have associated themselves with the community as it has developed.

The community has proved to be a very dynamic organization, continually growing in terms of membership and continually altering the ties linking one member to another. It is safe to assume that within the lead time necessary to construct a new plant and make it operative (three to four years) it will have altered still further. What is needed, then, is not so much a definition of present tariff barriers as a projection of future barriers. What will the community look like ten years from now? That is the question plant location must take into consideration. It is a crucial question, the answer to which could seriously influence the decisions made for Western Europe.

The enlarged European Economic Community has several levels of membership (see Table 16.1). First, there are the full members, i.e. those that take part in all of the economic and political aspects of the group as set out in the Treaty of Rome. On this level we may expect tariff-free trade of industrial products within an increasingly homogeneous industrial framework of laws governing mergers, competition and industrial standards. Closely associated with these countries will be the important group referred to in Table 16.1 as 'Free Trade Associates'. The national markets represented here will be virtually a part of the Common Market as regards industrial trade. Corporations planning their future expansion strategy must consider the present and future interrelations between these two groups. If history is any guide, the two will move even closer together, eventually forming a single industrial market of sixteen countries and a population of over 300 million people. This is not to deny

Table 16.1   E.E.C. structure

Levels of membership	Market relationship
I. *Full Members:* Belgium, France, Italy, Netherlands, Luxembourg, West Germany, Britain, Denmark, Ireland.	Free trade in industrial and agricultural products. Progress toward reduction of legal and monetary differences together with free movement of labour and capital.
II. *Free Trade Associates:* Austria, Finland, Sweden, Switzerland, Iceland, Portugal, Norway.	Free trade in industrial products between each other and countries in Group I.
III. *Mediterranean Associates:* Israel, Tunisia, Morocco, Algeria, Libya, Malta, Greece, Turkey, Egypt, Cyprus, Spain.	Selective reductions in trade barriers between countries at this level and those in Groups I and II.
IV. *Developing Country Associates (Lomé Convention):* Mauritania, Mali, Niger, Chad, Sudan, Ethiopia, Gambia, Guinea-Bissau, Senegal, Guinea, Upper Volta, Nigeria, Cameroon, Central African Republic, Uganda, Kenya, Somalia, Sierra Leone, Liberia, Ivory Coast, Ghana, Togo, Dahomey, Equatorial Guinea, Gabon, Congo, Zaire, Rwanda, Burundi, Tanzania, Zambia, Malawi, Botswana, Guyana, Madagascar, Swaziland, Lesotho, Jamaica, Western Samoa, Bahamas, Grenada, Trinidad and Tobago, Fiji, Barbados, Tonga, Mauritius.	Developing countries whose goods have preferential access to Common Market.

that real differences in taxes, social policies and location incentives will persist for at least another decade. It is this mixture of commonality with key areas of national difference, the precise combination changing over time, which represents perhaps the major planning challenge of the new E.E.C.

The other two levels of E.E.C. membership comprise less industrial countries. Level III countries have a number of differing treaty relations with the Level I group, which vary from one Level III country to another. In general these offer the possibility of preferential access to E.E.C. markets for the products of these countries while permitting access to their own markets for Level I exports in certain product categories. Level IV countries enjoy preferential access for many of their products (primarily agricultural products and raw materials) into Level I. In the past they have also offered entry into their markets at a preferential rate for exports from Level I, though some doubt attaches to future prospects for such 'reverse preferences'. Nevertheless, the affiliation of this important group of countries with the E.E.C. presents major opportunities for the supply of certain products from these countries on a tariff-free basis to plants located in Level I.

Looking further into the future, there is little doubt that the affiliation of these last two groups with the E.E.C. will open up additional possibilities. Particularly, it may be expected that some of the Level III group will apply for Level II membership, joining the industrial free-trade area while offering substantially lower wage costs to plants located there.

THEORY VERSUS PRACTICE

The enlarged E.E.C. brings together Europe's two major industrial centres — the northern European industrial complex beginning with Hamburg in the north and extending south through the Ruhr, Belgium and on towards Paris; and the British industrial complex. Many multi-national corporations already have plants located in one or other (and some in both) of these areas.

This poses a special problem. Theoretically, the removal of tariff barriers now taking place between these two industrial concentrations would seem to strengthen the case for exporting from one to the other, i.e. if you have a plant in one of the member countries (Level I or II), your logical way of reaching the new markets opened up by the enlarged community would seem to be by exporting, rather than investment in new plants and facilities.

It is strange, therefore, that one hears so much emphasis on the latter. One finds an increasing number of firms that have historically relied on exports to reach other members of the enlarged community now turning toward direct investment just when the barriers to such exports are being lifted.

British Leyland, for example, which has historically relied on exports to reach continental markets, prepared for British entry into the Community by embarking on an accelerated programme of plant acquisition and expansion. The same pattern is to be found in a number of corporate areas, including breweries, food companies and electronics. The rapid pace of merger negotiations and agreements with continental firms is still another aspect of the move to acquire foreign production facilities within the new tariff-free area.

The dominant motivating factor here is a perceived need to be closer to the market. With the British-initiated expansion, the E.E.C. will take on the dimensions of a true mass market. The more competitive situation this implies is already putting pressure on consumer-oriented companies to concentrate on a number of marketing variables, which, although sometimes omitted from formal calculations, are nevertheless assuming an increasingly important role:

1 *Delivery time.* Shorter delivery times are becoming an ever more important competitive variable. The wider choice of consumer products made available by the lowering of trade barriers has meant that the long-patient European consumer no longer has to wait as long for producers to supply his needs. The pressures on delivery times gives advantage to local-investment facilities over imports with their generally longer waiting period.

2 *Market feedback.* Company facilities located near the final consumer provide a better 'feel' for the market. Rapidly changing product requirements are behind the efforts of some companies to establish a local presence.

3 *Government sales.* For many products sold directly to Governments, it is still true that the company that wishes to sell in a particular country must produce in that

country. Current E.E.C. efforts and statements point in
the opposite direction, but experience has shown that it
will be many years before the plans to eliminate this bias
can provide a basis for action.

4   *Control.* Difficult to pin down, but nevertheless vital, is the
added control over marketing strategy the firm with its
own locally owned facilities is able to exercise. One of the
areas of greatest upheaval currently is the conversion from
reliance on import agents to wholly or partly owned sales
agencies.

In short, plant location is becoming an integral part of the
corporate marketing mix. As such, its adjustment to the new
business environment frequently calls for more rather than less
expansion within local European market areas.

FOREIGN EXCHANGE

Exchange-rate fluctuations are yet another factor encouraging
some companies to move abroad. The E.E.C. has been notably
unsuccessful in eliminating or significantly moderating such
fluctuations, and prospects for the future on this score are not
optimistic. Regardless of progress in other areas, trade within
E.E.C. member countries is still 'foreign trade' as regards currency. This will continue to be the case until some distant date
when national sovereignty over monetary matters may be yielded
to a central E.E.C. authority charged with managing what will in
effect be a single Common Market currency. Until then, exchange-
rate fluctuations will continue to become more, not less, important. Since the formation of such a group is directed towards the
increased exchange of products among member states, exporters
find that their investment abroad in terms of promotion expenditures, distribution facilities and inventories rapidly increases.

The most successful exporters assume the greatest risk. Resort
to forward cover, effective in short-term situations, is no solution
here; for it is the exporter's market position that represents his
most important investment and this cannot be hedged. Any
change in exchange rates is bound to exert an impact on the
foreign cost structure of his products within three to six months.

True, this presents the possibility of gains as well as losses.
Ultimately, however, each company must ask itself what business

it is in. Does its competence lie in manipulating different currency positions or is it based on certain skills and transferable
assets? If the latter, the prospect of eliminating foreign exchange-
rate risk by locating within the target market represents a consideration that will have to be balanced against other possibilities,
such as locating in low-wage countries.

BACKDOORS OF EUROPE

Although great strides have been made toward eliminating
Governmental differences between one member of the Common
Market and another, the distinctions that remain are substantial.
Differences in wages, regional incentives and other regulations
continue despite statements and efforts to the contrary. Careful
investigation of those areas sometimes referred to as 'backdoors'
has proved worthwhile for a substantial number of companies.
Moreover there is no short-term prospect that these preferential
regions will be eliminated. Areas such as the Channel Islands,
Ireland, the North of England and the Italian Mezzogiorno, will
continue to offer distinctive advantages in terms of tax and wage
differentials that the prospective investor cannot afford to
overlook.

   Investment incentives offered to companies locating within
their jurisdiction by different local and regional governments will
continue to play a major role. Management must exercise considerable judgement in evaluating the different types and amounts
of incentive. Although the stated E.E.C. policy is to standardize
such aid and to reduce discrepancies in locational incentives
among member countries, in practice the implementation of this
objective will be extremely difficult to enforce. Incentives to
companies locating in specific areas may take a bewildering
variety of forms, including programmes such as labour training
and housing, which are also frequently encompassed by national
programmes outside the scope of the Commission. There is no
subsitute here for on-the-spot investigation and talks with local
officials.

ENVIRONMENTAL CONSTRAINTS

One of the most important influences determining new-plant
location stems from the current wave of concern over the ques-

tion of pollution and associated environmental problems. The
full impact of this phenomenon is only now emerging in the form
of action and proposed E.E.C. legislation but its impact on industry is already much in evidence.

A West German electronics firm recently decided to cancel its
proposed plant in the Saar basin and locate instead in the less
industrial and less polluted Moselle region. Other companies
similarly situated have not always publicized their decisions,
but there is little doubt that this factor is playing an ever-larger
role in corporate-expansion considerations.

The lead here is being taken by local (i.e. national) authorities.
Holland, Germany and France, within the Community, have
instituted specific pollution-control programmes. Since such
measures were not anticipated by the Rome treaty, legislation at
the Community level has been slower in reaching implementation.
However, programmes now in process leave little doubt that this
will be a major future area of E.E.C. initiative, particularly with
reference to plants located in the Rhine basin and along other
major commercial waterways. The increasingly onerous penalties
on plant-connected pollution will provide still another incentive
for location in less congested regions.

A FRENCH CALIFORNIA

Looking toward the more distant future, one can detect signs of
substantial change in the industrial geography of Europe. The
basis for the present distribution of European industry is being
eroded. The present heavy concentration toward the north is due
largely to the location of coal and steel deposits there. However,
with the energy switch toward gas and oil and the diminished
emphasis on heavy metals, the rationale for this northward bias
is rapidly disappearing.

Will industry continue to concentrate in the north? For the
near- and middle-term future the answer is positive. Having
established a comprehensive infrastructure of transportation,
communication and skilled labour, the area cannot discard its
industry rapidly. Yet it would be foolish to overlook the vast
potential of Southern Europe as a new centre of industrial concentration based on the more advanced technologies. For those
companies requiring a high proportion of highly skilled manpower, i.e. electronics, scientific instruments, etc., the milder

climate and outdoor life-style of Southern Europe are likely to prove as attractive to the more mobile European of today as they have in the U.S. There are indications that this is already happening.

GEOGRAPHICAL FLEXIBILITY

There are then a number of forces at work on the European scene that may be depended upon drastically to affect strategic planning of corporate facilities. The growing freedom to locate production facilities in distant parts of the world while transferring the finished product to the local market place has already critically influenced the competitive position of many firms. Its impact will no doubt vary from one industry to another, but it would be dangerous to assume that its effects were limited to electronics and office equipment. Automobiles, machine tools, and all types of mechanical as well as electrical appliances are suitable candidates. Within the E.E.C. the affiliation of what we have termed here as Level III and Level IV countries presents additional incentive in this direction.

AVOIDING THE PLANNING PITFALLS

Where and how to expand plant capacity is only one aspect of the more general strategic problem posed for management by the changing business environment. None of the preceding comments should be construed as an argument against due consideration of other strategic alternatives – particularly exporting. That has already proved to be the source of dramatic sales gains for those firms abandoning (some of them for the first time) the notion that exports comprise a residual market. They have found that pruning and cultivation of previously neglected export agents and outlets can yield surprising dividends.

The more basic issue goes beyond the export/foreign investment trade-off. Logically, before this come a number of decisions bearing on the company's basic competitive reaction toward the forces set in motion by the widening of the market place. Faced with membership in the Common Market, corporate attitudes in the U.K. vary from 'protect the home market' to 'let's get the other fellow's customers'.

The precise point a company chooses along this spectrum will depend on its perceptions and priorities. The former re-action is probably the most common and most dangerous, since the pressure of the forces set loose by E.E.C. membership is entirely in the opposite direction, towards market interpene-tration. Also, the effort required to stop foreign producers from acquiring even a small segment of the home market can be dis-proportionate to results. Whatever stance the company chooses, whether defensive or aggressive, the impact of the E.E.C. will be to benefit those companies that can master the new strategy and to damage those that cannot.

No easy prescriptions can be offered for dealing with these new complexities. However, many firms would deal more com-petently with both new and more familiar problems by keeping in mind the most prevalent pitfalls in formulating their expansion strategy. These may be categorized under the following headings

Tunnel Vision

By arbitrarily directing expansion to one part of the world rather than another, management runs the risk of suboptimizing. The key word here is 'arbitrarily'. Through tradition, precedent or simply management bias, there is a distinct tendency in many companies to focus expansion in a particular part of the world. Often this is rationalized in terms of some corporate advantages or expertise. This is legitimate enough, where such geographic advantage in fact exists, but all too often the evident bias reflects institutional or other factors that have long disappeared. The concentration of British investment in the Commonwealth countries is one example. The factors that once conditioned such expansion have long since altered, yet many British firms have been slow to reflect such change in their expansion strategy. Only a careful weighting of the trade-offs between alternatives in all parts of the world can serve as a basis for rational decision-making in today's environment.

Passive Planning

Perhaps the most prevalent and painful mistakes begin as a res-ponse to outside initiative. Despite all the emphasis given today to forward planning and associated skills, most expansion still takes place as a response to external demands to 'look at this part of the world'. A foreign Government wants new corporate facilities to alleviate a local labour problem, or an export agent asks that a new plant may be allocated to his territory. These are legitimate requests, and the source of many profitable ventures, but the company that simply reacts to initiatives of this nature has in effect abdicated control.

Static Strategy

Whatever else may be said of the emerging foreign business environment, it does not present a static situation. Yet many companies proceed with expansion abroad as if it were indeed the case. The problems this generates are most obvious with reference to contractual commitments. All too often companies distribute their agencies abroad on a basis of assumed perpetuity of present conditions, with no provision for termination or review of contract. Having sprinkled the globe with long-term commitments, they then find alternative arrangements either extremely costly or impracticable.

CONCLUSION

We began by suggesting that current events in Europe and elsewhere are bringing about far-reaching changes in the global business environment, forcing companies to re-examine their basic strategy towards plant location. Today's fast-moving international markets require that company strategy anticipates fundamental change at the outset. Any particular corporate configuration in world markets must be regarded as a phase in an evolutionary process whose future characteristics may be anticipated today.

Part IV
Implementing Corporate Strategy

17 Corporate Planning and Organizational Change

Bernard Taylor

THE HALF-LIFE OF THE PLANNER

The accident rate among relatively young and apparently healthy corporate planners is uncomfortably high. In fact corporate planning has a reputation as a high-risk occupation. The 'half-life' of the corporate planner is a standing joke in the profession. To quote Michael Kami, who set up corporate planning at both IBM and Xerox Corporation: 'A good, competent Corporate Planner has a life of around three years. On the other hand, if the planner is really enthusiastic and committed, the operating management will usually see him out within the year.'

Yet top managements need corporate planners. If they did not exist they would have to be invented under another name, for in any successful organization there is a tendency for management to become complacent – to lose its edge. Corporate planners can help to keep managers on their toes, for they are 'change agents'. At their best they are the corporate philosophers who may speak the unspeakable or, at least, think the unthinkable.

In consequence corporate planners see their plans as the instruments for determining the corporate destiny. Unfortunately many relatively powerful managers have not yet read the corporate-planning textbooks, or, even worse, have read them but remain unconvinced of the truths present in corporate planning – and the turnover in planners is high.

THE CASE FOR PLANNING

Long-range or strategic planning has almost universal acceptance as a theory, and numerous studies have also established that companies using formal planning techniques perform better than companies relying on intuitive planning. Moreover companies that now use formal planning systems are more successful than they were previously, when they relied on more informal methods. The evidence on acquisitions is especially impressive. As might be expected, managements who develop specific objectives, and criteria for evaluation, tend to make fewer mistakes than those who use hunches, the old-boy network, and a strictly financial evaluation (see Chapter 1, p. 6).

The case for having objectives, a strategy and a plan seems obvious but is worth restating. Every management team needs to develop a consensus about the future of the enterprise, to determine the following:

1 *Purpose* — what size and type of organization it will be in five to ten years' time
2 *Goals* — the intermediate targets to be achieved
3 *Strategy* — what products or services are to be offered to which markets, and how resources are to be acquired and allocated
4 *Action programmes* — what specific projects need to be established, who will be responsible, and what resources will be required
5 *Appraisal* — a means of auditing the effectiveness of the organization against objective standards, and a system for monitoring changes in the environment which could have an important impact on the enterprise.
6 *Monitoring and Control* — a procedure for reviewing the whole process, to ensure that objectives, strategies and plans are kept realistic and up-to-date.

This is the theory and, so the argument runs, because of the pressures of day-to-day business, it is sometimes necessary to make special arrangements in the company to ensure that policy or strategy is not neglected — an executive committee of the board, a corporate-planning procedure to fit alongside the one-year budget and five-year operating plan, or even a full-time or part-time corporate planner to help introduce and coordinate the process.

A THEORY IN SEARCH OF A PRACTICE?

On the other hand, when researchers go out and investigate what is happening in practice, they are frequently surprised and disappointed at the poor progress that has been made. Let us take a few quotations, the first from a BIM study published in 1968:[1] 'Whatever may be said, few companies have implemented corporate planning, which is the acid test of acceptance. A number of executives reject it completely, either verbally or by their actions. Others pay lip service to it for a variety of reasons, the foremost of which is perhaps lack of comprehension of what corporate planning is really about.' The second comes from a Stanford Research Institute Survey in the U.S.A.:[2] 'Organised corporate long range planning is neither as well accepted, nor as well practised as suggested by the literature on the subject. Although much planning is done, the effort is often sporadic, it is lacking in co-ordination and it is less formalised and sophisticated than much of the literature suggests.' Finally, the third quotation is taken from a more recent study of corporate planning in thirty leading British companies, selected for their long experience of planning: 'Corporate Planning in major British companies is neither as well developed, nor as fully accepted as one might expect'.[3]

The fact is that the 'root and branch' total integrated corporate-planning system envisaged in management literature is rare, almost as rare as the much sought after total integrated information system. Researchers who look for the total system are doomed to disappointment. A recent study of objective-setting in British boardrooms for example reveals that the only objective that directors could agree on was 'profitability'.[4] One study revealed that even in companies with a national reputation for corporate planning one in three of the chief executives were not concerned with the development of corporate strategy, but simply with the reviewing of divisional plans and budgets.[3]

The evidence all points one way: formal strategic planning is rare. Planning is usually

1 *Partial*, e.g. extended budgeting, marketing planning, or economic forecasting.
2 *Operational*, i.e. an integration of divisional plans with no analysis of objectives, long-term trends, alternative strategies, etc.

CORPORATE PLANNING AS A PHILOSOPHY AND STYLE OF MANAGEMENT

To understand the problems of introducing corporate planning we must look behind the façade — the objectives, strategies and plans — to the philosophy, the management style, and the political system in which corporate planning plays a central role.

A Philosophy of Change

The first and fundamental problem about introducing corporate planning is that it is a philosophy of change. Corporate planning is most avidly taken up by organizations which face a crisis. A new book of case studies in corporate planning by the Society for Long Range Planning[5] clearly demonstrates this. Virtually every case begins with a crisis, and a change of top management, followed by a rapid assessment of the state of the enterprise, and the establishing of clear objectives, strategies and programmes of action aimed at ensuring the survival of the company.

The most recent study of corporate planning in Britain demonstrated the same fact. Corporate planning tends to be introduced because of some major threat. The traditional product/market is stable or declining. The company faces the risk of having its assets nationalized or cannot repatriate its profits from developing countries. A major technological change threatens to make some major products obsolete. The company has just been reorganized into semi-autonomous product divisions or subsidiary companies and the corporate staff are being asked to agree to major capital investments without prior discussion of the general strategy for the divisions.[3]

Of course, not all managements in a crisis choose corporate planning as a route to increased profitability and growth, but the best time to sell corporate planning to an organization is when profits are down, sales are static, and costs are rising. On the other hand, it is virtually impossible to persuade management to undertake a complete reappraisal of the company's operation if the business is doing well. For one thing, the managers are honestly too busy making sales, building up production capacity, and taking advantage of the profit opportunities which lie before them.

A Reorientation in Attitude

A second fundamental problem is that corporate planning forces the operating manager into a complete reassessment of his priorities and a fundamental change in his approach to his job. Of course, there is nothing new in the idea of developing long-term and short-term plans. This has always been part of management. What is new is the suggestion that these plans should be:

1   *Formulated for the enterprise as a whole* as well as for individual departments, divisions and operating units
2   *Written down, discussed and reviewed systematically* as part of a regular annual procedure, very much like the annual budget
3   *Concerned with formulating and implementing a full strategy for the future* rather than simply maintaining or expanding existing operations.

Most operating managers will have several kinds of long-range plans. The most common are:

1   *The five-year operating plan,* showing how present operations are likely to develop over the foreseeable future
2   *Project plans or product plans,* for new production and warehousing facilities, the introduction of new products, or the launching of existing products in new markets, etc.

Corporate planning means reassessing these in the light of a third type of plan:

3   *A divisional strategic plan.* This strategic plan is prepared by operating management within guidelines suggested by top management, and in discussion with specialist staff groups covering finance, marketing, production, personnel and research.

In addition top management leads in producing a fourth kind of plan, which might be called:

4   *A corporate development plan.* This will deal with new developments, acquisitions and mergers, diversification, and international moves, not envisaged in the divisional plans.

Research in Europe and the U.S.A. indicates that this kind of management approach does not come naturally to the present generation of managers. Kirby Warren, in a study of corporate planning in the U.S.A., concluded that operating managers tend to be selected because they take action. They are not analysts by nature and their whole experience and training pushes them towards taking decisions, not making plans.[6]

The General Electric Company has also found that the conventional management system, with its emphasis on short-term results, tends to inhibit managers from taking a broader or longer-term view of their business. If operating managers are to take corporate planning seriously, they must be selected, trained, motivated, appraised and rewarded, with this in mind. All too often the promotion or the salary increase goes to the manager who produces the best results in the short term, and then he moves on to another job unaware, and unconcerned, about the long-term implications of the decisions he has taken.

Top management, too, is likely to find difficulty adapting to the demands of corporate planning. As one president of a U.S. company put it, 'I am surprised if a week goes by without me receiving a request from an Operating Manager asking for guidance about what our objectives are, what are our priorities for capital investment, or what is our policy on a certain topic. I'm not Caesar or Napoleon. I want to know what *they* think.'

For top management corporate planning means the following:

1 Determining objectives, strategies and policies, so that divisional management and corporate staff can develop their plans within broad guidelines. Top management should *define* what new projects should be investigated, rather than reacting to projects that arise
2 Thinking ahead about the organization, so as to start new projects in good time
3 Considering new projects in the context of alternative strategies for the division and the company as a whole.

This means discussing divisional strategies at an early stage, before line management has become committed to a particular capital project. It also means trying to consider new projects for the whole company over a five to ten year period, *altogether* not one by one.

For management at all levels, then, corporate planning requires discipline, commitment, imagination, skill, and in particular a

questioning approach. It is not easy, after ten to fifteen years
with an organization, to question established practices, to set
more demanding targets and to try to look at the business objectively, in short to become reconciled to change as a way of
life.

Corporate planning usually demands a radical reorientation
in management style. Possibly this is why, in one study of corporate planning in major British companies, it was found that
in 36 per cent of firms there had been a change of chief executive, or a member of the main Board.[3] An experienced American
corporate planner concluded: 'Ultimately, the question reduces
to the unchanging character of human behaviour; without
changing a management it is not really safe to assume that significant changes can be made in the action pattern of the company.'

Changing the Political System

To read books and journals on planning, one might think that
it is a rational activity proceeding by logical scientific analysis
from the setting of objectives, through the appraisal of the firm
and the environment, to the evaluation of alternative strategies
against defined criteria and the establishing of action programmes
and budgets that are monitored and controlled on a regular basis.
In practice corporate planning is a political process. The successful corporate planner is essentially not a technician but a diplo-
mat, and a salesman. A recent study by Mumford & Pettigrew
makes it clear that strategic decisions are concerned with the
allocation of resources both in terms of finance and manpower,
and the status and position that goes with it.[7] Anyone who
seeks to make this process more rational inevitably takes his
career in his hands.

Corporate planning, like any other political process, depends
on negotiation, compromises and coalitions for its success, and
a good deal on the planner's own political resources — his status
and experience, the goodwill he has accumulated in the company,
the power of top management and the extent of their commitment to planning, and the support in the board and in operating
management. The corporate planner's first requirement is a solid
power base. Without this, he had better not start. With it, he

may succeed, provided he can demonstrate quickly to operating management that on balance they and their department or division may gain more in terms of resources and prestige than they would by following the traditional approach. From this point on, the rate of his progress will depend very much on the climate for change in the organization.

Introducing Major Changes Successfully

If corporate planning is a philosophy of change, can it then change an organization? The answer must surely be no. Corporate planning must be seen as part of a coordinated programme for change. The programme will probably include most if not all of the following:

1 Changes in management, and stronger leadership from the top
2 A change in organization structure, possibly the creation of semi-autonomous divisions and operating units
3 Improvements in the information system, e.g. better data on profitability and on certain markets
4 Internal training, and maybe the use of organization-development techniques
5 Alterations in appraisal and reward systems, and more emphasis by management on management development and product development.

'Success' Patterns in Organizational Change

After examining the records of a number of organizations that had introduced major changes successfully, Lawrence Greiner[8] listed the common factors as follows:

1 Internal and external pressure on top management
2 A new man appears as chief executive or consultant to the chief executive
3 Reappraisal of past practices and current problems
4 The top manager and the board are deeply committed to the re-examination
5 Line management participates in fact-finding and problem-solving to diagnose the organization's problems

6   The new man infuses new ideas and approaches to problems
      at several levels
7   Solutions are developed, tested and proved on a small scale
8   The change effort spreads with success and becomes part of
      the organization's way of life.

Today and Tomorrow

Most businesses are organized to manage their present operations
efficiently. This, after all, is the first priority – to stay in
business this year. Moreover it is probably inevitable that the
majority of managers will have this operation as their major
task. This demands a fairly narrow perspective, knowing the immediate environment of the firm and its industry. It also requires
a limited range of experience, because the manager is working
within a technology he knows well. The actions of his department tend to be directed towards the optimizing of immediate
profits, and within the group there is a high respect for conformity. Change and innovation are likely to disrupt the established
systems and lead to waste or delays.

On the other hand, as the pace of change in the environment
quickens and as companies grow in size and complexity, so it
becomes increasingly vital for businesses to cultivate the capacity
to adapt and innovate. This means making arrangements to ensure
the promotion of individuals and teams of managers who are concerned not so much with operating problems and present profits
but rather with the longer-term survival and development of
the enterprise.

They will require a broad experience in several industries
and environments. Their perspective must be multi-national, and
they need to be aware of social and political as well as economic
and technological trends. They will probably be concerned as
much with the acceptance of the firm in its social environment
as with its economic prosperity. They will be busy not so much
maintaining the present operations as in spawning new ventures,
and they will be looking for change and innovation rather than
stability and conformity.[9]

CONCLUSION

Corporate planning is a philosophy of change. It is not so much
a battery of techniques and systems as a style of management,

and the main benefits from planning derive from a continuing dialogue about the future of the organization, between top management and middle management, between line and staff, between divisions and head office, even between management and unions, or the company and its major suppliers or major customers. But to start the dialogue involves a dramatic re-orientation in management thinking — and a willingness to change.

REFERENCES

1 Hewkin, J. W. M. and Kempner, T. *Is Corporate Planning Necessary?* (BIM, December, 1968).
2 Ringbakk, K. A. *Organised Planning in Major U.S. Companies* (Stanford Research Institute, 1969).
3 Taylor, Bernard and Irving, Peter. 'Organised Planning in Major U.K. Companies', *Long Range Planning,* June 1971.
4 Norburn, D. and Grinyer, P. H. 'Directors without Direction', *Journal of General Management,* Winter 1974.
5 Baynes, P. (ed.). *Case Studies in Corporate Planning* (Pitman, 1973).
6 Warren, E. Kirby. *Long Range Planning: the Executive View-point* (Prentice-Hall, 1966).
7 Mumford, Enid and Pettigrew, Andrew. *Implementing Strategic Decisions* (Longman, 1974).
8 Greiner, L. 'Patterns of Organisational Change', *Harvard Business Review,* May–June 1967.
9 Ansoff, H. Igor, Declerk, Roger P. and Hayes, Robert L. *From Strategic Planning to Strategic Management,* Wiley, 1976.

18 Management Information Systems for Corporate Planning and Control

J. C. Higgins

INTRODUCTION

Corporate planning is concerned with (1) the setting of objectives for the organization, and (2) the development of plans to enable the organization to meet those objectives. Clearly both tasks necessitate the provision of suitable information, and the design of information systems that will enable the organization (1) to review its corporate plan at appropriate intervals, and (2) to monitor its progress against a given corporate plan and take control action where necessary.

A management information system may be defined as follows: 'A system that provides each manager in an organization with the information he needs in order to take decisions, to plan and to control within his particular area of responsibility in the organization.' It follows, therefore, that the planning and control requirements of an organization should have a major influence on the management-information system. The other major determinants, and clearly they interact, will be the external environment, the organizational structure, the job specifications of individual managers, and the prevailing management style. The definition above makes no explicit reference to the computer, and it should not be thought that a computer is a prerequisite before an organization can claim to have a management-information system. Nearly all small and the majority of medium-sized organizations make little use of the computer in their management-information system; indeed, in many large organi-

zations the computer's influence on managerial decision-taking
is negligible compared with its contribution at the data-processing
level.

THE CORPORATE PLANNING PROCESS

It will be helpful in discussing the information-system requirements for corporate planning if we first examine some of the
major features of the corporate planning process (Figure 18.1).

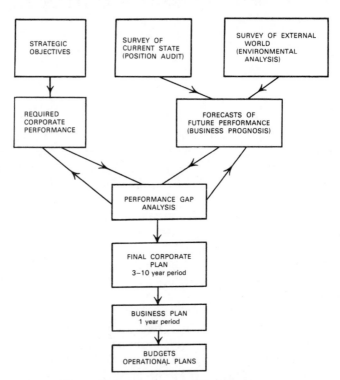

Figure 18.1   Corporate planning process.

Strategic objectives are discussed at length elsewhere in the
book, and it should be sufficient in this chapter merely to observe that they may be purely qualitative, e.g. to be technologically a leading innovator, or quantitative, e.g. to achieve a profits
growth of 10 per cent p.a. over the next five years. The next
stage is to specify the required corporate performance in terms

of such measures as market shares, profit contributions, manufacturing costs, etc.

In parallel the organization should carry out surveys of its
current state (position audit) and of the external world within
which it operates (environmental analysis). In carrying out the
first survey it may prove helpful to list at an early stage key
success functions (for a brewery, quality control and outlet
management might well be examples), and then attempt to assess
the organization's performance of these functions. Quantitatively
this assessment is not an easy task; the organization may choose
to analyse historical data and compare current with past performance, or, alternatively, it may try to develop more objective
measures of performance, and here the help of management
scientists can be invaluable. Ultimately the survey will have to
cover all the activities of the organization, though in less detail
than the key functions, and for many of these activities the
historical-comparison approach may have to suffice. The environmental survey will take in such factors as the structure and demand
characteristics of the industry within which the organization
operates, such Governmental influences as taxation and legislation peculiar to the industry, and technological aspects of the
industry.

Given satisfactory completion of these two surveys, the organization's future performance may now be projected. It is
usually best to project performance in the first instance on the
basis of no major changes in company policy, strategies and activities. The projected performance is now compared with the
required performance and, almost inevitably, there will be a
performance gap. Analysis of the reasons for this gap and the
preparation of strategies to reduce it represent a major task.
Finally, it is the responsibility of the top management of the
organization to select the most appropriate strategies from
the various alternatives prepared by the senior managers with
assistance from the corporate planners.

INFORMATION NEEDS FOR PLANNING AND CONTROL

Figure 18.2 illustrates the major categories of information needed
for planning and control. It will be noted that planning and
control need much more than purely accounting information,
even though this is, of course, of fundamental importance.

Internal Information

All organizations will possess some internal historical information, and this usually provides a major input for planning. Unfortunately we find all too often that the information systems
have developed piecemeal, and that records lack compatibility,
e.g. the warehouse may have kept bin cards for the last ten
years but sales have only preserved their monthly returns for
the last three years. Even the information provided by accountants, usually the most systematic and comprehensible of any
information category, may not be in the most appropriate
form for corporate-planning purposes. The introduction of
corporate planning may, in such an organization, have to rest
in the first phase of development on a somewhat untidy information system, but after a few cycles of the corporate-
planning process, and certainly within a space of five years,
the organization should have developed an efficient information system.

In general, internal information is used in planning only to
project historical trends. However, as mentioned earlier, there
is a second planning use — what we might call planning from
first principles. For example, we might attempt to estimate
the resources used in developing our own transport fleet from
an investigation of the basic system characteristics such as demand pattern by time and by location, average vehicle speed,
drop-times and so on. Clearly this type of planning takes us
immediately into the sphere of model-building.

Figure 18.2 indicates the major categories of information for
control purposes. For the majority of organizations that introduce corporate planning, after having established business planning and a sound budgetary system, their existing financial and
accounting control procedures provide a basis requiring only a
degree of modification rather than radical revision. As regards
non-accounting information, the systems designer should advise
the line managers concerned as to the most appropriate forms
of analysis and presentation: for example, for corporate control
purposes it may be appropriate that the marketing director
should receive monthly reports of the market shares of the
leading products and their main competitors shown in tabular
and in graphical form. In general for non-accounting information, both for planning and control purposes, it is extremely

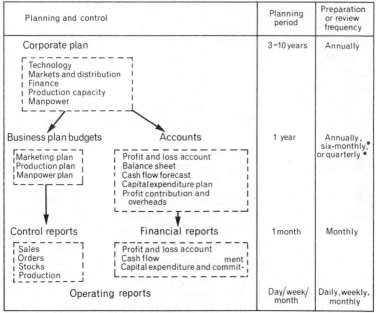

Planning and control	Planning period	Preparation or review frequency
Corporate plan	3–10 years	Annually
Technology Markets and distribution Finance Production capacity Manpower		
Business plan budgets **Accounts**	1 year	Annually, six-monthly,* or quarterly *
Marketing plan Production plan Manpower plan	Profit and loss account Balance sheet Cash flow forecast Capital expenditure plan Profit contribution and overheads	
Control reports **Financial reports**	1 month	Monthly
Sales Orders Stocks Production	Profit and loss account Cash flow ment Capital expenditure and commit-	
Operating reports	Day/week/ month	Daily, weekly, monthly

* Many organizations prefer to maintain the business plan for
the year and to revise the forecasts periodically.

Figure 18.2   Information categories for planning and control.

important that the information system is designed to suit the
organization and its managers; any tendency to impose a pro-
duction-line information system supposedly designed to encompass a range of different industries, markets and technologies
should be resisted.

Information on the Environment

As has already been indicated, at corporate-planning level
environmental information needs are manifest – behaviour of
the national economy, taxation, performance of major competitors, technology, and so on. The information system must
accumulate relevant information historically and be sensitive
to the current environment.

We will, therefore, require an information system that embraces a variety of sources and sensors ranging from Government statistics to what the chairman overheard at a club dinner,

and including critical studies of the annual reports of competitors. Information provided by the various inter-firm con-
parison studies is often very helpful.[1]

At tactical planning levels organizations acquire considerable
information, particularly on the marketing side, through direct
observation and contact, e.g. through salesmen. In addition it
would be naïve to minimize the information provided by
recruitment of staff from competitors, not least in technological
fields.

In general most organizations accept, perhaps too compla-
cently in many cases, a considerable degree of heterogeneity
and even haphazardness in their environmental information.
More effort could invariably be made, to the organization's
benefit, on identifying the key information categories, establishing on a routine monitoring basis those information sub-systems
for which this is feasible and necessary, and ensuring, as far as
possible, that information on the more significant chance events
is disseminated speedily to the people who are most likely to
need it. A well-designed marketing information sub-system[2] is
almost certain to pay off both at strategic and tactical levels,
and an increasing number of organizations require a technological/
research and development information sub-system for strategic
planning. In both fields forecasting requirements will influence
the information system's design.

Information and Models

At the beginning of the chapter it was pointed out that a
management information system is, or should be, the result of
a number of organizational requirements and influences; in that
sense it is itself a sub-system of a larger organizational/environ-
mental system. Ackoff[3] refers to a management information system as a sub-system of 'what might be called the *management
system*'. Clearly the more we understand the operation of the
management system, the better will be the design of the information system. The management sciences attempt to improve our
understanding of management systems by modelling those systems, in order to explain the behaviour of a given system and
to make predictions of future behaviour. Incidentally, it is
perhaps worth noting that, in planning, management scientists
provide two types of forecast, as follows:

1   Purely statistical forecasts that passively extrapolate into
       the future historical and current trends.
2   Forecasts or predictions based on explanatory models of
       the appropriate systems.

Our concern here is with the role of the management scientist
as corporate model-builder.[4] Few organizations would yet claim
to have adequately modelled their whole operations and structure, although increasingly particular areas of operation are
being successfully modelled.[5] Management scientists are well
aware of the needs for various types of information throughout
the modelling process. The building of a model creates information needs that organizations are frequently incapable of satisfying from their routine records and reports. Clearly if we model
a complete area of the business, such as the distribution system
or the sales-force operation, then we would almost always
expect this to produce significant changes in the information
system for that area; in many cases, the impact on the routine
information system has been considerable. In addition, the
model creates well-defined information requirements, of a
more one-off type, which have to be satisfied not only by
accountants and the appropriate line people but by such other
management-services people as market researchers, O. and M.
and work-study men, and industrial engineers. Figure 18.3 indicates the relations in simple terms for the area of marketing.

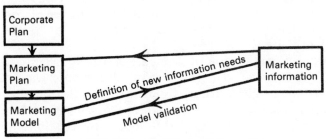

Figure 18.3   Plans, models and information.

Computer Packages for Corporate Planning

Simulation models may be designed for batch-processing or for
remote terminal use. Optimization models, in particular large
linear programming models of resource-allocation problems, are
usually run on batch-processing machines. In the last five years
or so a large number of computer packages have been designed

as aids to planning. They are particularly concerned with the following:

1 Projection of current performance
2 Selection of strategies
3 Allocation of resources.

Their use provides speed, accuracy appropriate to the level of planning, and a facility that enables both planners and decision-takers to examine the sensitivity of various possible decisions to changes in the values of variables and of assumptions. For example, a package would give a quick and appropriately accurate reply to a question such as 'What will happen to the profit contribution of product X if its sales decline by 2 per cent in year 2 instead of increasing 4 per cent?' Since the development of packages unites the accumulated total experience of many corporate planners, management scientists, systems analysts and programmers, and managers, their adoption by an organization can save considerable time, effort and cost. For example, Gershefski[6] found from a survey of 323 American organizations that the average time required to develop a working corporate model was $3\frac{1}{2}$ man-years, of which roughly 40 per cent was spent on developing the computer program. Furthermore some packages provide a psychological bonus in that they permit executives to communicate directly with the computer model by means of high-level language, which they can comprehend fairly readily. More detailed information on the use of computer models and systems in practice may be found in references 7 and 8 (p. 309).

Various classifications of such packages exist. One such[9] distinguishes between *computer models* and *computer modelling systems,* the former category would include inflexible single-purpose models, e.g. for investment analysis, while the latter category would require the user to specify the relations of his model and would include simple financial report generators. Figure 18.4 gives examples of three types of package.

Accuracy and Value of Information

Planners and management scientists recognize various types of inaccuracy in information, including errors of recording at data-base level, e.g. an incorrect invoice; processing errors, particu-

System	Gpos	Foresight	Capri
Company	On line decisions incorporated.	TSL Cybernet Services Computer Cooperatives.	METRA
Classification of system	Modelling system.	Financial report generator.	Computer model Inflexible.
Mode of use	On line or batch from Atkins and Cybernet Services.	On line or batch.	Batch CDC 6600 machine.
Forecasting and data analysis	Integrated into the system. Uses extensive methods such as multiple regression, exponential smoothing, time series, growth.	Simple forecasts built into the model by user as growth rates.	Forecasts input into the model.
Model building	Built by the user in Extended Fortran, with integrated subroutines. Number of time periods specified by user.	Consists of a high level language that defines row and col. relations of output report. Up to 20 time periods available.	Structured model used to optimize the best investment plan. Projects of up to 20 years permitted.
Structured investment techniques	NPV DCF ROI D/E analysis Capital expenditure.	DCF NPV	DCF Net Assets
MODEL ANALYSIS Reports	Specified by user. Up to 200 lines.	Defined in model by user. Up to 200 lines.	None
Consolidation	Yes	Yes	No
Sensitivity analysis	Backward and forward iteration. Excellent facilities.	Excellent facilities.	Only by re-running model.
Risk analysis	No	No	No

Figure 18.4   Computer packages for corporate planning (continued
on p. 308)

System	Gpos	Foresight	Capri
Plotting	Graphs Histograms	No	No
Optimization	Functional by iteration.	No	Main objective
APPLICATIONS	Multi-purpose corporate use.	Reports for budgeting.	Capital investment

Figure 18.4 (cont.)   Computer packages for corporate planning.

larly in manual or semi-automated systems; basic measurement errors, e.g. in timing a job; inaccuracies due to the aggregation assumptions; sampling errors, e.g. in inspection schemes or market research surveys; and errors in future estimates due to uncertainty. Clearly errors in the first three categories can usually be neglected for corporate planning and control purposes, as can aggregation inaccuracies in a sensibly designed, properly operated system. The statistical treatment of errors in market research is well-known: the greater the sample size the higher the degree of accuracy (for a sample size n, the error is proportional to $1/\sqrt{n}$). Forecasting errors may be evaluated statistically by standard techniques.

When we try to estimate the effects of uncertainty, we find the computer model invaluable. Management scientists developed the technique of sensitivity analysis[10] with respect to specific models and techniques (the best known is linear programming) well over a decade ago and the approach is now also used more broadly, as just indicated in the section on computer packages. The 'What if?' simulation technique allows us to compute the impact of possible errors due to uncertainty and to other causes.

In general we can usually obtain better information at greater cost, and we must always attempt to establish the value of improved information in terms of the effect on the quality of our decisions. For example, how much better will be our marketing strategy for a new product if we test market in two regions rather than one? Our thinking on such questions is frequently illuminated by the use of decision trees and Bayesian arguments.

REFERENCES

1 For a review of the area see Higgins, J. C. and Jackson, K. C. 'Essential Criteria for Valid Inter-Firm Comparisons', *Management Accounting,* June 1973.

2 For a sensible realistic account see Cox, D. F. and Good, R.E. 'How to Build a Marketing Information System', *Harvard Business Review,* May–June 1967.

3 Ackoff, R. L. *A Concept of Corporate Planning* (Wiley Interscience, 1970).

4 A number of aspects of the role of the management scientist in corporate planning are discussed in Higgins, J. C. 'Corporate Planning and Management Science', *Journal of Business Policy,* Spring 1972.

5 See, for example, Schrieber, A. N. (ed.). *Corporate Simulation Models* (University of Washington, 1970).

6 Gershefski, G. W. 'Corporate Models – the State of the Art', *Management Science,* 1970, 16, no. 6.

7 Wagle, B. V. and Jenkins, P. M. *The Development of a General Computer System to Aid the Corporate Planning Process,* IBM Report UKSC-0024, October 1971.

8 Grinyer, P. H. and Batt, C. D. 'Some Tentative Findings on Corporate Financial Simulation Models', *Operational Research Quarterly,* March 1974, vol. 25, no. 1.

9 Higgins, J. C. and Whitaker, D. 'Computer Aids to Corporate Planning', *Computer Bulletin,* September 1972.

10 Higgins, J. C. 'Accuracy and Value of Information for Planning and Control', *Long Range Planning,* August 1974.

19 Practical Problems in Corporate Planning: I Batchelors Foods

A. J. Goodall

One might define corporate planning as *making strategic decisions concerning the type of business to be entered into or
abandoned, allocating resources between new and old business,
growing through external acquisition or internal development,and
seeing to the direction of basic and applied research.* This definition closely describes the principles that have transformed, over
a period of twenty years, Batchelors Peas Limited from a virtually
one-product one-technology operation into the multi-product
multi-technology company represented today by Batchelors
Foods Limited.

It will be seen that the change of name is a significant point
in the progress of the company, for it was in 1953, as tin-plate
was freed from the restrictions of postwar rationing and conditions in the canning industry instantly became more competitive,
that Batchelors, in a study of the future working environment,
decided that their business rested not in canning alone, but in
the total processed-food market. This recognition of the future
was manifested in the change of name to Batchelors Foods
Limited.

The fact that Batchelors undertook the fundamental environment, strengths and weaknesses assessment twenty years ago
indicates perhaps that successful businesses were applying some
of the principles of corporate planning long before the term
came into common use, and supports the contention that corporate planning is but the application of logical process and for-
malization to older style acumen in a way that eases the evalua-

tion of options and the formulation of strategy in an increasingly complex situation.

Batchelors corporate planning has evolved from a simple base to a more systemized process today (see Figure 19.1), and the evolution continues. In this chapter some of the lessons learned by Batchelors in developing corporate planning over the years are set out. Whereas our early planning was without a specific horizon, we now work to a five-year term, which was chosen as a reasonable limit in the present stage of forecasting techniques in our type of business.

It is a point worth making early in this chapter that one of the lessons that was learned in this change of the corporate image, was that the execution of any plan depends on people. In preparing for the changes that may come from a determined execution of a corporate plan considerable attention must be paid to the problems of adapting personnel to consequent new circumstances in technologies, products, administrative procedures and markets. A salesman or a factory manager who has handled only one product group for years requires a lot of help in reorientating his thinking. If it is accepted that personnel are one of the resources of a business, then reallocating this resource effectively between the old and the new business is one of the skills of management implicit in introducing a corporate plan.

ASSESSING THE WORKING ENVIRONMENT

That a corporate-planning procedure starts with an assessment of the working environment for the company is well understood, and demonstrated in our initial approach, but there is a risk that the emphasis may fall so strongly on marketing factors that the true requirement to take every section of the business into account may be weakened. It is stressed, therefore, in our procedure that it is the working environment for all operations with which we must be concerned. It is indeed the backing for a *corporate* plan.

Our initial assessments were indeed very much marketing-orientated, but at that time the working environment was less complex than it is today. Now we attempt to undertake a comprehensive survey of all the changes in the working environment that can affect the operation of our business. Our experience is that this is a continuous monitoring process rather than a once-

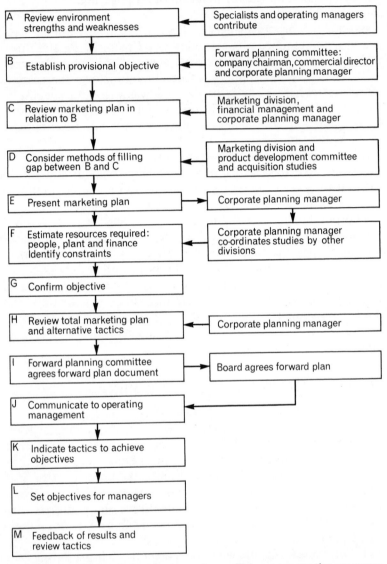

Figure 19.1   Forward planning procedures. This represents the processes for forward planning at Batchelors Foods Limited in an idealized form; in practice the procedure is less formal, i.e. the Forward Planning Committee is more a discussion group of appropriate members built around the nucleus shown as required.

only exercise, particularly in the present economic and legislative climate.

To aid our thinking we approach the problem under five broad headings:

1 Economic factors
2 Social changes
3 Industrial, trade and competitive changes
4 Technological changes
5 Political and legislative influences.

Obviously there is no hard and fast boundary between these groupings, for one is very much linked with another, but they represent a convenient systematic checklist. The input to this study comes now from both operating management and specialists, coordinated and stimulated in the study by the corporate-planning manager. The economic factors of interest are those that provide some parameter for assessing growth potential, including constraints, e.g. G.D.P. growth, consumer expenditure, personal disposable income, savings ratios, credit. We are equally interested in projections of construction costs, wages and salary movements.

Economic Factors

Economic changes at national level may not be completely reflected locally. Considerable importance is attached, therefore, to assessing changes in regional situations that can affect our business, particularly our factories, where labour availability, industrial relations, and movements may differ significantly from the national pattern.

Regional planning policies may well be seen to have a long-term effect upon the continued success of operations, e.g. by altering the direction of labour flow through new-town developments or changed communications. We have had a true example of this assessment of regional changes, leading to a decision to close a factory and redeploy the production, largely on the grounds that the original location would suffer in the long term from the siphoning of labour from the area to a major town expansion that had previously lost exported labour to our factory district.

As we are large-scale importers of raw materials, it is not sufficient to monitor the economic movements in the United Kingdom alone. We have also to build in awareness of the changes in the exporting countries and in world markets that may affect price, quality and availability. The changes consequent upon the accession of the United Kingdom to the E.E.C. have given added point to this section of our economic environmental study. For instance, the effects of the E.E.C. upon agricultural economics in the United Kingdom are typical new factors that we have had to add to our appraisal.

Social Changes

Closely linked with the economic factors are those under the social grouping, where changes in the age structure of the population, the raising of the school-leaving age, and the lowering of the age for marriage and family rearing may all affect both labour availability in factory and office and the pattern of markets. Again importance is attached to watching both local and national trends. Recruitment of a female labour force in an overspill area where the entering population is young presents very different problems from recruitment in a stabilized area. In reviewing this situation in depth we examine such factors as the age distribution recorded in the national census for the locality, the activity rates for women, and general information that will help us build up a picture of the sociology of our factory catchment area.

We want to know how people will spend, and whether there are possible changes in the spending power of sectors of the population arising, for example, from new social policies in pensions or other allowances. We are in fact interested in a wide variety of social factors, of which those mentioned are but examples of the type of information we can use in evaluating consumer change.

Social changes affect the choice of job that people will accept, while changes in business method require new skills. Both factors are reflected in the ratio of operators to staff, which has to be recognized in organizational structures, office accommodation and cost ratios.

Industrial, Trade and Competitive Changes

In an inflationary era the economic environment has become even more significant than it was when Batchelors first set out upon the planning associated with the strategy of product diversification, but paramount importance still remains in the ability to appreciate and interpret the trends of change in the structure of the trade through which we sell goods. It is almost as important that we should observe and understand the changes in the industry of which we are part and that largely forms our competition.

In our planning experience we have seen, and taken account of, the massive changes in the structure of the retail and distributive trades as independent shops and wholesalers have fallen in number with the growth of self-service, supermarkets, discount stores, cash-and-carry, and now possibly hypermarkets as a major development. The whole area of distribution requires monitoring for such factors as trends in method, central warehousing versus branch delivery, changes in the national road system or vehicle type, and the influence of the E.E.C. These are typical factors that we build into our environmental assessment.

As the trade structure has changed, so has the shape of the industry through mergers and takeovers, which have presented competitors of considerable resources in place of fragmentation. Our environment study, therefore, contains a series of competitor profiles that we may use later in building a strategy based upon an analysis of the company strengths and weaknesses.

Technological Changes

The food industry now has a strong technological base. There has been substantial progress in the last decade, particularly in processes for structured foods. Our task is to build into the picture of the working environment the likely effects of the technological advances against a time scale and in relation to our assessment of our competitors' abilities, i.e. their technical profiles. Delphi techniques have been used during these assessments.

Political and Legislative Influences

The last broad heading, political and legislative influences, has spread considerably throughout the number of sectors to be studied since we initiated our planning sequences. All the following have some effect upon the business:

E.E.C. regulations, tariffs, levies, quotas etc.

E.E.C. transport regulations
Food composition and labelling
Industrial Relations legislation
Factories Act revisions
Pollution control
Fair trading.

In addition it is necessary to take some account of the activities and potential success of pressure groups.

In this review of the areas of study for an assessment of the working environment, we use as a backing to our interpretation of the figures an accumulated bank of data relating to the past. We acknowledge, however, that in a time of very many fundamental changes, such as entry into the E.E.C., there is a need for great caution in drawing too heavily upon trends.

It will be clear that carrying out this survey adequately requires a concerted effort, both from specialists and operating management, but it serves the purpose also of bringing a wide range of people into the corporate-planning cycle at an early stage. Companies that do not have the supporting services of appropriate specialists will find that a number of consultants exist in this field to give equivalent supplementation of the input from operating management.

STRENGTHS AND WEAKNESSES ANALYSIS

In its early planning Bathelors identified its weakness as a fragmented product market in which it held no significant advantage over the competition. Its strength rested in the opportunity to develop in a wider market, by means of the internationally acquired expertise and the resources of Unilever, of which it had become a subsidiary during the war. From this realization stemmed the strategy of rationalization and diversification that is represented in the company today. The significant difference in the process then and now is that responsibility for making the strengths and weaknesses analysis initially rests much lower down the organization than in those early days.

We believe that in looking at products and markets the analysis starts now with Brand Management, whose members produce a basic discussion document covering the prospects and strategic options, including possible constraints, which they can see for their product group, taking account of the working environment that has been depicted for their area of operation. Similarly other operating managers will feed in their assessments of the future of their operations, preferably with some quantification of the probability of achieving certain levels of performance.

The objective of this analysis is to provide a clear knowledge of the assets that may be exploited and the problems and constraints that require resolution or recognition in the final strategic plan. It is worth stressing again that strengths and weaknesses analysis is a total company operation, not merely a marketing tool; it is as important to know that a production weakness is, say, growing competition for labour as it is to know that sales of a brand are subject to increasing competition.

OBJECTIVE

The success of a company depends on a complex of related factors. As in any company, we have an obligation to give our shareholder, in our case our parent company, the financial performance that is required to maintain its investment and faith in us, but this performance cannot be achieved without generating the goodwill of the trade, the consumer, employees and suppliers.

In compiling our first formal plan we set out not only our objective in terms of our position in the industry, but also a list of contributing secondary objectives without which our main purpose could not be fulfilled. In quantifying our primary objective as a target we have to take into account the fact that although we rely upon central funding, we have to think of ourselves as competing for finance to a degree similar to that of any public company.

We are concerned, therefore, in quantifying our financial objective to consider both return upon capital employed and cash flow, in association with a target increase in the significance of the company in the total processed-food market, assessed from the results of an analysis of competitor growth rates, and our interpretation of changes in the purchasing mechanisms of the trade and the consumer built up from our survey of the working environment. For the purpose of quantifying the development effort required from the various sections of the business to support this growth we translate this into a phased turnover target.

MARKETING PLAN

It is the responsibility of marketing management to produce a
preliminary marketing strategy based upon the strengths and
weaknesses of existing product groups.

This preliminary strategy is issued for comment by other
operating management with reference to feasibility in terms of
resources and confirmation of the meeting of the financial
criteria expressed in the objective. If there is seen to be a gap
in the achievement of the financial target, we re-examine the
tactics, including the time scale of development projects to
effect the necessary improvement. At this stage it is a conjoint
exercise by all operating sectors as an ongoing routine. This
again illustrates how, over the years, the corporate-planning
exercise has moved down to include operating management,
in providing the input and setting out possible alternative strategies for evaluation.

RESOURCE PLANNING

Reference has been made already to the depth study of factors
affecting labour availability to our factories, so that there is an
estimate for each unit of the maximum strength that it should
reasonably be able to maintain or build to over the planning
period. The practicability of phasing recruitment satisfactorily in relation to the production demand has to be
confirmed.

The marketing plan, evaluated in terms of the additional
categories of labour and staff required, is expressed in a schedule,
by department or operational division, ranging from factory
operators through salesmen to senior management. The demand
upon plant and buildings, both administrative and production,
is evaluated either in absolute terms for known developments
or by the use of ratios for less well defined projects expected
to come from development to national launch within the planning
period. Raw material requirements are interpreted, feasibility
of supply or constraints being identified.

When these evaluations have been completed, we are able to
start working out financial implications of the marketing plan
in relation to the objective.

FINANCIAL PLAN

The emphasis throughout this case study has been upon the input to the plan from operating management. There has been no question of a superimposed plan upon an unwilling management team.

It has been stressed that over the years we have moved to our present form of planning from a situation where the strategic thinking, as we would now term it, was done at the top alone with little bottom-up input. However, at the financial-plan stage the options and alternatives of shaping the total company strategy become the responsibility of the board, and ultimately that of the chairman. It is for the chairman and his board to decide in the light of all the evidence provided by the analysis of alternative strategies, and against the background of the working environment, the policy that will be pursued and the tactics to be employed, the degree to which development shall be from internal or external sources, and the direction of basic or applied research.

COMMUNICATION TO MANAGEMENT

Many members of the management team will have contributed to the input, but for implementation there must be a clear understanding of those parts of the plan that are to be their responsibility. Without that understanding the inter-working relations necessary to the attainment of our objective would not be achieved.

There are sections of the plan that remain the confidential and direct responsibility of the board. They may deal with external relations, as in acquisitions, or perhaps such highly emotive issues as redeployment, which require special timing for successful communication. The communication to management, therefore, is principally an action section relating to the strategies for existing business, and growth through internal development.

It is our practice to hold a management meeting at which the chairman, supported by appropriate board members, and the corporate-planning manager present the plan and review the background against which it has been formulated. They identify possible dangers of constraints and summarize the tactics to be employed.

Through a system of annual work plans for each manager in
the business it is possible to incorporate responsibilities for
actions required for implementation of the plan, and for the
board members to review progress with their managers. The
responsibility for implementing the plan through profit-
improvement programmes and similar measures is a corporate
duty of the board, using the services within the business to
provide the information that is appropriate to monitoring progress, but with the corporate-planning manager playing a major
role in continuously reviewing potential alternative strategies
independently from the operating divisions as an objective challenge to their proposals.

A completely new five-year planning cycle is set in motion
in alternate years; a review document, or a short-form plan,
is prepared in the intermediate years and rolls the plan forward
a year. This review takes account of changes that have occurred
in factors affecting the company over the previous twelve
months, and identifies new opportunities and problems.

Our corporate-planning process continues to evolve, not least
from the constructive comments contributed by managers at
divisional meetings taken by the corporate-planning manager at
the conclusion of each planning cycle for the purpose of reviewing the procedure and answering points of detail on the plan. It
is certainly our experience that a corporate plan is not a document to prepare once and follow slavishly. There must be constant review to take account of changes in the working environment and competitors' evolving strategies, for they may
fundamentally affect our own, despite all our attempts to understand their philosophies by evolving the competitor profiles.

After two decades of planning we can see with hindsight some
of the mistakes we have made. They came usually where hunches
were allowed to overrule logic, or where an analysis was not made
in sufficient depth.

We have entered and abandoned markets and rationalized our
canning activities to that sector where we are brand leader. We
have generated new business from internal development, while
acquisitions have represented external development. Certainly
we are a more diversified company than we were twenty years
ago, and significantly more profitable. This has been achieved
not by a definite decision to introduce corporate planning at
any point of time, but as the result of applying system and logic

to our thinking ever increasingly, and bringing the management team into the formulation of our strategy.

What we now do we acknowledge as corporate planning, but would stress once again that it all adds up to good sound business sense to support the inborn abilities of the management team by the use of logical processes, and the developing techniques of mathematical models for the evaluation of strategies as the number of options increases.

20 Practical Problems in Corporate Planning: II John Laing

F. H. Stokes

HISTORICAL FACTORS

In the early years of the century, after some sixty years as a
local builder in the North West, John Laing & Son found themselves in serious trouble with a contract that had gone wrong
and legal claims for damages to abutting properties which, if
successful, would bankrupt the partnership. Throughout the
long anxious period the young head of the firm was deeply
conscious of the other people who would be seriously affected
if he 'went under' — the staff and work force, many of them
long-serving employees, who were dependent for their livelihood
on the continuation of the firm; the customers whose projects
were unfinished, the suppliers to whom money was owed; and
the people who had provided the risk capital.

When the verdict went in his favour, John Laing, being a
deeply religious man, first thanked his Maker and then got down
to evolving a policy that would protect, as far as possible, those
other people who depended on or were creditors of the
firm. He resolved that henceforward his profits must be split
three ways — one-third for the taxman and those who had provided the funds, one-third for investment within the business,
and one-third for investment outside the business in a form
that could be realized to give protection against a future catas-
trophe similar to the one from which he had escaped so nar-
rowly.

At the same time he recognized that there were three groups

who must be satisfied and protected. They were his customers, his work force and the people who provided the capital and the credit. All three were essential to his business, for the dissatisfaction of any one group would spell the beginning of the end.

These thoughts were recorded as the guiding policy of the firm some sixty years ago. Changing times and conditions have required some adjustments to the details, but the principles remained to guide the planners when formal corporate planning was introduced in 1963.

By this time the small local building company had come a long way. It was one of the few 'national' contractors and, although turnovers were not then published, thought to be the second largest contracting firm in Britain. In addition it had its Property Development Division working in the Commercial sector, mainly but not entirely in the South East; a small 'Homes' Division developing estates and building houses for sale, and a Building Products Manufacturing Division. These were supported by a Property Investment Division, which managed a portfolio of properties valued at nearly £20M.

PLANNING CONSTRAINTS

The company had 'gone public' some ten years before, with family interests and charitable trusts holding sufficient shares to cause it to be a 'closed company' when that classification was established. While giving a considerable degree of security against the threat of takeover, this form of shareholding (particularly the charitable trusts) places a heavy responsibility on management to ensure a regular and increasing flow of dividends. In consequence there is a restriction on the adoption of strategies that might impair or intercept this flow − in other words, there is a constraint on the amount of risk that may be undertaken. In addition, if the security from takeover threat is to be maintained by the predominance of family and family-controlled shareholdings, the advantage of being able to buy other companies with one's own shares must be forgone. Again the means by which additional capital may be raised are restricted; as charitable and other trusts rarely have cash, the raising of additional capital by means of rights issues is almost excluded as an acceptable financial strategy.

Since external additional equity capital is almost ruled out, the only remaining sources of capital are fixed-interest borrowings, both long- and short-term. However, the permissible extent of borrowing, without incurring higher interest charges, is related to the amount of equity capital. In consequence the ploughing back of a high proportion of earnings, and indeed the maintenance of a high level of earnings, is of great importance if the company is to have enough growth to be attractive to and provide career opportunities for its staff. The experience of several years of planning has repeatedly demonstrated how important an understanding of the constraints imposed by the financial structure of the company and its shareholdings can be in limiting the acceptability of possible strategies.

THE SITUATION AT THE START OF PLANNING

Shortly before formal corporate planning was introduced, the company had decided to extend its manufacturing activities. Its main subsidiary, Thermalite, which manufactures and markets aerated concrete blocks with high thermal qualities, had gone through a long period of 'probation' before the market had accepted its products. This period had ended about 1960, and the expansion of the housing market found Thermalite short of capacity. A very large expansion programme was decided upon, and by 1963 capacity had expanded nearly fourfold.

The Government housing programme had, in fact, found the whole industry short of capacity, and the large contractors particularly were put under heavy pressure to provide facilities for continental-style industrialized building. Laing built three large factories to manufacture units for the construction of the Jespersen system. A new type of synthetic lightweight aggregate, invented in the company's research department, had begun to gain market acceptance and a new programme of expansion was put in hand.

Laings had recently acquired the business of Holloway Bros, contractors and property developers, with a number of subcontractor activities, but this business was by no means integrated into the Laing operations. The opportunity to acquire had come because Holloways had a poor recent record of profitability, and much needed to be done to make the new investment realize its potential.

The normal contracting business, too, was expanding rapidly.

It had, in fact, increased its turnover by nearly 70 per cent in three years.

Profits were at record levels when, in 1962, the board decided that, with the business expanding so rapidly, corporate planning was necessary if the wave of success was to be successfully ridden. A very small department was set up to undertake the task.

START-UP PROBLEMS

This department was faced with the difficulty that there was very little published work on corporate planning, and what there was referred to American practice in manufacturing companies. Laings were neither American nor primarily a manufacturing company, but there seemed no alternative to using the results of this experience as a basis for future innovations. Laings became members of the Long Range Planning Group of the Stanford Research Institute, and made the greatest possible use of the experience of the men there. In consequence the early efforts followed closely the methods advocated by Ansoff in his early writings.

The first task was to determine the group's objectives. The work and unpublished writings of Mr (later Sir John) Laing after his early experience provided the philosophy and the qualitative objectives. After much discussion it was decided that, for the first run through, quantitative objectives were not essential — a view that appears to have been sound. As experience comes, the quantitative forms of the objectives become increasingly necessary, but it does seem much more important to find out what the problems of the company really are than to debate whether the growth-rate objective should be 15 per cent or 20 per cent.

The divisions were given an objective of a return on capital of 20 per cent (a number picked at random), and were asked to prepare their plans for a five-year development period based on the assumption that they would be allowed to plough back all their after-tax profits. It was assumed, implicitly but not explicitly, that the net rental income from the property-investment portfolio would provide the dividend.

The results were astonishing. It seemed that not only did distance lend enchantment to the view but that all the divisional managers were wearing rose-coloured spectacles as well. Without

exception they expected their current problems to be solved
and no more to take their place.

Perhaps fortunately this state of euphoria did not persist very
long. The new Thermalite factories found difficulty in selling
their greatly increased output, a change of Government caused
a change of attitude to the desirability of industrialized housing,
the new acquisitions were becoming less rather than more profitable, and there were overvaluations in many of the contracting
activities. The profits had virtually disappeared – the outward
cash flows from the new investments had no profits to offset
them and the company's liquidity was declining rapidly. A
second round of the planning cycle, while still optimistic, suggested where the problems might lie and what needed to be
done to put things right.

EARLY RESULTS FROM PLANNING

Firstly, it became apparent that the traditional break-even graph
did not apply to contracting activities. These are highly dependent on the efficiency of middle management – the project
managers and their staff. Over-rapid expansion could easily
result in these men being overstretched without necessarily
appearing to be so, with the result that the very narrow profit
margin, traditional to the industry, could soon turn to a loss.
It was apparent that an upward limit of growth must be determined and a rigorous control on turnover established. This was
not the only control inadequacy; financial control through budgets was insufficient and needed the addition of short-term
planning to supplement it.

But the greatest shortcoming was undoubtedly the inability
to forecast the likely sequence of events, particularly the trends
in the markets the group served. This had been shown up
especially in the overoptimistic five-year plans and the over-
confidence they engendered in management.

The early and persistent failures of the national five-year
plans (on which the control of the economy depended) in Eastern
Europe was acknowledged to be caused by the planners' inability
to forecast. There seems little doubt that the period and degree
of detail in plans must be closely related to the level of accuracy
of forecasts.

It appeared to Laings that it was unreasonable to expect the men who managed the divisions, branches and regions to have the level of market-forecasting skill that planning demanded. Forecasting must be done centrally and fed from the centre to the operating units.

It appeared, too, that the traditional 'five-year plan' had no particular logic. It was considered that planning fell into two sectors — long-term or strategic, and short-term or tactical. Furthermore, if a plan is defined as being a statement of intention to take action, then the long-term strategic document was not strictly a 'plan' at all. Indeed, if the use of long-term plans suggested that decisions should be taken unnecessarily early, before the maximum and latest information was available, these 'plans' would defeat the object for which they had been prepared.

THE REVISED PROCEDURE

Laings reached the conclusion that there was no standard period for which plans should be prepared. In the contracting field, with most projects lasting less than two years, accurate forecasting beyond this period was impossible and, except in a most general way, undesirable. In the property-development field the period of the project was longer, and here a four- or five-year plan may have been more appropriate. In the manufacturing field very long term trend forecasts were possible, but detailed forecasts of much more than two years seemed unrealistic.

It was decided to abandon the five-year planning, substituting a long-term (ten to fifteen year) strategic review that would serve as the basis of change in company policy and a short-term operational plan for converting policy into action. This second document would also provide the principal basis for exercising control on the operating units.

The long-term strategic review is prepared in the Central Planning Department; members of its staff consult operating units and external agencies but the responsibility for its preparation and presentation to the chief executive is wholly theirs. The chief executive uses this document as the basis of his recommendations to the board for their decisions on policy changes, which must be conveyed to the operating units in time for the annual updating of their short-term action plans. (See Figure 20.1.)

	Divisions	Corporate Planning Department	Chief Executive	Board
JAN	Instructions to departments on implementation of Year 1 S.T. plan	Review of strategic market forecasts	Appraisal of group and divisional performance against plan and targets and need for change	
FEB				
MAR	Proposals for revisions to Year 1 S.T. plan and targets	Proposals for revisions to Year 1 S.T. plan and targets and special assignments		Agreement of S.T. plan and target change
APR	Departments prepare outine S.T. plan proposals for Year 2			
MAY	Proposals for revisions to Year 1 S.T. plan and targets	Proposals for revisions for Year 1 S.T. plans and targets	Proposals for strategic change	
JUNE		Preliminary work on S.T. plan for Year 2	Preparation of proposals for strategic change	Agreement of strategic and S.T. plan and target changes
JULY	Preparation of S.T. plan for Year 2	Implications of and plans for agreed strategic change		
AUG	Proposals for revisions to Year 1 S.T. plan and targets	Proposals for revisions to Year 1 S.T. plans and targets	Appraisal of group and divisional performance against plan and targets and need for change	
SEPT	Consultation with Corporate Planning department on revisions to S.T. plan required on consolidation			Agreement of S.T. plan and target changes
OCT		Preparation of Year 2 short term plan and divisional target proposals	Proposals for short term plan Year 2	
NOV	Discussions with departments on implementation of revised plan			Agreement of S.T. plan and targets Year 2
DEC		Discussions on implementation of S.T. plan as agreed		

THE SHORT-TERM PLAN

The short-term plans for operations are prepared by the individual units. These units are supplied with a list of mandatory assumptions whose main purpose is to ensure that all units are planning on the same basis in regard to world and national political and economic movements. The units are also supplied with optional assumptions (which they can discard) on trends in the construction industry and its main sectors. If these assumptions are not adopted, the operating unit is required to state why it has taken this action.

The units are supplied with information on agreed changes in group policy that might affect their activities, and an indication of the level of funds that will be available to them. Their objectives provide them with information on what they are expected to achieve. They must state what assumptions they have made in their plans, particularly how they expect their particular markets to behave; the availability and cost of labour, staff and raw materials; the operations of their competitors; and any other unknown factors that require to be forecast.

Units are responsible for strategic decisions affecting their own operations, subject to check and approval by superior authorities. A statement of strategic policy is included as a reminder, and to ensure that others who will see the plan are aware of changes.

The main part of the plan is the schedule of 'action to be taken'. Each item states what change of action is intended, its purpose, what resources (financial and other) are required, the expected return, who will be responsible for its implementation, and when it is to be done. Only items to be started in the next twelve months are included, but a separate schedule of ongoing special projects is given.

The financial effects of all these operations, existing and new, are brought together into a budget, which is prepared by quarters for the following year and as a whole for a second year. while changes in financial-resource requirements are given for a third year. The second year is included to allow provisional resource planning to be carried out in good time for the next cycle, while the financial needs of the third year supply an 'early warning' device.

The results are compared with the plan quarterly, and changes
to the plan, as a result of unforeseen events and problems, are
proposed at the quarterly review meetings. The effect of these
changes on the resource requirements for the following year
are also recorded and the availability checked.

THE STRATEGIC REVIEW

Any long-term forecast must be based on forecasts of the trends
in the national and international scene, and the Laing strategic
review conforms to this in that it uses a general economic model
to forecast fixed capital formation, of which construction forms
the bulk. This national forecast provides both a 'background'
and 'field of play' to which trends within the industry must be
related and have their limits of possibility shown.

The output of the construction industry has followed a strong
trend line, somewhat steeper than the graph of G.N.P., since the
industry got back to normal after World War II. In this the
U.K. has conformed to the same pattern as that found in most
European countries — strongly cyclical, with a period ranging
from three to six years and a variation from norm of less than
10 per cent. Order-placing follows a similar pattern with a larger
amplitude.

The variation from year to year, particularly in order-placing,
has given the industry a reputation for volatility, although the
trend line, the basis for long-range forecasting, is so stable.
This highlights one of the major problems of the long-range
forecaster — the clearing of the mind of short-term current
affairs, and concentration on the underlying long-term factors
that cause changes in the trend line. These can sometimes be
detected by econometric and statistical methods. There is, however, danger in using these methods alone, and it is rarely wise
to adopt the results produced unless it is possible to find basic
economic, social or sociological causes.

Within this general background the industry is broken down
into its main statistical headings — private and public housing,
public non-housing, private industrial and private other. The last
three have a number of main markets, and detailed consideration of each of these markets is given periodically. The time
cycle varies — the most important may be studied annually,
others every three to four years.

A similar treatment is accorded to the resources used in the industry. The likely labour availability is examined regularly, as are the principal materials used. At the same time, likely relative price trends, both of the materials themselves and of their cost in position in the building, are studied and forecast.

A feature of the contracting industry has always been its low concentration on sales. When the gaining of business traditionally depends almost entirely on price, while reputation and quality have an infinitesimal effect, it is understandable that the additional overheads brought by a sales force were thought to be expensive and unnecessary luxuries. The recent trend towards limited tender lists and negotiation of contracts has caused a changing attitude to sales staff, but there are still few market-researchers operating in contracting and even fewer market-planners.

Laing conformed to normal practice, but planning experience soon showed that economic and statistical analyses were insufficient and market-researchers were brought in to assess reaction to likely change, mainly within, but partly outside, the construction industry. This work has become an essential part of the forecasting process.

Finally, the effects the forecast changes will have on the business are drawn to the attention of the chief executive and suggestions of strategic change made. The means by which these changes are introduced into the action planning have already been described.

THE FUTURE

The purpose of planning is to forecast, assess and prepare for change. Change is inevitable and, on the whole, highly desirable. Planning methods are in no way exempt. (See Figure 20.2.)

As the planning process at Laings has passed from being a chore imposed by top management to a normal routine method of running the business at branch and regional level, as well as at the centre, changes have taken place and will take place. Subsidiary-company managements now understand, to a much greater extent, what is happening and likely to happen to the markets in which they operate. They now feel competent to take

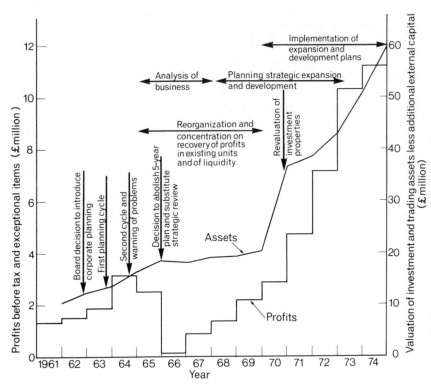

Figure 20.2   The progress of corporate planning in John Laing.

a full share in the formation of strategy. They have much to contribute and will progressively take a larger part in this important aspect of business.

It is not anomalous to say that greater decentralization and devolution of authority require closer control. A good planning system makes decentralization possible, provided that the control system is designed to give early warning to more senior management. Greater control does not mean more paper and more reports. It relates to the future rather than the past, and its real purpose is to avoid trouble rather than correct it.

The recording of the assumptions on which plans have been drawn up helps materially if the assumptions are regularly checked. The invalidity of an assumption can often be seen before its effect on the business is noticeable, and it is possible to take the necessary action to avoid trouble.

This is but one means by which control can be exercised through planning. Others are appearing. Their development is a major task for company planners.

21 Practical Problems in Corporate Planning: III Kent County Council

Clive A. Rugman

Local government is the main instrument of environmental or community management. The input of resources is on a scale that demands effectiye management. Total public expenditure is equal to some 60 per cent of Gross Domestic Product, and local-authority spending some 35 per cent of all public expenditure.

The community commonly requires from local government, at one and the same time, better local services and less expenditure. There is no yardstick such as profitability by which to measure and justify output. If only as a measure of self-protection, therefore, local government has had to examine the cost-effectiveness of its policies and management, which has put many authorities in the forefront of developing modern management systems.

The local-government reorganization of April 1974 occasioned a reappraisal of the whole management structure. This case study is concerned with the organizational changes that took place within Kent *before* local-government reorganization.

THE BACKGROUND

Traditionally, local government has seen itself from a 'service' viewpoint — providing a number of separate services, each requiring a separate department with specialist management qualified for its role. Kent was fairly typical of the larger counties in 1967. It would not be true to say that there was no coordination between departments. We ourselves, in education, were reliant upon the services of some other departments: for example, the County Architect's department designed our schools and the Supplies Department furnished and equipped them. We looked to the County Planning Officer for information about development and population, and had obvious overlaps in the care of young people with the Children's and Welfare Departments (now, since the implementation of Seebohm, part of the Social Services Department) and the Health Department.

Those departments central to the whole organization were the Treasurer's Department and the Clerk's Department. The Clerk, in addition to supplying the legal expertise to the County Council, operated such requirements for general management as were then carried out. One must also bear in mind that all departments were, of course, answerable to their committees, which were drawn from the membership of the County Council and subject to its policies. There were, on the other hand, twenty-three committees of the County Council and fifty-three sub-committees, many including additional members from outside the Council. With that number of committees and sub-committees there was a large measure of independence, and the task of giving the whole membership of the County Council a comprehensive view of its activities was a very difficult one.

There are those who would argue that this form of organization is not necessarily against the interest of the paying customer. Such an organization has been well summed up by Mr J. B. Woodham, Borough Treasurer of Teesside, as follows: 'My concept of a local authority is not that of a simple organism; rather is that of a federation of organisms needing a central "brain" for finance and an important, but limited range of general management services, and a number of decentralized "brains" for the operational aspects of service management.'

The opposite viewpoint is to take the environment as the starting point for the activities of local government. From the environment the local authority draws its input — men, money, values, ideas — and to the environment it gives its output. It requires members and officers to accept an all-round responsibility for the safety, health and well-being, both material and cultural, of people in different localities in so far as these objectives can be achieved by local action and local ini-

tiative within the framework of local policies and national
legislation.

Outside the realms of philosophy, however, it must be
accepted that at some point the service must be administered
by those with the professional expertise to do so. What is
debatable, if one can return to the original simile, is how
large the central 'brain' of the authority should be in relation
to the 'decentralized' brains, and to what extent and how
they should interact through a common nervous system.
Rather than enter that particular debate, we shall describe the
particular point within this spectrum at which Kent stands,
and give an interim report on how its management system is
operating.

THE POSITION IN KENT

The move towards restructuring followed the appointment of
Mr Malcolm Bains as County Clerk in 1970. Mr Bains was the
chairman of the study group appointed jointly by the Secretary
of State for the Environment and the local-authority associations
to examine management principles and structures in local government at both elected member and officer levels. The group's
report is, of course, the 'Bains Report'. Although it has gained
this title against Mr Bains' wishes, there is perhaps some justice
in that, since much of the report reflects what has been happening in Kent, where the introduction of a management system has brought together the professional departments in the
formulation of corporate policy.

The first move was the introduction of a Chief Officers Group
(COG), comprising a number of senior heads of departments —
the County Clerk, the Deputy County Clerk, the County
Treasurer, the County Education Officer, the Director of Social
Services, the County Surveyor, the County Planning Officer
and the County Medical Officer. It was, of course, a matter of
some delicacy to exclude some heads of department from this
group, but it is clear that the smaller departments, such as
Weights and Measures, Analysts and some of the functional
departments (Fire, Police, Supplies, for example) would not have
a role to play in a group that would be concerned with the general
strategic policy of the authority. In May 1971 the County Clerk
presented the Selection and Special Purposes Committee of the

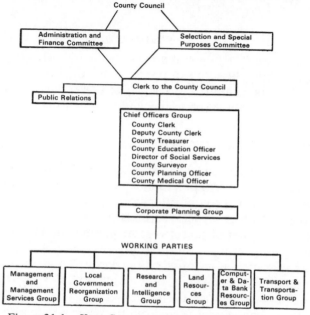

Figure 21.1   Kent County Council organization structure.

County Council with a structure that has since evolved to the form set out in Figure 21.1.

The terms of reference of the Chief Officers Group were the following:

1   To assist the County Clerk in formulating recommendations for consideration about matters of countywide significance. It was thought that those would not be many in number, but could include such matters as local-government reform, Maritime Industrial Development Area on the Medway, the Channel Tunnel, and employment and planning strategy for the county.

2   To act as a steering group and management-supervision body for county services generally. This would call for the preparation of objectives for submission to the County Council, formulation of recommendations on the determination of priorities and the setting of common standards where appropriate for the whole county service.

It would clearly not be practicable for heads of departments to give detailed attention to these topics and run their own departments at the same time. These aims were therefore to be achieved through a series of steering parties and working groups. The first and most important of these is the Corporate

Planning Group (C.P.G.), comprising the deputy officers from all departments. The terms of reference for the C.P.G. are to act as a steering committee on behalf of COG, and in this way to provide a link betweeen policy and structure planning.

THE KENT PLANNING GROUP ROLE

C.P.G.'s work includes identification and review of objectives; evaluation of short-term programmes aimed at achieving these objectives; consideration of priorities within those programmes as between different services; formulation of proposals for linking presentation of objectives, programmes and budgets; developing long-term plans (as far into the future as is considered necessary); monitoring and reviewing progress as against plans; and providing guidelines for all other working parties and receiving progress reports. C.P.G. in fact acts as a sieve, feeding up what has been examined and can be recommended for consideration by COG.

Another important aspect of C.P.G. is that it brings all departments into the corporate planning process at a fairly high level. This emphasis on participation is carried over into the five working groups supporting C.P.G. These look at manpower and management services, local-government reorganization, computer and data-bank resources, research and intelligence, world resources and (a proposed addition) transport and transportation.

Under the aegis of C.P.G. an examination has been carried out of the presentation and format of the budget and its relation to a revised statement of objectives. The County Council has for some years had a five-year forward revenue and capital estimates programme and manpower budget, with supporting statistics, and therefore the implications of spending in these three areas for the next five years are known in advance. Another innovation in 1970 was the submission of a statement of objectives as an indication of future policies. It must be admitted, however, that the presentation of the budget frequently defeats County Council members, both by its length and complexity, and efforts are being made to produce a new format based on a needs statement, as a means of assessing as closely as possible the requirements of the community and deciding how they can best be served by the Council.

The basic questions to be answered are the following:

1 What has been achieved so far?
2 What do we need to do in the future
   (a) To maintain existing standards of services
   (b) To provide for additional demands
   (c) To improve standards of services?

A major difficulty in setting down standards is the acceptance of a realistic base. There is a tendency, for example, to accept nothing but the best. On the education side there would be a reluctance to regard as acceptable conditions under which schoolchildren are accommodated in substandard or temporary accommodation, yet about a quarter of Kent's primary and secondary children are accommodated in this fashion.

Demanding the best in this instance, therefore, just shows the enormous gap, which there is no prospect of filling, between desire and the present availability of resources, except over a very long term. There are obvious difficulties politically in producing information in a way that may generate distress and controversy without accelerating an improvement in conditions. This is one of a number of examples in corporate planning where there needs to be a balance between the rival claims of philosophy and realism.

THE WORKING GROUPS

There are six working groups reporting to the Corporate Planning Group.

The Research and Intelligence Group

A number of major departments, including Education, the Planners, the Treasurers, the Roads Department, and the Police, have their own staff working on research or development projects. In addition there is a small Central Research and Intelligency Unit in the Clerk's Department. Most of them are in the course of their work concerned with the collection of statistics and other data as a basis for forward planning. Representatives of these units have been brought together within the Research and Intelligence Group on the principle of pooling expertise and avoiding duplicating departmental work. Its brief is to

determine the data requirements of the County Council for
policy formulation and efficient operation of its services; to
promote cooperation and consistency in the collection and
application of data and to encourage its general availability
between departments; and to coordinate research into specific
policy issues and current practices as directed by C.P.G.

In some respects at present the R. & I. group has tended to
concentrate on questions of long-term policy that have had
little impact to date. For example, it is considering the establishment of a common data base. Most county departments
have a basic need for information and statistics, particularly
in regard to the use of land and to population; but the search
for the form of a common core that could usefully be made
available to all departments, with the necessary provisions for
confidentiality, etc., is a tremendous undertaking, and no
doubt its translation into facts would require an enormous
expenditure in terms of manpower, hardware and software.

Many of the aims of this group are not immediate, so that
there could have been a danger of its deliberations losing contact with the departments its members represent and the financial restraints within which they operate. This is, however,
a danger of which the group's members are aware, and there is
recognition of the need to justify themselves by some immediate if limited returns as well as marking out paths towards the
hoped-for fields of Elysium.

The Computer and Data Bank Resources Group

The county computer has for some time been providing the
basic services for payment of salaries throughout the county,
including some local districts, and it has also been carrying
out applications for particular departments. The Computer
and Data Bank Resources Group has, as its brief, the recom-
mendation to C.P.G. of all computer applications for investigation and implementation, including details of additional resources and manpower equipment, if any, needed to implement
such recommendations. It also keeps departments informed of
developments in software and hardware and arranges talks
and demonstrations on computer topics. There is a clear overlap between its activities and those of the R. and I. Group. However, they each have their own separate areas, and the problem

has been met by their having a joint steering group that considers matters common to both.

In the course of the year the group produced a list of all computer applications in which departments had expressed an interest, and translated these into requirements of equipment and building to house them. The result was sufficiently frightening for C.P.G. and COG to lay down the degree of expansion that was likely to be acceptable within the short to medium term, and to indicate priorities within this period. This has resulted in a corporate approach to the use and development of the computer that has improved all departments' understanding of its services, potential and its cost.

One illustration of the benefits of joint planning in this field is the work that is going on to link together education and health requirements for information about children of pre-school age. The Health Department has computerized all its records of births, vaccinations, handicaps, etc. The Education Department obtain from this programme information about the numbers of children in each age group in zones sufficiently small to be related to individual school catchment areas. This information might also be of potential value to the Social Services Department. The joint steering group has served as a very useful forum of discussion for the development of this particular project. There was a danger that some members of the group regarded this as a possible basis for development into the Common Data Base project. It has been recognized, however that this was an instance of the best striving to kill the good; there is often benefit in implementing something that yields immediate, though limited, returns, even if it does not fulfil the ideal 'ultimate' requirement.

The Manpower and Management Services Group

The general brief of this group is to consider strategic questions concerning the acquisition, use, motivation, and development levels of the Council's manpower resources, and in particular to design procedures aimed at improvements under any of these heads; and also to consider any other matters where evaluation by the O. & M. work-study unit might be appropriate. This group has been chaired by the Deputy Education Officer, whose appointment has proved that groups gain from being

chaired by deputies from what, on the face of it, are unrelated
departments. By this means key people at senior level take part
in the general working of the authority.

The Local Government Reorganization Group

This group was called into being by the approach of local-
government reorganization. It has enabled the major departments to coordinate views on the implications of the new
legislation and has done much valuable work for the benefit
of individual departments, County Members and the County
Joint Committee of County Council and District Council
Representatives. It is difficult to envisage how the departments
could have undertaken this work except through some such
corporate group.

The Land Resources Group

The County Council is by far the largest owner of land and
property within its area. Traditionally, however, departments
have kept their premises very much to themselves and there
has been a reluctance to consider, for example, alternative or
'shared' uses by other departments. It is the function of the
group to examine land sources on a corporate basis. It prepares
a programme of land acquisitions, which is vital in an expanding
county like Kent, where more land is constantly required at
ever-rising prices. In this respect the group has been examining
the criteria for the choice of sites. Examinations have been
carried out into the joint use of sites and buildings by different
departments and reviews carried out in particular of property
in valuable central town sites, to see whether it would not be
sensible to sell certain of them and locate the establishments
displaced in a more rational and economic pattern elsewhere.
The Land Resources Group also has its own sub-group, which
keeps an eye on the acquisition of sites and the progress of
capital projects.

Bringing the departments together does not, of course, resolve all conflicts. But at least they know, at an early stage,
what the areas of conflict are. In building new schools we
have often had problems in meeting the aesthetic requirements
of the planning officer within the cost limits allowed by central
Government and access requirements stipulated by the County

Surveyor. Any problems of this sort are now discussed within the group and, if conflict still remains, can be quickly dealt with at C.P.G. or COG level. The process means a saving of time and the prevention of open confrontations in which County Council members debate the cases of rival heads of department. If differences still have to be reconciled by County Council members, at least the ground will have been well cleared in advance.

The Transport and Transportation Group

The formation of this group arises from the new County Council's responsibility for transport and transportation. The county has, of course, been concerned for some time with the problem of the decline of public transport services. In education we are now being forced into the position, in some areas, of providing our own bus service. Again, however, there is a need to take a broader look. There is, for example, no sense in allowing a rural bus service to perish for lack of subsidy if, as a corollary, the Education Department needs to provide its own bus service at a very much greater cost.

CONCLUSION

This case study has sought to give some idea of the work of the planning groups on the officer/management side. It is, of course, essential that this should be paralleled by and subject to the Committee structure for members as well. The County Council has a Selection and Special Purposes Committee that acts as a general policy committee. It is to this Committee that the recommendations of the Chief Officers Group normally go. It works in close association with the Administration and Finance Committee, which deals with the financial needs of the county. It is likely that in the new County Council these two committees will be combined to form the Policy and Resources Committee envisaged by the Bains Report. The process of reducing the number of committees has already reached a stage where, instead of the twenty-three committees and fifty-three sub-committees mentioned earlier, there are now seventeen and thirty respectively.

It would, however, be a mistake to think that there is some magic system of rationalization that will bring together all policy-making within a few all-powerful committees. In education, for example, the range of work is so wide that the existence of some sub-committees with narrow terms of reference is the most efficient way of despatching business. We have, for example, sub-committees for boarding education and university and further education awards, which deal with all difficult individual cases.

The pruning that has been done in Kent has been essentially pragmatic. So, too, has the assumption within the corporate policy structure of only such matters as have been genuinely inter-departmental. It is essential that the formulation of policy should not be regarded as solely within the competence of the corporate policy structure. Other committees and departments must continue to formulate policy for which they are responsible. Indeed, rather than drawing decision-making upwards, one would wish to see more decisions delegated to the lowest level at which they can be competently taken.

After their first year's work all groups were asked to assess and report upon their progress. It is perhaps not surprising to hear that none of them pronounced their own sentence of death. There is no doubt that the system is time-consuming, with highly paid officers taking part in long meetings, not all of which have been by any means productive. The specialist has to discipline himself to realize that his function there is not to learn about or to ask useless questions about someone else's job, which he is convinced he could do better himself.

The essential basis of tying in corporate planning within the 'line' management of departments is a feature distinct from the approach of many private enterprises. This approach has the advantage that, while enlarging the experience of officers and enabling them to make a more valuable contribution, they nevertheless remain responsible to real policies and conscious of real constraints.

FURTHER READING

1   *The New Local Authorities — Management and Structure* (the Bains Report), Report of the Study Group appointed jointly by the Secretary of State for the Environment and Local Authority Associations (H.M.S.O., 1972).

2   Stewart, J. D. *Management in Local Government: A Viewpoint* (London: Charles Knight, 1971).

22 Practical Problems in Corporate Planning: IV Williams & Glyn's Bank

Richard E. B. Lloyd

The best laid plans, wrote Burns, 'gang aft agley'. He might have said, too, that the best laid plans are not worth a scrap if the process of putting them into action is not itself of the highest order. Successfully organizing and implementing strategic planning is more important than any other part of the planning process. This chapter outlines the reasons for this belief, and then describes the way we carry out our own planning process at Williams & Glyn's Bank.

First, and most important, putting the plan into action is the only part of planning that contributes to growth in profits. One often hears criticism these days of large planning departments whose annual cost, because of expensive business graduates or professional planners, is high, and whose contribution to the company's profits is very indirect and hard to quantify. Probably the criticism arises because the planners spend too much time on conceptual work and general analysis, and too little on implementing action via the line divisions. Professional planners are important and have a place, but not every company needs them. Once line executives learn to raise their sights from short-term problems and solutions, they are capable of doing their own planning. Consequently, because they are undertaking most of the process themselves, one achieves greater commitment to the plan, and a more practical action programme.

Secondly, organizing and implementing the plan is probably

the most difficult part of the planning process, because it demands a wider variety of skills than just producing a plan. For instance, setting the company's objective as, say, 10 per cent per annum growth in earnings per share is not in itself a difficult process; the difficulty is in implementing courses of action, motivating managers and controlling results so as to achieve this objective.

Finally, business success depends, like stock-market investment, on timing. You can choose the right objectives, know the right stocks to buy, and excel at investment analysis, but all this will be worthless unless your timing is right, and your investment decisions are put into action in the market. In the same way correct timing, which we consider to be an integral part of organizing and implementing strategic planning, is vital to business success.

FORMATION OF THE BANK

The nature of our own planning process cannot be appreciated unless the background to the formation of our bank in 1970 is outlined. The character of the bank, in fact, evolved through a heavy process of planning over two or more years.

Formed from three old-established banks of differing character, Williams & Glyn's Bank came about mainly as a result of the merger of two Scottish parents in 1967–8. One of these, the Royal Bank of Scotland, owned both Williams Deacon's and Glyn Mills & Co., while the other, the National Commercial Bank of Scotland, owned the National Bank, which after the sale of its Irish business in 1966 to the Bank of Ireland Group, was left with thirty-seven branches in England.

All three English banks were small enough to share an entrepreneurial approach to business but had very different management styles. Glyn Mills, for instance, worked in some ways like a partnership with merchant-banking overtones; most of its executive directors sat in one room — The Parlour — and there were only four branches, all in London, each with a large degree of autonomy. The National Bank had an intimate style of management revolving closely round the general manager himself; it being a small bank, he could influence, in a highly personal way, all his branch managers. Williams Deacon's by contrast had 283 branches, was based in Manchester and had a

strongly centralized and authoritative management, with a
mainly non-executive board. All three banks were profit-
orientated, seldom missed business opportunities, and had each
its own strong connections with particular groups or market
sectors.

The new bank, however, did not spring fully formed like
Athene from the head of Zeus. First of all, study groups drawn
from the three English banks and both Scottish parents were
set up in 1968, to consider three possible alternatives, only
one of which envisaged a full merger of the three English banks.
There was no rush into a single merged bank; the alternatives
were dealt with thoroughly and empirically for nearly twelve
months, until the thinking of the directors of the three banks
and the holding company developed into gradual acceptance
of the idea of a single new bank. During this period (December
1968 to February 1969) considerable priority was given to
objectives and organizational structure in discussions about
the alternative strategies open to the three banks.

STRUCTURE OF NEW BANK

The organizational structure was given the earliest priority
during this formative stage of thinking. It was considered vital
to balance the desirability of logical tidiness and accountability, on the one hand, with the available executives and their
particular abilities, on the other. With this in mind, various
forms of organization for the new bank were discussed from
December 1968 to February 1969 — that is, for some four
months before it was finally decided by the group to go for
a single English entity. The structures proposed avoided committee responsibility and 'one over one' relations. In discussing
and obtaining agreement on the organization, a pragmatic approach was adopted in order that all executives responsible for
divisions had a fair allocation of responsibility. Consultants
were not called in at any stage to advise on structure.

As part of the organizational structure, a chief personnel
executive was from the outset to be recruited at board level
from outside to advise on personnel work. He was to provide
a personnel skill at the highest level and to persuade the line
divisional heads to become the 'employers' of their own staff,
rather than to rely on the staff departments.

A further problem on structure was how best to preserve the goodwill of the existing banks' staffs and customers. To achieve this, it was initially proposed that the National Bank branches, Williams Deacon's branches and Glyn's branches should each be organized in separate divisions, despite overlapping between all three banks in the south and between the National and Williams Deacon's in the north. Logic demanded a regionalized structure, but it was initially intended that this should follow as a second stage to be implemented after one or two years of the new Bank's life, so that customers and staff could continue to deal at first with those they knew.

In March 1970, however, one year after the announcement of the intention to undertake a full merger, and six months before the implementation was to begin in September, the future banking divisional heads agreed to a much more radical structure — a regional split between banking divisions, which meant breaking up and reallocating the branch organizations of the constituent banks. By thus hastening slowly during the planning stage, general agreement was gradually achieved for a far more radical structure than would have been possible at the outset.

In the light of the lessons we learned about implementing our plans for this merger, the following points are worth noting:

1   The style of planning had been participatory throughout the whole process. Line divisions had been brought into the business of designing strategy for the bank and in discussing the output of the Planning Division, whose role was advisory rather than directive.

2   The majority of those taking part in the strategic-planning process were of an age where they were able to take a long view of what was required. In other words, having some fifteen to twenty-five years still to go before bowing out from the executive scene, our top management had and have greater commitment and greater willingness to accept risk than they would if they were nearer retirement.

3   There was no pressure to produce plans or profit forecasts to fend off unwelcome bidders, as is sometimes the case in mergers and acquisitions where public shareholders have to be considered.

4   The absence of public shareholders also meant that there
    was time for second thoughts, since a deal on share prices
    was not relevant.

All the above factors contributed to a successfully implemented
merger.

PLANNING PROCESS

We turn now to consider our current planning process, and to
draw out certain observations about organizing and implementing strategy. First of all, one hears so much these days about
the importance of good communications that it may seem trite
to reiterate this point. Nevertheless care should be taken to
ensure that the right people receive the right messages, and that
enough of the decision-makers in ordinary middle management
are brought into the discussions leading to the formulation of
plans. In our case, in 1970 and 1971 our corporate plan was
used not just as a summary of action to be taken but also as a
means whereby each division would learn what other divisions
intended to do. We call this the 'open' approach to planning. In
1970 and 1971 we held a major top-management conference at
which each divisional contribution to the plan was extensively
discussed by other divisions. About fifty people were present
each time, including some senior 'in-line' branch managers. Subsequently the corporate plan itself, the first issue a ninety-page
document, was printed and issued to all branch managers, together with the strong suggestion that they communicate the
key features to their own staff. We did this as part of a conscious effort to build a new single bank out of the constituent
parts, by encouraging all levels of management to participate
in the planning process.
    Another part of our effort was directed towards the intro-
duction of management by objectives. This is serving us well in
two ways: first, by ensuring that each manager in the bank is
clear about the extent of his job and his targets in the new
scheme of things, and second, by providing a vehicle for each
level of management to communicate bank plans and policy
through a regular programme of review meetings between the
manager and his deputy director or director. In fact, when it
comes to detailed implementation of strategy, we find the

system of M.B.O. to be of great value through its discipline of
setting objectives, working out action plans, and regularly reviewing progress.

In our planning process we have been through a kind of self-
appraisal as a bank, looking at our strengths and weaknesses, especially in the light of the new competitive banking scene. We
have also extended our planning outlook to five years, super-
seding our original concentration on such short-term matters
as naturally concerned us in the merger and post-merger period.

PLANNING PROCEDURE

In previous years divisions used to write their own contribution
to the corporate plan, which was then discussed and edited
centrally, agreement being reached with the divisions about any
major changes. Once the merger was completely behind us and
its immediate objectives achieved, it was appropriate to continue
to speed the process of change in a more radical way.

In 1972, therefore, we formed small working parties each
under the chairmanship of an executive director or deputy
director, with one of our planning team as secretary. The other
members, who were usually drawn from more than one division,
were of senior managerial rank or above. Each working party
tackled one of our major business areas — for instance, City
banking — with a brief to come up with three things: first, a
summary of likely developments in the market and competitors'
action over the period 1972–7; next an analysis of where our
bank stood in relation to these markets; and finally recommendations on strategy and courses of action open to us.

These findings were then discussed at a two-day conference
of executive directors, with each working party presenting its
points to the conference. Some fifty or more decisions were
reached in those two days, although sometimes it was only a
decision to make a further study of the problem. The major
strategic issues then went in the form of recommendations before the full board of our bank during April 1972. In the next
stage, running to the end of June, each division prepared a five-
year operational plan, based on the outcome of the two-day
conference and the recommendations to the board. The final
stage was the production of divisional budgets before the end
of our financial year in September. A similar process took place

in 1973, although we extended the timetable so as to digest over three or four months the working parties' proposals.

While we have full-time planners, they work with and through divisional management. We believe that those responsible for implementation gain a greater commitment to their plans by shepherding them through the various stages and by defending them against sundry and sometimes unexpected critics. The planners' task is to enable divisional executives to broaden their horizons. They also have to gain a consensus of opinion about what will happen in the market, and they must be able to keep people informed about competitors' actions.

Our present planning has now become much more of a two-stage approach — first, strategy formulation in working parties that submit their reports to conferences of the executive directors, and, second, implementation through divisional operating plans and budgets. In the first stage there is a lot of discussion within the groups, but in the second one gets down to detail, and this has to be left to divisional management without undue interference. All the same, these detailed plans and budgets have to be agreed by the chief executive with the divisional head concerned.

CONCLUSIONS

In our experience of organizing and implementing strategic planning the following points stand out:

1   In terms of gaining acceptance at director level for a specific strategy, we try to get a complete consensus of opinion, even if this takes a long time, because we believe that if one were to force change without acceptance, the strategic moves would be made with less impact and less conviction.

2   Full-time planners have an important part to play, as advisers and catalysts, but should not attempt to undertake someone else's planning for them.

3   It is difficult to prevent people from discussing points of detail in the early stage of strategy formulation, when they ought to be comparing alternative strategies. But then it is so tempting to talk about what is familiar — and so much easier.

4   One should not expect everyone to take to this 'open' approach easily, but, once established, it helps build up mutual understanding and assistance.
5   Plans only have a value if action results from them. If no action results, they are merely pipe dreams.

23 Practical Problems in Corporate Planning: V British Nuclear Fuels

Neville R. Geary

INTRODUCTION

British Nuclear Fuels Ltd has been in existence since April 1971. A strategic-planning operation was set up in the months leading to the formation of the company and has played a major role during the succeeding and formative period. This chapter presents an account of the state of strategic or corporate planning in BNFL at the present time. It is not necessary to state the reasons for seeking to have a strategic-planning operation in a company; such reasons have been set down clearly and at length in the earlier chapters. In implementation, however, there have been considerable differences between what is often propounded and what has actually happened in BNFL. To what extent this may be due to features peculiar to BNFL or to shortcomings in the theoretical approach is a matter for personal judgement.

It must be recognized that since this is an account of a real system in which people are seeking to tackle real problems, both commercial and personal discretion must limit the extent and depth of what can be said.

WHAT IS BNFL?

British Nuclear Fuels Ltd was set up by the Atomic Energy Act (1970) and is comprised of staff, premises and plant of the former Production Group of the United Kingdom Atomic Energy Authority. In the first year of its operation (1971–2) it

had a total equity of £18m, 9,000 employees, a turnover of
£64m, of which £6m was from exports, and a net profit of £4m.

BNFL's business is the sale of fuel services to the operators
of nuclear power stations both in the U.K. and overseas. To do
this BNFL takes uranium ore concentrates from mining companies throughout the world, and prepares pure uranium com-
pounds. The concentration of the uranium − 235 isotope (the
isotope that can undergo fission in a nuclear reactor) is increased
by the gaseous diffusion or centrifuge processes, and the material
is assembled into precision-designed fuel elements. These elements are sold to the power companies, who irradiate them in
reactors. In this process the fissile (U−235) content of the element is partially spent and quantities of the fissile material
plutonium, together with the very radioactive fission products,
are formed. BNFL then undertakes the transport of these radioactive elements to the plant at which they are processed. The
residual uranium and the plutonium are extracted and fabricated
into new fuel elements. The fission products are reduced in bulk
and placed in permanent safe storage.

To carry out this work BNFL operates three factories in the
North West of England from a headquarters and design centre
near Warrington. It also operates two small nuclear power stations, which sell power to the electricity generating boards.

For clarity, it should be emphasized that BNFL is not primarily concerned with nuclear research, which is the responsibility of the United Kingdom Atomic Energy Authority; nor
with the design and sale of British nuclear reactors, the business
of British Nuclear Design and Construction Limited; nor with
the preparation and marketing of radioisotopes for medical and
industrial purposes, which is principally carried out by the
Radio Chemical Centre Limited.

FEATURES OF BNFL IMPORTANT TO STRATEGIC PLANNING

There are a number of features, both of the structure of BNFL
and of the ambience in which it operates, which can be identified and must be taken into account by the strategic planner.
Some of these are typical of modern technical industry while
others are peculiar to the nuclear energy industry or unique to
BNFL itself.

Technology

It almost goes without saying that the nuclear fuel industry is a
'high technology' industry. During its formative years all its
technology was blanketed by military security and today, more
than a quarter of a century after the first reactor was brought
into operation, some aspects are still, quite rightly, secret. Due,
in part to this, and in part to the unusual nature of the technology and materials, BNFL has had to develop a substantial
reliance on itself and has been able to benefit from the 'spin-
off' of other industries only to a limited degree. For example,
the gas centrifuge, developed for U–235 separation, has little
in common with ordinary high-speed centrifuge technology.

Compactness

A plant capable of producing nuclear fuel, which for electricity
production is equivalent to the output of several coalmines, is
complex and requires quite substantial capital, but it occupies
the space equivalent of a modest sized factory. On the other
hand, the financial consequences, to electricity producers and
consumers, of a failure to bring a power station into operation
owing to non-delivery of fuel would be much greater than the
value of the fuel itself. Quite small decisions regarding the plant
must therefore be given a weighting far greater than their immediate financial importance.

Time Scale

Because of the 'high technology' content of its work and the
substantial time scale on which the nuclear power industry
operates, many of BNFL's investments, particularly those in
R. and D., have unusually long pay-back periods. In the intervening years problems of cash flow and manpower deployment
require close attention. This is a problem that is familiar in
many sectors of the 'energy business'.

Input Material and Product

Strategic planning for any industry must reflect the nature of
the input and output materials. The fundamental raw material
for the nuclear energy industry is uranium. Metal markets are

notoriously erratic; in this respect the uranium market is worse
than most others. Because of the participation of Governments
in the nuclear energy field, there has been, throughout the
world, a high level of national control of both the procurement
and sale of uranium. Purchases have tended to be large, infrequent and long-term, while attitudes to stocks have alterna-
ted between anxiety over assurance of future supplies and concern over present surpluses. There is similar alternation in the
uranium mining industry, which frequently forecasts world
shortage but seems to find new uranium reserves whenever it
looks for them.

The output of the nuclear industry is energy and here there
is no greater stability of forecast. The national demand for
energy depends on national economic growth. The number of
power stations to be constructed depends, further, on the ratio
of peak to base load and the margins of surplus capacity required. The fraction of power stations to be nuclear depends
not only on the favour with which the nuclear industry is
regarded, but also on the position of coal, oil and hydro power.
An economic recession, a hard winter, a coal strike, an oil find,
a move to conserve upland valleys and the late construction of
a nuclear power station can all cause significant fluctuations in
the forecast demand for nuclear fuel.

BNFL's Home Market

BNFL's trading is dominated by sales of fuel cycle services to
the Central Electricity Generating Board. This single customer/
single vendor relation is one that can be developed to the significant benefit of both (as has been shown in several other industries). This arrangement is not backed by any statute or regulation and could be broken by any commercial entrepreneur who
believed he could compete. It is, contrary to what might be the
first impression, far from being a 'cosy' situation or one that
can be allowed to lead to any degree of complacency. It requires
most careful strategic planning and imposes unusual characteristics on that planning.

While the success of a nuclear programme must require the
efficient supply of successful nuclear fuel services, it must be
recognized that the supplier of these services has little influence
on the size of the nuclear reactor market.

The total effect of these factors is to impose, on BNFL, an unusual emphasis on being able to respond in a flexible and optimal manner to changes in the environment, rather than on seeking to reshape the environment itself. This must be reflected in planning operations.

BNFL's Export Market

Other considerations apply in the export field, which is keenly competitive and in which BNFL has had a significant level of success. Here, however, a new factor arises to distort 'normal' commercial strategy. The role Governments have played in the uranium field has already been mentioned. There is similar intervention in fuel-fabrication areas. Once a Government has a national airline, the next thing it wants is a national nuclear fuel industry. Barriers, both overt, in the form of tariffs, and covert, in the form of pressures through grants, loans and national regulations, are used to discourage the import of fully fabricated nuclear fuel, no matter what the economic arguments might be. A company seeking to derive the maximum benefit from an expanding world market must, therefore, be prepared to plan flexibly and in terms of multinational organizations, joint companies, licences, etc.

Public Obligations

BNFL has a wide range of public obligations, both because it is in the nuclear industry and because the British Government will always be one of its major shareholders. Obligations in relation to safety, defence and international agreements, such as the Non-Proliferation Treaty, are obvious. There are, however, others. For example, it would be naïve to imagine that the Government would regard, with equanimity, a decision by BNFL to withdraw from magnox fuel fabrication leaving nearly 5,000 MW of electricity generating capacity 'high and dry'.

Management

Ultimately, any strategic plan has to be implemented through management. It must, therefore, be credible to the management and take account of its structure and characteristics.

Unusual Features

1   The staff structure and many of the staff themselves have
    their antecedents in the civil service. This has advantages
    as well as disadvantages.
2   Without exception the managers are numerate, and most
    have a technical background. They are, therefore, recep-
    tive to the concept of strategic planning but are prepared
    to let nothing get by 'on the nod'.

STRATEGIC PLANNING IN BNFL

The Function of Strategic Planning

The prime purpose of all planning is to aid the decision which
has to be taken today. It is obvious that planning has failed if
the decision is taken too late; it is less frequently recognized
that it is also failure to allow the decision to be taken too early,
perhaps in advance of the full information. The correct identification of the timing of company decisions in the light of the
forecast pattern of events can therefore be said to be a prime
requirement. In relation to such company decisions, strategic
planning might be said to be 'The application of objective and
quantitative criteria to decision-making previously tackled by
experience, intuition or prejudice'. This definition was in fact
given of Operational Research.[1] In BNFL strategic planning is
regarded as an application and extension of the operational-
research approach. This does not mean that the work is carried
out by the Operational Research Section; the position of that
section in the planning operation is discussed below. Nor does
this refer to the use of standard O.R. techniques, though these
have their place. BNFL's predecessor the Production Group of
the U.K.A.E.A. had its own long-range planning methods, which
were particularly attuned to meeting the financial forecasting
requirements of the Treasury. In seeking to build on, and
modify these to meet the requirements of the new company
the following practical constraints could be recognized for the
strategic-planning operation:

1   It had to be shaped to the business, structure and manage-
    ment of the company; only if it was fully adapted to
    present conditions could it attempt, validly, to identify
    the need for change.

2   It had to be introduced progressively and benefit from ex-
    perience and modification as it proceeded; like any other
    new aspect of management, it had to prove itself and
    gain acceptance before it could call for wider allocation
    of effort or command a more influential role.
3   It had to be able not only to identify new problems but to
    be capable of assisting with existing problems, and of
    providing a framework against which a continuum of
    decisions could be taken. Further, it had not only to be
    directed to the larger initiation problems, such as merger
    or diversification, but had also to guide delineation and
    implementation of everyday policy and to do this to a
    level that made it clear where the responsibilities lay
    within the middle-management structure.

The basic demands on strategic-planning operation could be
seen as (1) to forecast the future to which the company's present policies would carry it; (2) to identify the problems which
such a future presents; (3) to formulate or, in certain specialist
areas, to have formulated, the alternative courses of action that
may be taken to meet the problem; (4) to determine the date
on which a decision on these alternatives must be taken; and
(5) to ensure that, at the appropriate time, those responsible for
making such a decision are aware of this responsibility and are
aware, as far as is possible, of the full range of consequences
flowing from the decision.

The Position of Strategic Planning

In accounts of corporate-planning methods it is possible to
distinguish a number of basic attitudes, as follows:

1   *Planning for the shareholder.* In this the shareholder, as
    the owner of the company, is considered to have over-
    riding rights. This allows an attractively simple approach
    in which the present and future return to the shareholder
    is the sole objective function.
2   *Planning for the whole management.* This may be described
    as consensus planning and is perhaps an extension to
    M.B.O. In the balance of advantages and disadvantages of
    this approach an important feature is the danger that the

planning, because of the level at which it is done, may
tend to become tactical rather than strategic.

3   *Planning for the board.* This inevitably places the planning
    section in an isolated position away from the normal
    management structure; it is difficult to avoid the impres-
    sion of élitism.

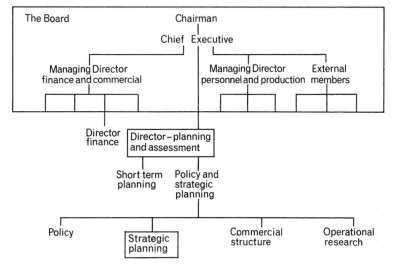

Figure 23.1   Planning structure of BNFL.

4   *Planning for the chief executive.* There is some degree of
    identity between approaches 3 and 4. The latter, how-
    ever, recognizes the peculiar responsibility the chief
    executive holds for advising the board on the company's
    long-term future. This also allows the planning section
    to operate as a normal section of management reporting
    'up the line'.

In BNFL the last of these approaches is adopted and a structure
(which is shown as Figure 23.1) is adopted to implement this.
The figure shows the all-important direct line through to the
chief executive and also the vital link with the finance branch.

    The four functions within the policy and strategic planning
area are the following:

1   *Strategic planning.* This is the central planning section,

responsible for the assembly and coordination of data, the preparation and analysis of forecasts, and the assembly of plans; and for ensuring that actions are placed and implemented in pursuit of these plans.

2   *Policy.* This covers two functions, which are, in practice, almost identical: (a) the interpretation of events both within and without the company to the Planning Section and the interpretation of the plans to the company; and (b) the analysis of *ad hoc* policy problems as they arise, in order to advise a course of action in the light of company plans. This is the main interface between strategic planning and the company. The relation is shown in Figure 23.2.

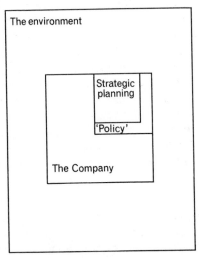

Figure 23.2   The interface between strategic planning and the company.

3   *Commercial structure.* Attention has already been drawn to the important role of commercial arrangements such as joint companies and licences in BNFL's export endeavours. It has been found necessary, in order to give realism to plans, to have a small specialist section advising in this area.

4   *Operational research.* As had been indicated above, strategic planning in BNFL is regarded as being the major application of the operational-research philosophy. In addition,

however, the O.R. section itself must act in a supporting role as the chief 'toolmakers' for the planning work.

PLANNING METHODS IN USE

The relation of the strategic-planning cycle to the operations of the company are shown in a simplified form in Figure 23.3. The following should be noted:

1 While the diagram presents a 'once through' picture of the planning cycle, there are many loops and iterations (e.g. the exchange with the chief executive is continuous) and the frequency of issue of all documents is not the same.
2 No 'assumptions' document is issued formally, but papers, setting out the assumptions in different areas used in each final form of the forecast, are circulated at working levels to ensure consistency in detailed planning.
3 No 'plan', as such, is issued. The object of the exercise is to identify problems for solution and the time by which such a solution is required. Once such a solution has been propounded, its implications will be worked out and included in the next company forecast. It will then cease to appear as a 'problem' unless changing circumstances render the solution inappropriate.
4 The setting of objectives is not the initial stage in the planning cycle.

This last point is at variance with the view 'First Set Your Objectives'. The logic of deciding where you want to go before finding out how to get there seems so obvious as to have an immediate appeal and, to assist the 'traveller', philosophical and semantic structures have been suggested to define and relate 'objectives', 'goals', 'targets', 'aims' and other criteria. In recent years, however, one has encountered a number of planning practitioners whose approach is that 'objectives' are not the raw material of strategic planning but one of its products.

This is not surprising when it is recalled that it has long been recognized, in operational research, that the formulation of a problem and the setting of objective functions are a major part of any task. Further this part of the work has frequently

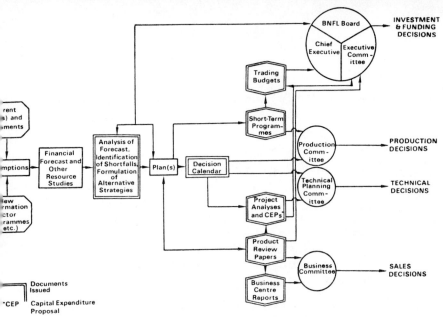

Figure 23.3   The strategic planning cycle.

to be undertaken iteratively, and often the nature of the problem
is finally resolved only immediately before the solution is
reached. There are thus, in simple terms, two distinct approaches:
(1) that of having quantifiable firm objectives set, probably
from outside the planning operation, as the instructions to that
operation; and (2) that of seeking to discern in each emerging
situation or opportunity the optimal course of action for the
company, recognizing the many dimensions on which the
health of the company depends and defining objectives accordingly.

The balance between these approaches is probably held by
the extent to which the company operates within an environment that may be 'shaped' by such actions as marketing, as opposed to one in which emphasis must be placed on a flexible
response to events and opportunities. As has been stated above,
for a majority of BNFL's operations, the latter is the case.

PLANNING STAGES VIS-A-VIS DEMANDS

The five basic demands on the strategic-planning system have
been set out above. In the following sections the way in which
these impinge on the stages of the planning operation illustrated
in Figure 23.3, are discussed.

Forecasts

Forecasts are intended to show the future to which the company's present policies would carry it. Forecasts of the total nuclear fuel-cycle services market are built up country by country by considering:

1   The declared nuclear building programme of that country
2   The fraction of the forecast energy requirement which (1) represents
3   The performance of the nuclear construction industry in that country and elsewhere
4   The competition, and other trade and political factors, which may affect the fraction of the market BNFL may capture in that country.

Other approaches, using mathematical models generating such forecasts from considerations of the general economy of the country in question, have been considered but have not appeared to offer any advantages. Discussions have shown that this conclusion has been reached in other organizations concerned in the world energy market.

These forecasts are used to develop, in appropriate detail, production, construction and R. and D. programmes, and calls for resources such as finance, operating manpower, uranium and engineering are calculated. It has been found necessary for the forecasts to span a nine-year period, though for some aspects a further horizon must be taken in order to determine the course of events within the span.

A plan is, of course, only a forecast derived from new rather than existing assumptions. Thus, for both the preparation of the original forecast and for the examination of major alternative plans, the mechanism of deriving a forecast covering a wide range of sections within the company has to be brought into operation rapidly and efficiently. To aid this, the process has been formulated as a network and normal methods of critical path control applied. A much simplified representation of the structure of the network is shown as Figure 23.4.

Forecast Analysis

Experience has shown that there was little to be gained by the issue of the detailed and voluminous full company forecast.

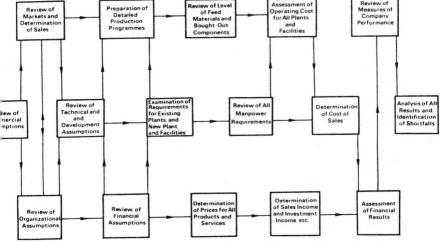

Figure 23.4   Simplified network for company forecast.

What has now been adopted is the preparation of a summary in which the forecast performance of the company is examined (both as a whole and by activity area) against a wide range of the accepted criteria, such as return on capital, continuity of funding, and self-financing ratios. Comparisons are then made (1) with the world nuclear industry, and (2) with what is published or known about other companies in the U.K. and elsewhere. In making these comparisons the greatest caution is exercised, since, apart from any deliberate policy of concealment, there are widely differing definitions and accountancy conventions.

In this analysis, and in discussion of it within the management of the company, certain aspects of performance which will give rise to concern will be revealed. Similar need for concern may be revealed by sensitivity determinations within the forecast. Since no forecast can be better than the assumptions on which it is based, the first step is to re-examine the assumptions that generate the concern. If the assumptions are found to be valid, it is then necessary to determine the sectors of the company's operations within which a solution should be sought; identify, as far as possible, the time scale for action; and ensure that appropriate actions are put in hand. It will be recognized that these steps correspond to formal 'gap analysis'. It is of interest to note that, in introducing this planning operation, one difficulty was that of having it accepted that there could be company-forecast documents in which unresolved problems were presented for which, because the time was inappropriate, no solution was being sought; the temptation to search for an 'instant' if, even, non-optimal solution, to any problem appeared to be deeply rooted.

Decision Calendar

Ultimately, having set the general strategy or range of strategies, one must coordinate all major decisions in the company within

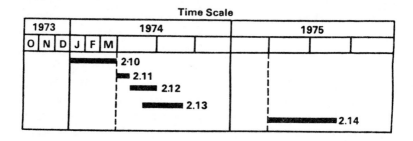

HVZ FUEL

2.10   HVZ fuel

Study to be concluded by April 1974 on market size, price, probable share.

2.11   HVZ fuel

Decision required in April 1974 on whether to enter HVZ fuel fabrication market. If decided positive, CEP (2.12) and CEP (2.13) would be submitted giving limited capacity in the short term. Study (2.10) must be reviewed before building a new plant CEP (2.14) the earliest date for which, against present market forecasts, being 1975.

2.12   Extensions to fuel jobbing shop

Capital expenditure proposal	Class of proposal	Handover
mid 1974, £0·25m.	New plant/extension	1974

Would provide capacity for manufacturing 100 te U pa.

2.13   Ventilation system for fuel jobbing shop

Capital expenditure proposal	Class or proposal	Handover
mid 1974, £0·15m.	Amenity/safety	1974

Necessary if 2.12 is approved to make building safe when higher throughput of fissile material is achieved.

2.14   HVZ fuel fabrication plant

Capital expenditure proposal	Class of proposal	Handover
mid 1975, £3m.	New plant/extension	1977

For a 400 te U pa. plant.

Figure 23.5   B.N.F.L. proprietary: decision calendar.

the context of the strategic-planning operations, and show both the time when these decisions have to be taken and the timing of the necessary studies. This is done by the Planning Section, through a document called the decision calendar. This shows in detail all the major decisions to be taken over a period of the next $2\frac{1}{2}$ years and highlights those on which a decision is required in the next six months. A sample (fictitious) page is shown as Figure 23.5.

Other Planning Activities

Clearly many other detailed planning activities are required and are carried out by other groups in the company. The relation of some of these activities to the strategic planning cycle is shown in Figure 23.3.

The nature of the product-review papers should perhaps be explained. Where, through the forecast and the decision calendar, the need for a major decision (e.g. marketing or capital) is identified, a detailed survey of all aspects (market, technology, finance, etc.) of the relevant activity area is carried out. This is presented to the board as a comprehensive background to, and explanation of, the decision it is asked to take, together with the expected consequences of the alternate courses of action. The product reviews subsequently provide much of the detailed 'building material' for future forecasts. (It should be noted that the title 'product review' is used loosely for this type of document even when no tangible product is actually involved.)

CONCLUSIONS

To date, certain aspects of a strategic-planning machine have been introduced into BNFL and an outline account of this is set out above. The process is far from complete but is sufficiently advanced to allow some assessment to be made of achievement.

No examples of problems revealed, solutions propounded or even the types of field within which strategic planning has operated have been given in this chapter. As was indicated in the introduction, the nature of strategic planning is such that, if it is a success within a company, its work must be treated with the greatest discretion. Even if such examples could be given, they would do little to substantiate claims of success for a planning operation with an horizon of at least nine years and which has been in existence for less.

Some measure of achievement against the initial requirements indicated at the beginning of the chapter may, however, be judged:

1   The planning operation that has been set up has proved to be adequately shaped and adjusted to the business of the company, so that it has proved valid in meeting immediate and short-term problems; there is therefore some confidence that it will prove equally satisfactory as a tool for the more distant future. In particular the method of allowing objectives to be formulated from the planning process rather than specifying these at the outset has worked well.

2   The strategic-planning operation has been accepted and used by the chief executive, the managing directors and the board in dealing with major problems of the company. There have, of course, been matters on which the strategic-planning section has either not sought or has not secured the role which, in future, it might wish to play.

3   The methods chosen to determine the immediate and short-term implications of strategic future questions have proved satisfactory, and have gained acceptance with senior and middle management. This is important not only because such acceptance is obviously necessary if planning is to be carried into action but also because the cooperation and approval of such staff are necessary to the planning work itself.

REFERENCE

1 Rothschild, Lord, in *Nature,* 13 October 1972, vol. 239, p. 373.

Postscript: From Corporate Planning to Policy Analysis

Bernard Taylor

INTRODUCTION

Formal strategic-planning systems were first introduced in the mid-1960s in the form of corporate planning along the lines advocated by Igor Ansoff, the Stanford Research Institute, McKinsey and others, and in the shape of program budgeting and planning systems, principally through the influence of Robert McNamara and President Johnson.

During the past decade, in various guises, the strategic planning approach has spread throughout the developed world and into the Third World, too. The methodology has been adopted and adapted to large and small private companies, to financial institutions, to public corporations and to regional and central government.

The last ten years have brought radical changes in the environment — new social and political pressures, shortages of energy and other resources, hyper-inflation and increased employee participation in decision-making. In recent years, too, numerous surveys and empirical studies have been made to describe and evaluate the impact of formal planning in different types of organizations.

In ten years of strategic planning what have we learned? Can we identify different types and styles of planning? Are there certain situations where internal pressures and external uncertainties make systematic planning virtually impossible? Do we need new concepts and new approaches? In this postscript we make the following suggestions:

1   The concept of comprehensive formal planning will develop

to encompass the notion of policy analysis, which may be applied with benefit to almost every type of enterprise.

2   We may use the results of a substantial amount of new thinking and research into long-range planning in the private and the public sector to diagnose policy problems in different types of organization.

3   Having analysed the position of the enterprise and its management, we should be able to suggest ways of improving the decision-making process and helping the organization to adjust more successfully to its environment.

PROBLEMS WITH FORMAL PLANNING

Research into comprehensive formal planning systems indicates that they are rarely as comprehensive as is sometimes suggested. The typical formal planning system suffers from the following defects:

1   It tends to be partial rather than comprehensive.
2   It is concerned with extended budgets and forecasts rather than action programmes.
3   It concentrates on operations as opposed to objectives and strategies.

The Conference Board came to the following conclusion in a recent study: 'It is clear that much planning – indeed in some companies practically all planning – is accomplished outside the context of a formal planning routine. At a large holding company for instance "large questions of strategy are not encompassed in the routine but are resolved by judgements reached in the policy committee".'[1]

Igor Ansoff after fifteen years' experience with strategic planning concludes:

Today only a handful of leading firms employ strategic planning to manage their forward growth thrusts. A majority still employ the simpler and earlier long-range planning techniques which are based on extrapolation of the past and lack the systematic generation and analysis of alternatives characteristic of strategic planning. Experience in companies has shown that the precepts of strategic planning are difficult to translate into practice. Not only is the translation difficult but attempts to install rigorous strategic discipline typically run into 'resistance to planning' – an organisational inertia which appears to frustrate the efforts and, given the opportunity, to reject the planning effort as a foreign antibody.

He quotes a typical experience in a billion-dollar American company, which prepared a six-inch thick corporate strategic plan: 'The planning effort so exhausted the planning staff and so depleted its goodwill with operating managers that no effort was made at subsequent revisions.'[2]

On the basis of wide-ranging studies of strategy-making in public and private organizations in Canada, Mintzberg wrote:

> Planning is not a panacea for the problems of strategy-making. As obvious as this seems, there is little recognition of it in planning books or by planners. Instead one finds a focus on abstract, simple models of the planning process that take no cognisance of other modes of strategy-making. Little wonder then that one finds so much frustration among formal planners. Rather than seeking panaceas we should recognise that the model used must fit the situation. An unpredictable environment suggests use of the adaptive mode just as the presence of a powerful leader may enable the organisation to best achieve its goals through the entrepreneurial mode.[3]

Yehezkel Dror, writing on the basis of experience in policy-making for U.S. Government agencies makes the same point:

> Many of the proponents of comprehensive planning seem to assume explicitly or implicitly that comprehensive planning is an ideal mode of direction for all types of systems, and should therefore be encouraged as much as possible. This opinion stems from a lack of familiarity with other types of system direction which often are not only more efficient but are also more effective.[4] . . . Even on the relatively small scale of city planning, comprehensive planning has not yet provided any convincing solutions for basic problems of transportation, air pollution, and recreation (not to mention more difficult problems of youth culture, community relations, etc).[5]

After examining planning systems in twenty-five American financial institutions, Israel Unterman found the following problems in operating comprehensive planning:

1. Few top executives have been trained to integrate and assess a host of many kinds of factor. The top man by experience and background is usually a specialist not a generalist. It takes a most exceptional skill to use what Peter Drucker calls a 'holistic' approach. Relatively few executives have this ability.
2. Even when the process is operational there are some ongoing problems . . . When profit centres become highly successful there is a tendency to overlook the total plan and the holistic process is not enforced.[6]

Dror in relation to the public sector and Ansoff in relation to business both reach the same conclusion. Dror finds, 'There is a growing awareness that efforts to improve decision-making in organisations through methods such as analysis and Planning-Programming—Budgeting cannot succeed unless accompanied by broader organisational changes.'[7] Ansoff suggests that 'a particular type of planning (or more accurately decision-making) can be seen as *part* of a complex vector of managerial capabilities which are required to support entrepreneurial activity within the firm . . . unless the other components are aligned to accept its results, strategic planning can be a distortion of the capability vector, akin to a rubber band being stretched while its two ends are held fixed. Like the band the capability tends to snap back once the distorting force is removed'.[8] (See Figure Ps. 1.) The problem as expressed by Dror is 'how to introduce

---

Managers

1. Values and attitudes
2. Skills and
3. Behaviour
4. Depth of management

Structure

5. Authority
6. Job definition
7. Rewards
8. Work structure
9. Power structure
10. Information
11. Self-renewal of structure

Process

12. *Ad hoc* decision-making
13. Systematic decision-making
14. Problem anticipation
15. Planning
16. Implementation
17. Control
18. Management technology
19. Computer application

Source: H. Igor Ansoff, from *Strategic Planning to Strategic Management,* Wiley, 1976

PS.1   Managerial capability components.

urgently needed improvements in decision-making while avoiding the possible boomerang effects of comprehensive formal planning systems'.[9]

Why have comprehensive formal planning systems met with only qualified success? The main reasons indicated by our research[10] seem to be the following:

1   Managements find the planning process rather unnatural; it is incompatible with their normal style, which is intuitive and spontaneous rather than analytical and explicit. They are prepared to accept the discipline in a crisis, when the survival of the organization is at stake, but once the crisis is past, they are likely to revert to their usual style of *ad hoc* decision-making.

2   The process is expensive in time and money. The expense can often be justified for a specific analysis, e.g. the British Steel Corporation's ten-year strategy, or the British Rail Freight Model, but once the crucial decisions have been analysed and the resources produced, the plan is unlikely to be updated.

3   Up to this point at least formal planning systems have over-emphasized certain aspects of management, i.e. the economic and the quantitative, and they have undervalued or omitted other considerations, e.g. the socio-political, the entrepreneurial and the creative aspects of strategy. In formal planning, strategy is all too often reduced to a game in resource allocation rather than an investigation of the character of the enterprise and its future.

4   It is becoming increasingly obvious that formal planning systems are more appropriate to large complex organizations, which have the need for explicit written communications, than to small entrepreneurial enterprises, where communication tends to be informal.

POLICY ANALYSIS

It is curious that planners, of all people, should be accused of refusing to consider alternative planning systems in favour of concentrating on a unique solution or 'the one best way', as follows:

1   Explicit and usually quantitative objectives and strategies

2   A comprehensive forecast of environmental changes
3   An assessment of resources and opportunities
4   Operational plans and budgets
5   A periodic review and control procedure.

Managers are naturally suspicious of panaceas, particularly those in which a great deal of calculation is based on sometimes questionable premises.

The role of PPBS and comprehensive corporate planning seems to be under question, but there are still the following problems to solve:

1   How to direct management attention to certain strategic issues that may be critical to the future of the organization
2   How to assist the decision-makers in taking these decisions, as systematically as possible and with the best available information.

Yehezkel Dror suggests that we should adopt policy analysis as a discipline (Figure Ps. 2). Policy analysis supplements formal planning by considering alternatives. It is 'an approach and methodology for design and identification of preferable alternatives in respect to complex policy issues'.[11] The 'new' features of policy analysis not included in formal planning systems are that increased attention would be given to the following:

1   The political aspects of policy-making, i.e. power inside and outside the organization.
2   Qualitative considerations (instead of viewing all decision-making as resource allocation).
3   Encouraging innovative and creative thinking
4   Attempts to change the organizational climate
5   Speculative thinking on the future as an essential background for current policy-making.

'The approach should be looser and less rigid but nevertheless systematic.'[12]

On the basis of his studies Rhenman stresses the importance of non-quantitative, socio-political factors:

> Neither size nor technology, nor administrative set-up is the most important in understanding organisation problems. It appears that an understanding of the value system (often known by men on the

	Systems analysis	*Policy analysis*
Criteria	Economic-efficient allocation of resources	Economic + Social and political effectiveness
Emphasis	Quantitative	Qualitative and innovative + quantitative where possible
Methods	Economic analysis quantitative models	Economic analysis + qualitative models, futures thinking and intuition
Expected Results	Better decisions on limited issues. Boomerang effect on complex issues.	Slightly better decisions on complex issues better information for, and education of, decision makers
Location	Financial Groups	Near decision-makers

Source: adapted from Y. Dror, *Ventures in Policy Sciences,* Elsevier, New York, 1971.

PS.2   Comparison of systems analysis and policy analysis.

spot as company policy) should provide the basic scheme for anyone trying to discover how organisational problems arise and how they can be solved. The value system is also closely linked to the power system. The most serious organisational problems arise from dissonance between the organisation's value environment and its own value system.[13]

Mintzberg makes the point that the usual definition of the word 'strategy' encourages the notion that strategies are also systematic plans made in advance of resource commitments. By defining strategy as 'a pattern in a stream of significant decisions', we can analyse those strategies that are planned in advance and then implemented, and those, perhaps unintended, strategies that evolve from decisions taken over a period of time.[14]

The vital difference between formal planning systems and policy analysis lies in this word *decisions*. It is important that a planner or policy analyst should measure his effectiveness not in terms of whether he succeeds in selling, installing and operating a sophisticated planning system, but whether he helps the decision-makers (e.g. the chief executive or the board) to identify their strategic problems and tackle them more effectively. He should focus on the end, decisions and action, rather than on a particular means (e.g. program budgeting or some other package). In doing this he should allow for intuition, flair and expert opinion as well as facts and figures and he should recognize that decisions must be politically feasible as well as economically justified.

The best planners have always done this. As Dror points out, formal planning has made very important contributions, 'but much of this contribution may have been due more to the wisdom, sophistication and open-mindedness of the few outstanding practitioners and their readiness to fight organizational inertia, than to their defined professional tools'.[15] Unfortunately, outstanding men are not always available, and it is safer to change the professional tools.

Guidelines for Policy Analysis

One advantage of the unique solution is that, however impractical it may prove to be in application, it is easy to explain and relatively easy to learn. The new corporate planner or policy analyst needs a more sophisticated approach. In essence he will need to be like the organization development specialist, a man with expertise in understanding certain types of problem but with no set solution. He will, however, have some theories and guidelines, such as the Harvard Stages of Corporate Development and Arthur D. Little's 'Strategy Centers' approach, described in Chapter 10. Various other attempts have been made to classify different types of enterprises from the point of view of strategy formulation.

Eric Rhenmen suggests a classification based on whether an enterprise does or does not have 'internal goals' (relating to its own future) or 'external goals' (relating to what it will provide for society or another organization). See Figures Ps. 3 and 4. Yehezkel Dror divides policy-making groups into three — the

Internal goals / External goals	WITHOUT internal goals	WITH internal goals
Without external goals	MARGINAL ORGANIZATIONS e.g. small entrepreneur	CORPORATIONS e.g. large companies
With external goals	APPENDIX ORGANIZATION e.g. sales company, government agency	INSTITUTIONS e.g. Public corporations, co-operative societies

Source: Eric Rhenman, *Organisation Theory for Long Range Planning.* John Wiley, London, 1973 (p. 55)

, PS.3   Types of organizations.

simple hierarchy, the complex hierarchy and the polycentric structure with autonomous units.

As Henry Mintzberg has pointed out, there are three theories concerning strategy-making in management literature. These are the entrepreneurial approach, characterized by bold strokes and individual decision-making; the traditional bureaucratic method of incremental, disjointed decisions, sometimes referred to as 'muddling through'; and the formal planning approach which involves developing explicit strategies and maing use of planning procedures (Figure Ps. 5).

William Newman has suggested that organizations may be divided according to the kinds of change they have to cope with. Change may be frequent or infrequent, precedented or unprecedented, and organizations tend to develop stable or flexible organizational structures and systems to cope with the type of rate of change they have to deal with (see Figure Ps. 6).[16]

FACTORS AFFECTING POLICY-MAKING

What guidance can we offer the corporate planner or policy analyst in his attempt to improve the quality of strategic deci-

	Marginal	Appendix	Corporations	Institutions
Value environment	Free	Political	Free	Mixed
Goals	None	External	Internal	External & internal
Power system	Centralized	Parent organization	Centralized (Limited)	Management and supporting groups
Defence system (inertia)	Weak	Protects organization from parent	Strong	Internal and external coalitions
Key skills	Rapid adaptation	Good link with parent	Development of new systems	System development + social awareness
Adaptation to environment	Mapping e.g. market research	Matching (cooperation)	Dominance (innovation)	Joint consultation

Source: Adapted from Eric Rhenman, *Organisation Theory for Long Range Planning*, Wiley, London, 1973 (Page 109).

PS.4   Organization for long-range planning.

sions in his organization? Current research into policy-making offers a number of valuable insights.

Decision-Space

First he should ask *What can this management team decide?* What are the limits of their authority? What other decisions can they influence? There is little point in devising strategies you have not the economic and political resources to implement. This point is particularly relevant in an organization whose freedom of action is circumscribed in some way.

A local authority may find, for example, that 95 per cent of its budget is already committed to carrying out its statutory duties. One might also question the wisdom of a local council preparing plans for developing the community in its area when

	Entrepreneurial	*Adaptive*	*Planning*
Environment	Yielding	Complex dynamic	Predictable stable
Organization	Young or strong leadership	Established	Large
Power	Entrepreneur	Coalition/ bargaining	Management
Horizon	Long term	Short term	Long term
Flexibility	Flexible	Adaptive	Constrained
Decisions	Bold moves	Incremental steps	Global strategies
Decision links	Loose	Disjointed	Integrated
Orientation	Proactive	Reactive	Proactive and reactive

Source: Henry Mintzberg, 'Strategy-making in Three Modes, *California Management Review,* Winter 1973.

PS.5   Strategy-making and management style.

	INFREQUENT	FREQUENT
PRECEDENTED	STABLE e.g. public utility	REGULATED FLEXIBILITY e.g. job shop
UNPRECEDENTED	TASK FORCE e.g. building contractor	ADAPTIVE e.g. research lab., advertising agency

Source: William Newman (unpublished)

PS.6   The management process: type of change.

it can affect only a small part of community life, the major decisions coming under the control of central Government, the Regional Water Board, the Area Health Authority, private property developers and local industry. The council's purpose must surely be to *influence* these other decision-makers.

The management of a unit within a large organization may find itself in a similar position. For example, the management of a large colliery in the National Coal Board may control assets of £30 million and a work force of several thousand, but its powers are very closely defined. The major decisions on prices and markets, wages and industrial relations, even the major investments in equipment and supplies, are largely made at headquarters, or sometimes by Government.

On the other hand, in a divisionalized company, the management often invent their own constraints. Several years ago the Boeing Aircraft Company corporate-planning group checked with divisional management what they believed was the scope of their authority. The group found that the divisional management had invented over forty central policy constraints which did not in fact exist.

Role

A related question is *What is the role of the organization?* In business a parent organization may have assigned a specific task to one of its subsidiaries. For example, a marketing subsidiary for an international oil company recently saw substantial profit potential in selling a wide range of bought-in accessories to motorists, only to discover, of course, that the parent organization regarded the subsidiary mainly as an outlet for its petrol.

In public-service organizations the role of the unit is usually specified by legislation. For example, in Britain a water board has an obligation to supply water, a hospital to provide medical treatment, and a local council to provide schooling. Nationalized industries exist to supply goods or services as required, to operate 'in the public interest' and 'to break-even taking one year with another'.

These are the rules of the game — the requirements of the stake-holders and the expectations of the owners — and managements need to be quite clear about the conditions under which they operate. These rules or expectations may be changed, but they are not normally the subject of negotiation.

Predictability

Some activities, like research or creative tasks such as advertising, are by their nature unpredictable. Other operations, such as banking, insurance and electricity generation, tend to be more stable predictable activities. The planner should ask himself *How predictable is this activity?*

He should not expect to establish as detailed a planning system for a division concerned with property development as for his other divisions in engineering contracting, housebuilding and building products. (See p. 327.) If he is in oil or mining he must recognize the uncertainties associated with geological exploration. The source of uncertainty may not be in the technology but in the environment. For example, under the Conservatives the management of the Greater London Council produced very detailed plans for new motorways round London, only to find that a Labour Council was returned at the next election and the plan was immediately shelved.

As Rhenman found in his research, the small businessman is often in a highly unpredictable situation, at the mercy of his suppliers and his clients. His remedy lies not in specific detailed plans but in flexibility – keeping his options open.

It is significant, too, how, during the energy crisis and the commodity shortages, large companies have put their long-term plans and their computer models on one side and regressed or reverted to intuitive *ad hoc* decision-making. There is no room for fine tuning when the uncertainties are so gross. As one planner from the electricity industry expressed it, 'We are preparing robust plans – plans which will be right whatever happens. It is better to be approximately right, than precisely wrong'.

In an uncertain situation, as Mintzberg has pointed out, the most suitable method of strategy-making is 'muddling through', that is making decisions incrementally on the best available information but trying not to pre-empt any long-term strategies. In a politically unstable situation the position is similarly precarious; there is no point in producing detailed long-term plans, for what are needed are broad policies that can be changed when the next party arrives in power.

Power Structure

Another vital factor to consider in improving the policy-making process is *Who has the power?* – not only who has the power to make the final decision, but who is in a position to influence the decision. The influencers may be labelled the 'decision-makers', in contrast to the 'decision-takers'. Power may be distributed among the following:

1 *The single individual or cabinet.* The role of the individual decision-maker has been greatly underemphasized in planning literature. In almost every kind of enterprise it is possible to find individuals who manage the power system so well that the necessary procedure is a mere formality and they in fact make the final decisions. This results in what Dror has called 'presidential policy-making'. He refers to former President Nixon and his inner policy group, and to the British cabinet under, for example, Winston Churchill.

   In business it is common for chief executives to keep certain decisions in their own hands. Lord Heyworth of Unilever is said to have concentrated on major investment decisions and key staff appointments. Umberto Agnelli of Fiat pays special attention to management development and international operations. Despite the impressive planning that exists in ITT, Harold Geneen appears to deal personally with acquisitions such as Sheraton Hotels and Avis Rentacar.

2 *The bureaucracy.* In large organizations, however, it is more common to find that power and influence are distributed widely throughout the organization. The Harvard research into stages of corporate development indicates that decision-making is critically influenced by the following:

   (a) Diversity of the product range – single or dominant product, related products, and unrelated products
   (b) The type of organizational structure – functional or integrated, divisionalized, or conglomerate
   (c) The international orientation – sales branch, local assembly, or subsidiary company.

   Investigations into resource allocation in divisionalized structures indicate that the definition of projects is made in operating units and the board typically has a ratifying function. More formal planning systems have been introduced in decentralized structures very much with an eye to enabling the board to discuss possible alternative strategies *before* divisions commit themselves to specific proposals.

In the most complex corporate structure there are at least three types of power groups, as follows:

1 National or regional groups
2 Product divisions
3 Functional hierarchies, e.g. personnel and finance.

The decision-making process has to be organized so as to enable all these groups to influence key decisions.

3 *The coalition.* As with the single decision-maker, there are occasions in most organizations when there is no identifiable hierarchy. No one is in a position to take complete control, and decisions are the result of negotiation and bargaining between rival factions. A hospital management committee, for instance, may require to reconcile the conflicting and sometimes incompatible demands of the medical profession, the nursing profession, the administrators, and community interests.

In private companies, too, it sometimes happens that the board is divided between the supporters of different divisions or departments. Attempts have been made to appoint boards or executive committees that can take a more detached view, but there is always the risk that, as Du Pont have found, this may mean that top managemen is too isolated from company operations.[17] In the absence of a single powerful individual it seems inevitable that key decisions should be arrived at frequently through some form of bargaining or horse-trading.

In these kinds of situations Mintzberg has suggested that incremental *ad hoc* decision-making is likely to take over. The development of explicit objectives and policies will frequently explode the coalition by making conflicts in values and aspirations overt rather than implicit. The leader can only unite his coalition on specific issues and by careful negotiation. This may be one reason why strategic planning seems to have made little or no progress in such areas of conflict as industrial relations.

Management Style

A question closely related to the power structure is *What is the management style?* This depends largely on the leader, the activity, and the tradition of the organization. Entrepreneurs typically are confident individuals who prefer to make their own decisions. They are not inclined to ask for advice or to discuss their decisions, except with a few intimates. In a family firm the management style is apt to change abruptly when the younger generation (which is less experienced) succeeds to the chief executive's role. A similar situation sometimes arises when a small private company that has been managed by an autocrat is taken over by a large company that appoints its own chief executive.

Growth is an additional reason for a change of style. In the early stages of developing a business the charisma of personal drive may carry the day, but at the point where explosive growth gives way to planned expansion competitors begin to reduce the margins and customers start to think about making the product themselves. Then the priorities shift, the sophisticated managers take over and the entrepreneur is obliged to manage in collaboration with a team of specialists in cost control, production control, stock control, and various other controls.

The choice of management style may also be made on ethical considerations. For all its behavioural-science connotations, 'participative management' and Maslow's hierarchy of needs are very firmly based in the Christian morality of individual 'self-actualization'. Kirby Warren contrasts the two distinct managerial philosophies symbolized in the autocratic/centralized and the participative/decentralized styles (see Figure Ps. 7). The autocratic style is based firmly in the Protestant work ethic. It follows the classical tradition of management in giving priority to the efficient solution of organizational problems. The heir to this tradition is the management scientist with his computer models, and the systems analyst with his flow charts. On the other hand, the participative/decentralized style emphasizes the need to satisfy the needs of the individual employee, and design the job and the work situation in such a way that the worker achieves maximum job satisfaction and opportunities for personal growth.

In reality managers tend to choose managerial styles somewhere between these extremes. But clearly the strategy-making activity is affected very significantly by the style of the top-management group. For example, Birds Eye, the largest British manufacturer of frozen foods, recently chose to introduce a

	Centralized/ autocratic	Decentralized/ participative
Keys to efficiency	Expertise, perspective, coordination, control	Motivation, commitment, flexibility, creativity
Focus	Anticipate, identify and solve organizational problems efficiently	— Understand and anticipate individual needs — Design work systems to meet them
System elements	— Detailed forecasts, plans, controls — specialization, simplification — systems planning to reintegrate — disciplined use of management system	— Involvement in key decisions — change/diversity — job enrichment development
Why people work?	— Increased leisure and material goods — childrens future etc.	— Job satisfaction — personal development, etc.

Source: Kirby Warren, Columbia University.

PS.7   Management philosophies.

form of organizational development based on the managerial grid. When asked who was responsible for planning, the Assistant Chairman replied that 400 managers were. In 1972 the board appointed a '1977 Committee' to develop a plan for the next five years, and each department was called upon to examine the implications for research, marketing, distribution, production, etc., based on certain assumptions about the growth in turnover and profits.

In some cases — as in a far-flung multi-national company — the federal nature of the business dictates that strategy formulation must take place on the spot. It is inconceivable that a central management team in London should dictate the strategy for Metal Box in India, for the United Africa Company in Nigeria or for British Oxygen in Australia.

On a smaller scale, it may be necessary to leave the strategy to the branch manager in a retail business. In a recent article the

deputy chairman of W. H. Smith, Britain's leading chain of book-
shops, explained that the organization had adopted a system
of planning called 'Participative Planning'. 'The key fuel for the
planning process', he wrote, 'is the Provisional Planning Issue.
This provides in effect an organized method of collecting and
recording ideas and comments on a standard form. Every PPI
is read and considered by a planning team.'[18] This seems a very
appropriate procedure for a retailer, because the business essentially consists of a federation of small businesses, each with a
very different environment. To plan in London for a branch in
Dundee or Cardiff would make little sense. In the conglomerate,
too, a decentralized form of decision-making seems to be sensible, because the industrial holding company is essentially a
financial investment group, with a portfolio of companies rather
than shares. The successful conglomerate management tends to
centralize a few financial decisions and rely very largely on the
entrepreneurial flair of managing directors in subsidiaries. Control is largely financial, and little attempt is made to provide
central services; rather, the central-management team tries to
act as a sounding board and a control on the chief executives
of the subsidiaries.[19]

Extrapolation and Forecasting

It is of course reasonable, as a starting point, for the corporate
planner to ask for a simple extrapolation from the present position. This after all is not threatening, and experience in Government and in business suggests that this kind of extended budgeting comes naturally to managers who are used to developing
budgets. The corporate planner asks simply, 'Where will the
organization be in X year's time if we carry on with our present
policies?' Stanford Research Institute call this 'the momentum
line', and when contrasted with top management's targets, it
often serves to alert management to the fact that profits are
tending to decline and market shares are falling. The gap between the goals and the likely achievement can draw attention
to the need for action to expand present activities, to develop
new products, to penetrate new markets, or to seek new resources.

The British Government, too, has a similar system, known
as P.E.S.C. (the Public Expenditure Survey Committee), which

provides ministers and officials with a means of examining
the future implications of present policies in the shape of a
five-year budget. A further development of this procedure, used
both by Stanford Research Institute and by the British Government, is to ask managers or administrators themselves to identify the policy issues requiring investigation. In the case of
S.R.I. they ask managers to suggest the critical issues for investigation, and then form project teams to investigate them and
develop action programmes. In British Government practice the
procedure is called programme analysis and review. Again, the
policy issues are suggested by the departments concerned,
policies are put forward to the Cabinet by the ministers
and departments carry out their own special studies with the
help of the Treasury. In recent years the formation a Think
Tank has provided additional commentaries for the benefit of
the Cabinet.

CRITICAL ISSUES

The question of policy issues is worthy of special attention.
However it is raised, the planner needs to ask, *What are the
strategic issues for this organization?* The original designs for
strategic planning were produced by management scientists and
economists, so that they were concerned largely with 'resource
allocation', i.e. capital budgeting. They appeared in the mid-
1960s when marketing was in vogue, and they viewed strategy
largely as a 'game' played by alternating investments in products
and markets. Since then, even in business, the game has changed,
and in attempting to apply formal planning systems to non-
business activities the product/market viewpoint has appeared
increasingly inflexible. Take, for example, the situation of a
nationalized industry that is limited by statute to operate in the
'Coal Industry' or 'Electricity Supply' in the U.K. In these cases
the product-market strategy models of Ansoff seem to have
limited application. Take the case of a local authority trying to
apply corporate management, and ask what its services are and
what its market is. In many cases, e.g. social services, where the
potential market seems to be 'open-minded', the objective must
be to allocate priorities rather than to expand the service beyond
the available resources. In recent years a number of British researchers have demonstrated the limitations of Ansoff's initial

model. David Farmer has pointed to the need to consider resource restraints such as raw materials and supplies.[20] David
Norburn found that boards of directors had no explicit objectives except a vague idea about 'profitability'.[21] Susan Birley
discovered that boards of directors rarely developed explicit
strategies for acquisitions.[22]

Ian MacMillan pointed out that Ansoff's approach tended
to ignore political considerations. He noted that 'In practice
top managers are fully aware of these shortcomings (in current
theoretical approaches) and in fact do formulate informal political strategies'.[23]

In looking for the 'key decisions' the planner should be asking
the question, 'What does it take to succeed in this business?' and
also 'Why do enterprises fail?' The rules for success usually include
maintaining satisfactory relations with *all* the 'stakeholders'. This
means not just the shareholders and financiers, but the customers
and distributors, the employees and unions, and suppliers of raw
materials, components and new technology — and, increasingly, a
variety of Government bodies and community groups.

It is rarely feasible to research and plan in great detail for
all these relations; however, it is sensible to aim to satisfy the
minimum requirements of each stakeholder group and to
develop appropriate research and planning capabilities for the
critical areas. At the moment, for example, it would seem
reasonable for large corporations to improve their planning
and forecasting for supply markets, and to appoint specialists
who can help top management to plan for social and political
change.

ORGANIZATIONAL CHANGE

A more ambitious question for the planner is *How can we
change this organization?*[24] As Ansoff has pointed out, it is
not sufficient to plan for expansion and diversification without
making corresponding plans to change the organization. For
example, Lockheed might plan to diversify from defence contracts into commercial aircraft but the organization would be
courting disaster if top management did not at the same time
plan to introduce commercial attitudes to quality and cost.

Similarly, it would be unreasonable for British Government laboratories, such as Harwell, to plan a changeover from government-funded research to contract research for industry without trying to change the attitudes of scientists who joined the laboratory precisely because it offered the opportunity to work for the civil service rather than for business.

All too often top management finds that new strategies are frustrated because they cut across established values and attitudes within the organization. In the commercial banks, for instance, top management are attempting to market a comprehensive range of financial services through existing branch networks. However, the idea of selling units in a unit trust belonging to the bank conflicts directly with the professional ethics of the branch manager, who feels his first loyalty must be to his client. Equally, the branch manager is often ill-equipped to advise on investment, taxation, insurance and mortgages. Before these services can be offered, he needs to be trained and to be provided with specialist advisers.

In evolving 'strategies for organizational change' the corporate planner will have to work closely with specialist staff who are skilled in organizational development and management education.

Certain companies, too, have accepted that if managers are to take a wider, longer-term view of their responsibilities, then it will be necessary to make extensive changes in the managemen system. As Clifford Springer, of the General Electric Company, points out: 'Some of our managers are not yet accustomed to thinking strategically about their businesses'.[25] In consequence the central management group has set about redesigning other elements of the management to support the formal planning procedure. New information is being made available from an environmental forecasting group, which has analysed the economic and social trends likely to affect the company. Staff attending company courses are being trained in 'strategic management', and staff specialists are also examining the appraisal and reward system to ensure that managers who act in the long-term interests of the company are rewarded for staff development or community relations, in the same way they might expect to be rewarded for increasing the return on investment of their division in the short term.

INNOVATION

A related question is *How can we foster innovation?* Academics and managers alike seem to be agreed that a central problem in strategy-making and organizational change is to develop creative and innovative activity. This is not so difficult in small enterprises, which have an excellent record for fostering new ideas. Indeed it is clear from an examination of the literature that small units offer just the kind of informal situation in which new activities can thrive. However, large organizations seem almost of necessity to produce formal systems that can stifle creativity by requiring detailed measurement at too early a stage.

Ansoff suggests that a major difficulty in developing an innovative organization arises from the fact that innovators do not exist easily alongside bureaucrats. Since, in most established organizations, the majority of staff are concerned with servicing and maintaining ongoing operations, the innovators appear as a deviant culture with different values and norms of behaviour. As a consequence they tend to be rejected by the dominant power group, unless special arrangements are made to foster and protect them. Ansoff labels the innovators 'strategic managers' and the managers of the ongoing operations 'operating managers'.

In an ideal world every operating manager would be an innovator as well, but in practice we find that the innovator is frequently a different person with a distinctive personality. Hence one popular way of fostering innovation is by establishing separate Corporate Development Diversification or New Venture groups — either at headquarters or, more rarely, in divisions. In either case these departments are tender plants requiring constant protection by top management. Another approach is to put the innovative activity into a separate company where it is less subject to scrutiny. At the same time it is difficult for top management used to managing established operations to understand the difficulties of planning for relatively speculative operations.

STRATEGIES FOR PLANNING

In this postscript we have suggested that after a decade of experience with formal planning systems it should be possible for planners to develop beyond the systems-analysis or management-scientist's view of corporate planning as a formal exercise in resource allocation to more flexible planning approaches. Instead of trying to sell, install and maintain formalized planning procedures, the planner should be attempting to improve the quality of strategic decision-making by whatever means seems to be most appropriate. It is clear from numerous research studies that comprehensive formal planning systems can produce strong resistance from management, principally because they require a highly disciplined approach and they can be expensive in time and money.

It is evident from the studies that have been carried out into long-range planning that formal planning systems are not a panacea for strategy-making in all situations, and it is a much safer policy for the planner to consider a wide range of alternative 'strategies for planning'. He will have a number of approaches and techniques to call on, including the following:

1   Extended budgeting
2   Coordinated planning for certain key areas, e.g. finance, facilities or manpower (possibly using computers)
3   Special studies on critical policy issues, including futures research
4   Assistance in comprehensive programmes for management development and organizational change
5   The use of task forces and project teams for new ventures and diversification.

There are no doubt many other approaches, variants and combinations that may be used according to the situation. (See Figure Ps. 8).

Finally, it would seem that the planner's best approach would not be the mechanic's, with a ready-made solution, but the doctor's, through a diagnosis; and the kinds of question he might ask would probably include the following:

1   What are the limits to the authority of the management team?
2   What is the role of the organization as prescribed by its owners or 'stakeholders'?
3   Who has the power to make strategic decisions
    (a) An individual or policy committee?
    (b) A management team or several teams?
    (c) An uneasy coalition of conflicting interest groups?

4   What is the prevailing management style — how participative or authoritarian?

5   Where will our present policies lead us and how do these results compare with any established goals?

6   What are the key strategic issues for the organization and do we need to develop new capabilities to deal with them?

7   How can we change the organization — in what directions and by what means?

8   How can we foster creativity and innovation and maintain it over time?

There is nothing very new about these recommendations. This is the kind of process that good experienced planning specialists and consultants use in handling strategy problems. The new factor is that management theorists and researchers are beginning to catch up with the practitioners. This means that in training new planners and in working with managers we should be able increasingly to be more explicit about our craft. Possibly — as Yehezkel Dror suggests — we should be educating now a new profession of policy analysts.

Figure PS.8   Strategies for Planning

---

1. **Operational Planning Only**
   strategy is determined elsewhere

2. **Extended Budgeting**
   extrapolating the consequences of present policies

3. **Ad hoc Analysis of Policy Issues**
   selected by management

4. **Special Studies using Research**
   e.g. attitude surveys and future studies

5. **Co-ordinated Planning for Key Areas**
   e.g. facilities or manpower (possibly with computer analysis)

6. **New Venture Groups**
   e.g. Diversification Task Force, Corporate Development Unit

7. **Strategic Management**
   attempt to promote extrepreneurial attitudes by organization development etc.

8. **Comprehensive Strategic Planning**
   e.g. following a merger or in a crisis situation

9. **Contingency Planning**
   to prepare for the unexpected e.g. a natural disaster or a failure of supply

---

REFERENCES

1 *Planning and the Chief Executive* (New York: Conference Board, 1972).
2 Ansoff, H. Igor *et al. From Strategic Planning to Strategic Management* (Vanderbilt University, 1973).
3 Mintzberg, Henry. 'Strategy-making in Three Modes', *California Management Review,* Winter 1973, pp. 44–53.
4 Dror, Yehezkel. *Ventures in Policy Sciences* (New York: Elsevier, 1971), p. 118.
5 Ibid., p. 127.
6 Unterman, Israel. 'American Finance: Three Views of Strategy', *Journal of General Management,* 1974, vol. 1, no. 3.
7 Dror, op. cit., p. 38.
8 Ansoff, op. cit., p. 12.
9 Dror, op. cit., p. 230.
10 Taylor, Bernard and Irving, Peter. 'Organised Planning in Major U.K. Companies', *Long Range Planning,* June 1971.
11 Dror, op. cit., p. 230.
12 Ibid., p. 231.
13 Rhenman, Eric. *Organization Theory for Long Range Planning* (London: Wiley, 1972), p. 67.
14 Mintzberg, Henry. 'Research on Strategy-making', McGill University Paper, Montreal, 1972.
15 Dror, op. cit., p. 231.
16 See also Jurkovich, Ray. 'A Core Typology of Organisational Environments', *Administrative Science Quarterly,* September 1974, pp. 380–94.
17 See 'Refining Du Pont's Managerial Process', *International Management,* October 1973.
18 Bennett, P. W. 'Participation in Planning', *Journal of General Management,* Autumn 1974.
19 See Berg, Norman E. 'What's Different about Conglomerate Management?', *Harvard Business Review,* November–December 1969.
20 Farmer, D. H. 'Purchasing Myopia', *Journal of General Management,* Winter 1974.
21 Norburn, David and Grinyer, Peter H. 'Directors without Direction', *Journal of General Management,* Winter 1974.
22 Birley, Susan. Unpublished Ph.D. Thesis, London Graduate School of Business, 1974.

23 MacMillan, Ian C. 'Business Strategies for Political Action', *Journal of General Management,* Autumn 1974.
24 Ansoff, op. cit., p. 12.
25 Springer, C. H. 'Strategic Management in General Electric', *Operations Research,* November–December 1973. See also Taylor, B. 'Introducing Strategic Management', *Long Range Planning,* September 1973.

Index

400

INDEX

Patents, 188, 192
Payment by results, 217–18
Performance, 6
  evaluation, 8
  gap, 300, 301
  measurement, 175
Personnel, see Labour
Piecework, 222
Planning, Programming and Budgeting
    System, 3
Plant
  delays in installation, 204
  European locations, 274–5
  location, 204
  nuclear fuel industry, 355
  obsolescence, 204–5
Policy analysis, 370, 373–7
  difference from formal planning,
      375–6
  guidelines, 376–7
Policy formulation, 361
Political change, 8
  business risks, 37, 40
  increasing the sensitivity of
      management, 39–40
  monitoring, 11
Political programmes
  acceptability of company policies, 105
  development, 35–6, 39
  implementation, 36–7
  policy analysis, 374
Pollution control, 30
  legislation, 21, 29
  public opinion surveys, 33
Portfolio management, 166–70
Pressure groups, 11, 20, 116
  effect on management thought, 21
  in General Electric's analysis, 34
Price/earnings ratio, 147
Price-fixing, 28
Prices
  commodity, 237, 314
  determination, 124
  government controls, 21, 29
  relative to competing products, 128
  study on attitude to controls, 32
Private enterprise philosophy, 14–16
Probability, 109
  distributions, 51–2
  in forecasting, 48–9
  of benchmark forecasts, 109
  use of models, 50
  used in investment decisions, 50–3
Probability-diffusion matrix, 109–11, 116
Procurement planning, 238
Product divisions, 175
Product/market analysis, 264–5
Production, 69, 196–213
  capability analysis, 209–12
  capacity, 201
  corporate investment, 199, 201

effect of government intervention, 207
  of newly-developed products, 193
Products, 8, 316
  life-cycle, 149–50, 155, 207
  obsolescence, 157, 181, 196
  performance and use, 124
  planning life-cycles to maintain profits,
      183
  quality compared with competitors,
      128, 172
Profit and loss accounts, 131, 132
Profit centres, 134, 175, 177
Profit Impact of Market Strategy, 172–3
Profitability, 144, 149
  factors which influence, 172
Profits, 130
  assessing profitability, 131
  cyclical pattern, 63–5
  government controls, 22–3
  impact of bought-in components, 238
  related to social acceptability, 39
  used for social projects, 23–4, 102
Programmes Analysis Unit, 76
Property investment, 140, 142
Protestantism, 15
Public authorities' expenditure, 70
Public Expenditure Survey Committee,
    386
Purchasing, 8, 237–42
  see also Supplies
Recreational activities, 30
Recycling, 240–1, 243
  forward integration of firms, 250
  water in steelmaking, 248
Redundancy payments, 21
Regional policies, 21
Religious basis of private enterprise, 15
Research and development, 8, 81
  appraising competition, 189
  choice of offensive, defensive,
      absorptive strategies, 188–9
  cost-benefit, 187–8
  critical factors in strategy, 186–90
  decision-making, 194–5
  finance, 193
  'knowledge explosion', 180
  marketing approach, 182, 191, 193
  project selection, 192–4
  research groups in local government,
      339–40
  resource allocations, 184, 185–6
  strategy, 182–90
  strategy formulation, 180–1
  strategy related to company strengths,
      190–2
  United States effort, 189
Resources, 237–55
  allocation, 9
  appraisal, 7
  availability of nuclear fuels, 355–6
  backwards integration, 239